# Preface

In January 2000, I sat in Dr. Jim Hendler's Defense Advanced Research Projects Agency (DARPA) office as he used his whiteboard to introduce me to Semantic Web concepts. Less than two years later, early on September 11, 2001, I was in the same DARPA building describing our ideas for using Semantic Web technologies for representing anti-terrorism intelligence information, not realizing the greater importance those recommendations would have later that same morning. I continue to believe that the Semantic Web has incredible potential and that OWL will enable a new generation of web technology. I created this book to help others use OWL to create new information representation solutions.

## Intended Audience

This book is written primarily for XML data engineers, web application developers, and database engineers that want to leverage the power of the Semantic Web by representing their information using the Web Ontology Language - OWL. Representing information in OWL enables Semantic Web applications and services to process and interpret content. Readers should already have a working knowledge of the Extensible Markup Language (XML).

## Acknowledgments

The cover and section title page artwork were created by Andres Arbelaez. Christina Hammock provided technical editing support. I appreciate the management and data engineering professionals at Dynamics Research Corporation (DRC) for their support in developing this text. DRC performed OWL research as part the DARPA DAML program and is using OWL on multiple projects. Dr. Larry O'Brien, Ben DaCosta, Karen Fraser, Dr. William Gerber, and Wayne Randolph are DRC employees that volunteered to provide technical reviews of this text. Mike Dean, the world's foremost expert on OWL, provided the foreword and technical review support. Jack Sheehan, a data engineering evangelist, has consistently challenged me to pursue new technology solutions. DRC's research was funded with the support of several Marks (i.e., Mark Greaves, Mark Gorniak, and Mark Nelson) and this book has been written with the technical and moral support of another Mark, my brother, Dr. Mark Lacy. My favorite author, my dad, Edward A. Lacy, provided invaluable encouragement.

# OWL:
## Representing Information Using the Web Ontology Language

Lee W. Lacy

© Copyright 2005 Lee W. Lacy.
All rights reserved. No part of this publication may be reproduced, stored in a retrieval system, or transmitted, in any form or by any means, electronic, mechanical, photocopying, recording, or otherwise, without the written prior permission of the author.

Note for Librarians: a cataloguing record for this book that includes Dewey Decimal Classification and US Library of Congress numbers is available from the Library and Archives of Canada. The complete cataloguing record can be obtained from their online database at:
www.collectionscanada.ca/amicus/index-e.html
ISBN 1-4120-3448-5
Printed in Victoria, BC, Canada

# TRAFFORD

*Offices in Canada, USA, Ireland, UK and Spain*
This book was published *on-demand* in cooperation with Trafford Publishing. On-demand publishing is a unique process and service of making a book available for retail sale to the public taking advantage of on-demand manufacturing and Internet marketing. On-demand publishing includes promotions, retail sales, manufacturing, order fulfilment, accounting and collecting royalties on behalf of the author.

**Book sales for North America and international:**
Trafford Publishing, 6E–2333 Government St.,
Victoria, BC v8t 4p4 CANADA
phone 250 383 6864 (toll-free 1 888 232 4444)
fax 250 383 6804; email to orders@trafford.com

**Book sales in Europe:**
Trafford Publishing (UK) Ltd., Enterprise House, Wistaston Road Business Centre,
Wistaston Road, Crewe, Cheshire cw2 7rp UNITED KINGDOM
phone 01270 251 396 (local rate 0845 230 9601)
facsimile 01270 254 983; orders.uk@trafford.com

**Order online at:**
www.trafford.com/robots/04-1276.html

10 9 8 7 6 5 4 3 2

# Foreword by Mike Dean

I've had the pleasure of working with Lee Lacy and the team at Dynamics Research Corporation (DRC) since the beginning of the DARPA Agent Markup Language (DAML) program in August 2000. They've focused on producing Semantic Web content, ontologies and instance data, for others to use – a critical requirement for bootstrapping the Semantic Web. In addition to describing the technical details of the Semantic Web in clear, understandable language, this book draws on this considerable experience in modeling and deploying real world data. Replete with best practices and examples, it provides a pragmatic introduction to the Semantic Web.

The Semantic Web is an international effort to make the vast data resources of the World Wide Web available in a format amenable to automated processing by intelligent agents and other computer programs. As more data becomes available on the Semantic Web, we experience the network effect of increased connectivity and are increasingly able to build applications through reuse rather than from scratch. A lot of reference data is available already. Soon, we'll expect web sites to provide data in Semantic Web formats and will be able to concentrate on adding our unique personal data and mapping common classes and properties between ontologies specific to our own communities of interest.

Semantic Web technology is scalable, from embedded uses to personal scale applications on a single computer to workgroups and intranets to the global Internet. The architectural principles of URI naming, the graph data model, extensibility, and machine-accessible descriptions provide a solid foundation. Application developers will often select among other features, balancing their needs for expressivity, completeness, and performance. A variety of high quality software tools are now available, most as open source. Methodologies and design patterns are emerging.

The Semantic Web is here. This book provides the tools to understand, explore, and contribute to it. I hope you enjoy working with the Semantic Web as much as I have.

Mike Dean
Ann Arbor, Michigan
October 2004

## *Purpose*

The Semantic Web is the next generation web that will support automated processing of information. Intelligent agents and other software access information marked up using OWL. The Semantic Web relies on information marked up in a computer-understandable manner. Marking up data, information, and knowledge for use in the Semantic Web is an investment that mirrors the development of HyperText Markup Language (HTML) pages that have enabled the current web. The ability to effectively represent information in OWL will provide new career and business opportunities for those that master its use.

Understanding component technologies of the Semantic Web's architecture supports using OWL to represent information for use by Semantic Web applications. By understanding the underlying technologies, OWL becomes much clearer and easier to use.

The intention of this book is to help people correctly mark up information for use by Semantic Web applications. Correctly applying OWL is critical to developing effective and quality Semantic Web applications.

## *Disclaimer*

Much of the content of this text is available from various World Wide Web Consortium (W3C) documents. However, this text presents OWL explanations in a more easily understood order in a single document. Although this book attempts to capture the latest resolution of various language issues, it is important to check the newsgroups for ongoing discussions of various Resource Description Framework (RDF) and OWL issues. The author attempted to make sure that syntax specifications and examples are correct, but the possibility remains that mistakes occurred that may lead to frustration in trying to implement examples. If mistakes are identified, they should be e-mailed to: owlbook@lacydatasystems.com.

## *Fast Forward*

Readers already familiar with basic Semantic Web concepts can skip Section 1 and proceed directly to Section 2. Readers already familiar with Uniform Resource Identifiers (URIs), XML, RDF, and RDF Schema (RDFS) technologies can skip directly to Section 3 to learn about OWL.

*Outline*

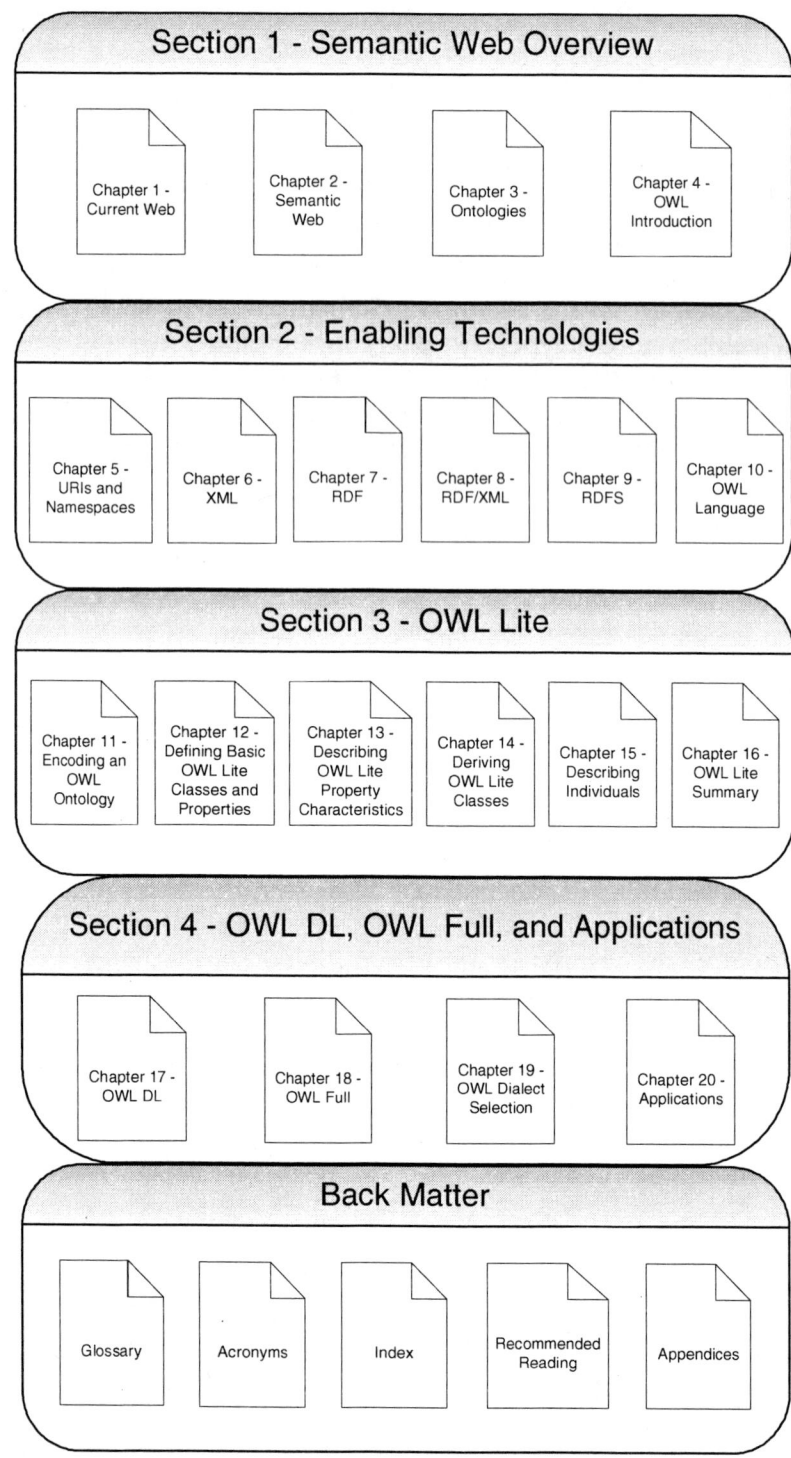

# Table of Contents

1 Current Web .................................................................................................... 1
   1.1    Current Web History ............................................................................ 1
   1.2    Current Web Characteristics ............................................................... 2
       1.2.1    Current Web Features .................................................................. 2
       1.2.2    Current Web Benefits .................................................................. 3
       1.2.3    Current Web Applications .......................................................... 3
   1.3    Why the Current Web is not Enough ................................................. 4
       1.3.1    Information Must be Structured ................................................ 4
       1.3.2    Finding Requires Metadata ........................................................ 5
       1.3.3    Semantics Must be Explicit ......................................................... 6
   1.4    Current Web Summary ........................................................................ 6
2 Semantic Web Introduction ........................................................................... 7
   2.1    Web Information Representation Challenges .................................. 8
       2.1.1    Increased Need for Information Representation ................... 8
       2.1.2    Ambiguous Human Descriptions ............................................. 8
       2.1.3    Software Demands for Specificity ............................................. 9
   2.2    Requirements for a Web Information Representation Solution .... 9
       2.2.1    Minimizing Human Investment .............................................. 10
       2.2.2    Satisfying Computer Requirements ....................................... 12
       2.2.3    Compromise ................................................................................ 14
   2.3    Semantic Web to the Rescue .............................................................. 15
       2.3.1    Semantic Web History ............................................................... 16
       2.3.2    Semantic Web Vision ................................................................. 16
       2.3.3    Populating the Semantic Web .................................................. 18
       2.3.4    Use Cases ..................................................................................... 19
       2.3.5    Appropriate Applications ......................................................... 22
   2.4    Semantic Web Introduction Summary ............................................ 23
3 Ontologies – Enablers of the Semantic Web ............................................ 25
   3.1    Ontology Definitions .......................................................................... 25
       3.1.1    Computer Science Definition ................................................... 25
       3.1.2    Types of Ontologies ................................................................... 26
       3.1.3    Gruber Definition ....................................................................... 27
       3.1.4    OWL-Specific Ontology Definitions ....................................... 27
   3.2    Ontology Features ............................................................................... 29
       3.2.1    Common Understanding of a Domain ................................... 29
       3.2.2    Explicit Semantics ...................................................................... 29
       3.2.3    Expressiveness ............................................................................ 30

## Table of Contents

    3.2.4     Sharing Information ............................................................................... 30
  3.3     Ontology Development Issues ................................................................. 31
  3.4     Describing Semantics ................................................................................ 32
    3.4.1     Information Representation Building Blocks .................................. 32
    3.4.2     Relating Information Representation Constructs .......................... 34
    3.4.3     Semantic Relationships within Building Blocks ............................ 36
    3.4.4     Semantics Summary .......................................................................... 40
  3.5     Ontology Languages .................................................................................. 41
    3.5.1     Frame-Based Systems ........................................................................ 41
    3.5.2     Description Logics ............................................................................. 41
  3.6     Ontologies Summary ................................................................................ 42
4    OWL Introduction ............................................................................................. 43
  4.1     OWL Features ............................................................................................. 43
  4.2     Semantic Web's Layered Architecture .................................................... 44
  4.3     Technology Support for the Layers ........................................................ 45
  4.4     OWL Introduction Summary .................................................................. 46
5    URIs and Namespaces ..................................................................................... 49
  5.1     Absolute URIs ............................................................................................ 49
  5.2     URI References .......................................................................................... 53
  5.3     XML Namespaces (xmlns) ....................................................................... 56
  5.4     Specifying an Alternative Base URI (xml:base) .................................... 58
  5.5     URIs and Namespace Summary ............................................................. 60
6    XML ..................................................................................................................... 61
  6.1     XML Overview ........................................................................................... 62
    6.1.1     XML Features ..................................................................................... 64
    6.1.2     Syntax and Structure ......................................................................... 64
    6.1.3     XML Declaration ............................................................................... 65
    6.1.4     Elements ............................................................................................. 65
    6.1.5     XML Element Attributes ................................................................... 65
  6.2     XML Schema Datatypes ........................................................................... 69
    6.2.1     User Defined Datatypes ................................................................... 70
    6.2.2     Built-in OWL Datatypes ................................................................... 70
  6.3     XML Summary ........................................................................................... 71
  6.4     Why XML is not Enough .......................................................................... 73
7    RDF ...................................................................................................................... 75
  7.1     RDF Overview ........................................................................................... 76
    7.1.1     Metadata ............................................................................................. 76
    7.1.2     RDF Purpose ...................................................................................... 76
    7.1.3     RDF Specification .............................................................................. 77

# Table of Contents

| | | |
|---|---|---|
| 7.2 | RDF Features | 78 |
| 7.3 | RDF Data Model | 78 |
| 7.3.1 | Resources | 79 |
| 7.3.2 | Literals | 80 |
| 7.3.3 | Statements | 80 |
| 7.4 | RDF Summary | 82 |
| 7.5 | Why RDF is not Enough | 82 |
| 8 | RDF/XML | 83 |
| 8.1 | RDF/XML Overview | 83 |
| 8.1.1 | Relation to XML | 84 |
| 8.1.2 | RDF/XML Specifications | 84 |
| 8.2 | RDF Syntax Features (Using XML) | 85 |
| 8.3 | RDF/XML Documents | 85 |
| 8.3.1 | File Header (rdf:RDF) | 85 |
| 8.3.2 | Resource Names | 86 |
| 8.3.3 | RDF/XML Statements (rdf:Description) | 86 |
| 8.3.4 | Describing the Subject of an RDF Statement | 88 |
| 8.3.5 | Describing a Statement's Property | 90 |
| 8.3.6 | Describing a Statement Value | 90 |
| 8.3.7 | Compound Property Values | 106 |
| 8.3.8 | Striped Syntax | 108 |
| 8.3.9 | RDF Description Summary | 109 |
| 8.4 | RDF/XML Summary | 109 |
| 8.5 | Why RDF/XML is not Enough | 110 |
| 9 | RDFS | 111 |
| 9.1 | RDFS Overview | 111 |
| 9.2 | RDFS Features | 112 |
| 9.3 | RDFS Classes | 113 |
| 9.3.1 | RDFS Class Concept | 113 |
| 9.3.2 | Predefined RDFS Classes | 113 |
| 9.4 | Individuals | 117 |
| 9.5 | Properties | 117 |
| 9.5.1 | Vocabulary for RDF Core Properties | 118 |
| 9.5.2 | RDFS Clarification Properties | 125 |
| 9.5.3 | RDFS Container Classes and Properties | 126 |
| 9.5.4 | RDFS Documentation Properties | 128 |
| 9.6 | RDFS Summary | 131 |
| 9.7 | Why RDFS is not Enough | 132 |
| 10 | OWL Language | 133 |

# Table of Contents

- 10.1 OWL Overview ........................................................... 133
  - 10.1.1 OWL Definition .................................................. 133
  - 10.1.2 OWL History ..................................................... 134
  - 10.1.3 OWL Specification ............................................... 135
  - 10.1.4 OWL Features .................................................... 137
- 10.2 OWL Species ............................................................ 137
  - 10.2.1 OWL Full ......................................................... 138
  - 10.2.2 OWL DL ........................................................... 138
  - 10.2.3 OWL Lite ......................................................... 138
  - 10.2.4 OWL Species Summary .............................................. 139
- 10.3 OWL Language Summary ................................................... 140
- 11 Encoding an OWL Ontology .................................................. 143
  - 11.1 OWL Ontology File Structure ........................................ 143
  - 11.2 OWL Header ......................................................... 145
    - 11.2.1 XML Declaration and RDF Start Tag .............................. 145
    - 11.2.2 Namespaces for OWL Ontology Files .............................. 147
    - 11.2.3 Ontology Element (owl:Ontology) ................................ 150
    - 11.2.4 OWL Header Summary ............................................. 165
  - 11.3 Body ............................................................... 165
  - 11.4 Footer - Closing Tag ............................................... 166
  - 11.5 OWL Encoding Summary ............................................... 166
- 12 Defining Basic OWL Lite Classes and Properties ............................ 167
  - 12.1 Defining a Simple Named Class (owl:Class) .......................... 167
  - 12.2 Predefined OWL Classes (Extreme Classes) ........................... 168
    - 12.2.1 Thing Class (owl:Thing) ........................................ 168
    - 12.2.2 Nothing Class (owl:Nothing) .................................... 169
  - 12.3 Describing OWL Lite Properties ..................................... 169
    - 12.3.1 Datatype Properties (owl:DatatypeProperty) ..................... 170
    - 12.3.2 Object Properties (owl:ObjectProperty) ......................... 171
    - 12.3.3 Annotation Properties (owl:AnnotationProperty) ................. 173
    - 12.3.4 Ontology properties (owl:OntologyProperty) ..................... 173
  - 12.4 Basic OWL Lite Classes and Properties Summary ...................... 174
- 13 Describing OWL Lite Property Characteristics .............................. 175
  - 13.1 Defining Global Property Restrictions .............................. 175
    - 13.1.1 Functional Property (owl:FunctionalProperty) ................... 175
    - 13.1.2 Inverse Functional Property (owl:inverseFunctionalProperty) .... 177
  - 13.2 Relating Properties ................................................ 178
    - 13.2.1 Stating Property Equivalence (owl:equivalentProperty) .......... 178
    - 13.2.2 Identifying Inverse Properties (owl:inverseOf Property) ........ 179

## Table of Contents

- 13.3 Inference Shortcuts .................................................................. 181
  - 13.3.1 Transitive Properties (owl:TransitiveProperty) ............................. 181
  - 13.3.2 Symmetric Properties (owl:SymmetricProperty) ........................ 183
- 13.4 Local Property Restrictions (owl:Restriction/owl:onProperty) ............. 184
  - 13.4.1 Value Constraints ........................................................... 186
  - 13.4.2 OWL Lite Restricted Cardinality ...................................... 188
- 13.5 OWL Lite Property Characteristics Summary ........................................ 194
- 14 Deriving OWL Lite Classes ........................................................... 197
  - 14.1 Simple Named Subclass (rdfs:subClassOf) ............................................. 197
  - 14.2 Class Equivalency (owl:equivalentClass) ............................................ 199
  - 14.3 OWL Lite Intersection (owl:intersectionOf) ........................................... 201
  - 14.4 Derived OWL Lite Classes Summary ..................................................... 202
- 15 Describing Individuals ................................................................. 203
  - 15.1 Determining an Individual .............................................................. 203
    - 15.1.1 Individual vs. Instance .............................................................. 203
    - 15.1.2 Class vs. Individual ................................................................ 204
    - 15.1.3 Leaves of a Taxonomy ............................................................. 205
  - 15.2 Encoding an Instance File .............................................................. 205
  - 15.3 Instantiating Individuals ............................................................... 206
    - 15.3.1 Naming Individuals .................................................................. 207
    - 15.3.2 Joining a Class ........................................................................ 207
  - 15.4 Describing an Individual .................................................................. 208
    - 15.4.1 Associating Property Values at Instantiation ............................... 208
    - 15.4.2 Describing Existing Individuals .................................................. 209
    - 15.4.3 Automating Descriptions of Individuals ...................................... 210
  - 15.5 Relating Individuals ....................................................................... 210
    - 15.5.1 Equivalent Individuals (owl:sameAs) .......................................... 210
    - 15.5.2 Differentiating Individuals (owl:differentFrom) ........................... 211
    - 15.5.3 Differentiating Groups of Individuals (owl:AllDifferent/owl:distinctMembers) ............................................. 212
  - 15.6 Describing Individuals Summary ..................................................... 213
- 16 OWL Lite Summary ........................................................................ 215
  - 16.1 OWL Lite Constructs .................................................................... 215
  - 16.2 OWL Lite Restrictions .................................................................. 216
- 17 OWL DL ......................................................................................... 221
  - 17.1 OWL DL Restrictions ................................................................... 221
    - 17.1.1 OWL DL Vocabulary .................................................................. 223
  - 17.2 Complex Classes / Class Expressions ............................................ 224
    - 17.2.1 Enumerated Classes (owl:oneOf) ............................................. 225

## Table of Contents

    17.2.2    Disjoint Classes (owl:disjointWith) ................................................226
    17.2.3    Boolean Class Combinations ........................................................227
  17.3    Requiring a Property Value (owl:hasValue) ........................................232
  17.4    Enumerated Data Values (owl:DataRange) .........................................234
  17.5    OWL DL Summary ..............................................................................235
18    OWL Full ..................................................................................................237
  18.1    OWL Full's Differing Perspective/Relaxation ......................................237
    18.1.1    Type Separation ...........................................................................237
    18.1.2    Individuals ...................................................................................237
    18.1.3    Classes as Individuals .................................................................238
    18.1.4    Properties .....................................................................................238
    18.1.5    Property Restrictions ..................................................................238
  18.2    OWL Full Summary ...........................................................................239
19    OWL Dialect Selection ..........................................................................241
  19.1    Choosing Your Weapon ....................................................................241
  19.2    Migrating XML and RDF Implementations to OWL ......................242
  19.3    Language Selection Summary ..........................................................243
  19.4    Satisfaction of Information Representation Requirements ...................243
  19.5    OWL Dialect Selection Summary ......................................................247
20    Applications ............................................................................................249
  20.1    Application Example ..........................................................................249
    20.1.1    OWL Lite Solution .......................................................................251
  20.2    Supporting Applications ....................................................................258
    20.2.1    Inappropriate Applications .........................................................258
    20.2.2    Appropriate Applications ...........................................................259
  20.3    Applications Summary .......................................................................259

# List of Tables

Table 5-1. URI Authoritative Description .................................................................. 50
Table 5-2. URIref Forms.............................................................................................. 53
Table 5-3. URI Authoritative Description .................................................................. 56
Table 5-4. Alternative Base URI Authoritative Description...................................... 59
Table 6-1. XML Authoritative Description................................................................. 64
Table 6-2. Authoritative "xml:lang" Support Documents ......................................... 66
Table 6-3. XML Schema Authoritative Description................................................... 69
Table 6-4. XML Schema Namespace........................................................................... 70
Table 6-5. XML Schema Datatypes used in OWL...................................................... 71
Table 7-1. RDF Authoritative Description.................................................................. 77
Table 7-2. RDF Statement Forms................................................................................ 81
Table 7-3. Examples of RDF Statements .................................................................... 81
Table 8-1. RDF/XML Authoritative Description....................................................... 84
Table 8-2. RDF Namespace and Mime Type.............................................................. 84
Table 8-3. Statement Forms ......................................................................................... 87
Table 9-1. RDFS Authoritative Description.............................................................. 112
Table 9-2. RDFS Namespace...................................................................................... 112
Table 9-3. RDFS Predefined Classes ......................................................................... 117
Table 10-1. OWL Authoritative Description ............................................................ 136
Table 10-2. OWL Namespace and Mime Type ........................................................ 137
Table 10-3. OWL Species Summary.......................................................................... 139
Table 11-1. Recommended Namespace Abbreviations........................................... 149
Table 11-2. Versioning Constructs ............................................................................ 160
Table 13-1. MinCardinality Value Interpretation .................................................... 189
Table 13-2. MaxCardinality Value Interpretation ................................................... 191
Table 13-3. Absolute Cardinality Value Interpretation .......................................... 192
Table 13-4. Cardinality Summary ............................................................................. 193
Table 13-5. Using Appropriate Cardinality Statements and Values ..................... 193
Table 13-6. Property Characteristic Summary ........................................................ 195
Table 16-1. OWL Lite Constructs .............................................................................. 216
Table 16-2. OWL Lite Restriction Summary............................................................. 218
Table 17-1. Set Operator Summary........................................................................... 232
Table 19-1. Criteria Summary ................................................................................... 243
Table 19-2. Supporting Information Representation Building Blocks ................... 244
Table 19-3. Information Representation Construct Relationships......................... 245
Table 19-4. Ontology Requirement Satisfaction...................................................... 245

## Table of Contents

Table 19-5. OWL Full Requirement Satisfaction ...................................................... 246
Table 19-6. OWL Dialect Comparison ..................................................................... 247
Table A-1. RDF Construct Descriptions in RDF Documentation .......................... 273
Table A-2. RDFS and XML Construct Descriptions in RDF Documentation ........ 274
Table A-3. RDFS and XML Construct Descriptions in OWL Documentation ...... 275
Table A-4. OWL Class Construct Descriptions in OWL Documentation .............. 276
Table A-5. OWL Property Construct Descriptions in OWL Documentation ........ 277
Table A-6. RDF(S) Property Domains and Ranges ................................................. 278
Table A-7. OWL Property Domains and Ranges .................................................... 279

# List of Figures

Figure 2-1. Representing Information using a Language...... 14
Figure 2-2. Sir Tim Berners-Lee...... 17
Figure 3-1. Knowledge Base...... 26
Figure 3-2. Gruber Ontology Definition...... 28
Figure 3-3. Representation Building Blocks...... 32
Figure 3-4. Relationships between Building Blocks...... 34
Figure 3-5. Individual/Class Relationship...... 35
Figure 3-6. Individual/Property Relationship...... 35
Figure 3-7. Class/Property Relationship...... 36
Figure 3-8. Taxonomical Hierarchy of Classes...... 38
Figure 4-1. Semantic Web's Layered Architecture...... 44
Figure 5-1. Symbol/Reference Layer...... 49
Figure 5-2. Types of URIs...... 51
Figure 5-3. URIref Fragments Identify Portions of Resources...... 55
Figure 6-1. Transport/Syntax Layer...... 61
Figure 6-2. Markup Language Evolution...... 62
Figure 6-3. Sample Menu...... 63
Figure 6-4. XML Schema Datatypes used in OWL (graphical view)...... 72
Figure 7-1. Basic Relational Language Layer...... 75
Figure 7-2. RDF Statement Components...... 81
Figure 7-3. RDF Model View...... 82
Figure 8-1. Basic Relational Language Layer...... 83
Figure 8-2. RDF/XML Statement Options...... 87
Figure 8-3. TypedNode Syntax Abbreviation...... 94
Figure 8-4. Example li to Numbered Property Translations...... 98
Figure 8-5. Example List Structures...... 105
Figure 9-1. RDFS Portion of the Ontological Primitive Layer...... 111
Figure 9-2. Subclass Transitivity...... 119
Figure 10-1. Logical Layer...... 133
Figure 10-2. Dr. James Hendler...... 134
Figure 10-3. Species Relationships...... 140
Figure 11-1. Ontology Language Layer...... 143
Figure 11-2. Imports and Namespace Dependency Relationships...... 144
Figure 11-3. Ontology File Structure...... 146
Figure 11-4. versionInfo Property...... 152
Figure 11-5. priorVersion Property...... 154

## Table of Contents

Figure 11-6. backwardCompatibleWith Property ..................................................155
Figure 11-7. incompatibleWith Property ............................................................157
Figure 11-8. Imports Relationship .....................................................................161
Figure 11-9. Transitivity of Imports ..................................................................163
Figure 11-10. Header Concepts..........................................................................165
Figure 12-1. Property Types...............................................................................169
Figure 12-2. OWL Lite Classes and Properties ....................................................174
Figure 13-1. Functional Property......................................................................175
Figure 13-2. InverseFunctionalProperty .............................................................178
Figure 14-1. Intersection....................................................................................201
Figure 14-2. OWL Lite Derived Classes ..............................................................202
Figure 15-1. Individuals Portion of the Ontological Primitive Layer ..................203
Figure 15-2. Constructs for Describing Individuals.............................................214
Figure 16-1. OWL Concept Type Separation Taxonomy......................................217
Figure 17-1. Ontology Languages Layer.............................................................221
Figure 17-2. Class Expression Components........................................................224
Figure 17-3. Complement of a Class...................................................................231
Figure 19-1. OWL Dialects ................................................................................242
Figure 19-2. OWL Extends RDF ........................................................................247
Figure 19-3. RDF Document Relationships........................................................248
Figure 20-1. Application Layer..........................................................................249
Figure 20-2. Use Case Data Flow Diagram .........................................................250
Figure 20-3. Hours of Operation Ontology.........................................................251
Figure 20-4. Compliant Data Relationship to Ontology .....................................255
Figure 20-5. Sample Open Hours ......................................................................256

x

# Section 1

# Semantic Web Overview

Section 1 – Semantic Web Overview

---

Section 1 provides an overview of the Semantic Web. It provides context and introduces terminology and concepts. This section provides a foundation before discussing specific language constructs.

Chapter 1 – Current Web – provides historical context on the current web, and describes its features and shortcomings.

Chapter 2 – Semantic Web – describes the challenges of representing information on the web, requirements for a satisfactory solution, and how the Semantic Web satisfies these requirements.

Chapter 3 – Ontologies – defines the concept of ontologies, describes their purposes, and describes semantic relationships, ontology features, and ontology languages.

Chapter 4 – OWL Introduction – introduces the Web Ontology Language, its features, the Semantic Web's layered architecture, and the technologies that support OWL.

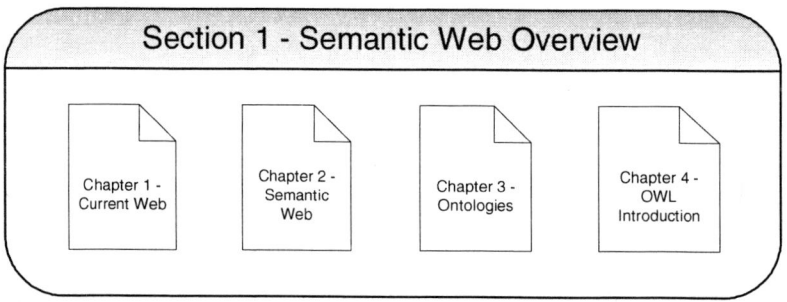

> "The Internet? Is that thing still around?," Homer Simpson, The Simpsons, Episode "Thirty Minutes Over Tokyo," original FOX air date 5/16/1999.

# 1 Current Web

In recent years we have witnessed an explosion of new capabilities on the World Wide Web. The World Wide Web is a relatively new technology that is continually maturing. A new evolution of the web, the Semantic Web, promises to deliver even more exciting applications. A description of the current web provides context for Semantic Web discussions.

The current web is fundamentally a publishing medium similar to a gigantic library. It is currently dominated by pages marked up using the Hypertext Markup Language (HTML). These pages are accessible using Uniform Resource Locators (URLs) (e.g., "http://www.w3c.org"). The current web primarily supports human readers that use browsers (e.g., Internet Explorer) to access and display the HTML pages.

This chapter describes the current web in terms of its history, characteristics, and shortfalls.

## 1.1 Current Web History

The Defense Advanced Research Projects Agency (DARPA) helped pioneer the Internet infrastructure. Early adopters of Internet technology struggled with cumbersome user interfaces and tools. Limited applications took advantage of the newly networked systems. Then, Tim Berners-Lee developed the Hypertext Transfer Protocol (HTTP) and Hypertext Markup Language (HTML). He pioneered the current web by marking up text using HTML and serving up files using HTTP from servers connected on the Internet. Adoption of these technologies occurred at an amazing rate and Berners-Lee's contributions were recognized in 2004 with knighthood. Encoding information into HTML syntax was a critical step in supporting the web's initial focus of providing simple structured documents connected with hyperlinks.

Section 1 – Semantic Web Overview

The evolution of the current web represents one of the most significant technological achievements in history. The standardization of protocols (e.g., TCP/IP) and languages such as HTML and the Extensible Markup Language (XML) enabled a technological revolution because interoperability was guaranteed at various levels of the web's layered network architecture.

The web became a "killer app" by adding hyperlinks to documents and allowing easy sharing of information. The availability of word processing software allowed everyone to become an author. The web allowed everyone to become a publisher. This led to exponential growth in available content as HTML files were populated on the web.

Despite its already incredible history, the web continues to mature and evolve. It is still a relatively new technology that has potential for moving beyond humans reading documents in browsers.

## *1.2 Current Web Characteristics*

The current web has been described from a variety of perspectives. It has become so ubiquitous that we often forget how quickly we have come to rely on it to access information, perform transactions, and communicate. Characterizing the web are its features, benefits, and supported applications.

### 1.2.1 Current Web Features

The current web is primarily a diverse document-centric set of distributed hyperlinked HTML pages that form a virtual repository of information. The decentralized content of the web's millions of pages is constantly growing as new content is added. Geographically-dispersed authors generate and maintain these pages using simple authoring tools without a central controlling authority. Software automatically generates some web content "on-the-fly" from databases. The communication of HTML pages is enabled by open standards, many of which are managed by the World Wide Web Consortium (W3C). HTML pages can be viewed using browsers on a variety of devices almost anywhere at any time. These pages are primarily intended for human access and reading.

## 1.2.2 Current Web Benefits

The web became popular quickly because it fulfilled users' needs and provided them with benefits. The web's approach to sharing information was far superior to using private networks and point to point interfaces. The web reduced information access time and transaction times. The web made transactions cheaper (through self-service) and virtually eliminated the costs of communicating hypermedia to the world. Many communities benefited from the web. For example, the open source movement was empowered by web technology, resulting in lower application development costs and an early web-like philosophy of sharing information.

## 1.2.3 Current Web Applications

Most web content developers target their information for direct human processing (reading). For the most part, the web is a medium where HTML documents are served up to browsers so that they can be read by humans. The current web is like a huge global library of documents available for reading.

Human users access web information for a variety of purposes (e.g., e-commerce, recreation, education). The current web's features and benefits have resulted in the development of a variety of applications including transaction-related applications (e.g., financial services, on-line stores and auctions), access to multimedia repositories and sharing (e.g., pornography, music), and communicating information and advertising (e.g., prescription drug sites).

A variety of technologies are used to generate content in the current web. Relatively few HTML pages are still generated by hand. Most web sites are created using authoring tools. Many HTML and XML documents, especially those associated with the large e-commerce sites, are generated from databases.

The web has enabled communication and collaboration among diverse communities and is an incredible success based on the number of available HTML documents and the number of human browsers.

Section 1 – Semantic Web Overview

## 1.3  Why the Current Web is not Enough

Although the current web is truly incredible, it does not provide enough structure to support advanced computer processing of content. We increasingly depend on the web to manage our lives and our businesses. However, not enough of the information on the web is connected to other information to allow for complex queries or updates of information. We need better information representations on the web to enable more advanced applications.

The current web's simplicity enabled its growth. HTML documents are easily authored with few constraints on document syntax. However, this simplicity results in too much variation for efficient software access. So far, people and software have been primarily marking up HTML documents with formatting instructions. What is needed is accompanying information that explains the meaning (semantics) of the information. Semantics are required for efficient automated interpretation of structured web content. The current web can be improved with structured information, metadata for finding information, and explicit semantics.

### 1.3.1  Information Must be Structured

The current web is too document-centric to support information representation. The bulk of the information currently shared on the web is semi-structured HTML documents containing free-form (i.e., unstructured) text. While this publishing process is very effective for communicating to humans, it does not support distributing data and information representation for automatic processing by computers.

Natural Language Parsing (NLP) is a complex computational challenge. NLP is a relatively easy process for humans (albeit with ambiguity), but is very difficult for software. Therefore, rather than presenting HTML-formatted text to human readers, information must be represented in structured forms for computer parsers. Computers need carefully structured and well-designed information representations if they are to unambiguously interpret the information. The structured information contained in databases should be shared in a computer parseable manner.

The current web is a victim of its own success. Finding, creating, and maintaining information is a difficult problem with weakly structured information representations. Users can no longer easily navigate the web's exploding landscape. It must be terraformed to allow automated software agents to explore its expanses, prospecting for nuggets of information. By carefully structuring information, exciting new functionality is possible because software will be enabled to provide more sophisticated applications.

## 1.3.2 Finding Requires Metadata

The amount of information on the current web makes human searches and integration of information impractical. Sophisticated keyword search engines are available for the current web. However, it is difficult for search engines to provide a small set of relevant and complete responses.

There is a key difference between searching for popular uses of textual phrases (traditional approach) and finding specific answers to a person's questions (the goal). Search engines focus on finding candidate web documents that might contain the desired content. Search engines typically provide lists of hyperlinks rather than specific responses to queries. Query engines should "find" the answers to users' questions. For example, a user might want to "find" the lowest price for a serving of Key lime pie at restaurants within 5 miles. The user does not want to read through thousands of websites describing restaurants to identify the local restaurants and then look for menu items by reading the text on the web pages. Instead, a query engine should be able to filter for the restaurants within 5 miles, access their menus, compare the prices, and return the desired price.

A related problem with accessing information on the web is finding authoritative sources. Humans and computers alike need to have some level of confidence or "trust" in the answers that are returned. Software needs to explain how it derives answers. Just like students, query answerers need to "show their work".

Section 1 – Semantic Web Overview

### 1.3.3  Semantics Must be Explicit

Semantics provide a description of a concept's meaning. New techniques are emerging for providing encoded hints with information to help computers understand more about the described information. Exposing the semantics of information enables software to effectively manipulate the information. Computers need to be able to infer new facts (inference) instead of simply displaying the original inputs. Explicit semantics support integration by identifying opportunities for semantic joins. Semantic joins link multiple distributed information representations.

## 1.4  *Current Web Summary*

The current web is primarily a document-centric communication service focused on the needs of human readers using browsers. The web has provided incredible features and benefits that have changed our world. However, current web technologies are insufficient to support more sophisticated computing requirements.

New web technology is needed to structure information, improve searches, and expose the semantics of the information. Once these requirements are satisfied, exciting new applications become possible. Providing these applications is the purpose behind the Semantic Web. The next chapter introduces Semantic Web concepts.

> "The Semantic Web is not a separate Web but an extension of the current one, in which information is given well-defined meaning, better enabling computers and people to work in cooperation." Tim Berners-Lee, James Hendler, and Ora Lassila, "The Semantic Web", Scientific American, May 2001.

# 2 Semantic Web Introduction

The previous chapter described the web experience currently encountered by the vast majority of its users. A new evolution of the web is underway. The name given to this new web is the Semantic Web, a web that is empowered by structured information representations that are marked up to provide explicit semantics.

Imagine a web that contained information representations that supported new software applications that were previously impossible. The data and information we use to manage our lives and our businesses could be linked together to provide new services and finally help us realize the goal of computers performing complex tasks and answering difficult questions.

For example, imagine being able to query the web for a nearby restaurant that serves your favorite pie, and will be open for at least another hour.

This type of query requires joining together data and information that is currently located in disparate non-communicating islands of information. Although the desired answer may be obtainable, it would require extensive searching and reading.

The Semantic Web supports information representations that allow software to "connect the dots" and even inference additional information that is not already explicitly stated. The information representations to support the example use case above requires computer processable descriptions of information about restaurants and their hours of operation, locations, and menus.

Section 1 – Semantic Web Overview

This chapter describes web information representation challenges, requirements for a satisfactory solution, and Semantic Web high-level concepts that satisfy those requirements.

## 2.1  Web Information Representation Challenges

As the web continues to evolve and mature, an increasing amount of information is available to human readers and computer applications. This information enables new functionality, but also introduces significant information representation challenges. Resolving these issues will avoid a variety of problems if the right solutions can be developed. Existing challenges include the increased need for information representation, the ambiguity of human descriptions, and the specificity of software data structures.

### 2.1.1  Increased Need for Information Representation

The volume of knowledge and information that humans develop and record continues to grow. This has resulted in rapidly increasing amounts of information to represent and communicate. Along with growing amounts of information are growing expectations from users for access to information on the web. Satisfying these expectations requires additional web features over and above the features provided by existing HTML, database, and XML solutions.

### 2.1.2  Ambiguous Human Descriptions

Formats that humans use to represent information are as diverse as the humans that represent the information. Specialized domains are often used to categorize information. In addition to regional language differences, domains of expertise often sport their own terminology. It is difficult to gain widespread acceptance for a particular vocabulary. Standards organizations work tirelessly to reach consensus on terminology within their respective communities of interest. Domain specialists tend to define their own sublanguages.

Human expressivity and creativity result in difficulty standardizing on a common language for information representation. Heterogeneous knowledge representation is human nature. However, we can agree on using the same language for expressing languages (metalanguage).

Chapter 2 - Semantic Web Introduction

In order to support the information representation requirements of expressive humans, we need a set of language features that can represent information from a variety of domains.

### 2.1.3 Software Demands for Specificity

Computers require structure and consistency. Structured information eases the processing requirements and is especially necessary to perform inferencing operations. Inferencing is the process of taking multiple facts and deriving new information not previously explicitly provided. Software agents need computer-understandable information to perform complex applications.

Computers are typically intolerant of ambiguity and require context for the interpreted information representations. Despite the existence of technologies such as "fuzzy logic" that deal with ranges of values rather than exact matches, computers tend to be reduced to their base nature of requiring binary values. Software applications need consistent, well-formed, logical content.

## 2.2 *Requirements for a Web Information Representation Solution*

As new techniques for overcoming information representation challenges are developed, there are information representation requirements that must be satisfied. Consider these requirements from the perspective of humans and computers.

A major challenge in providing more expressive information representations on the web is balancing the tradeoff between supporting humans' needs for expressivity and software's need for specificity. Developing a web information representation solution involves compromising between the needs of humans and computers. Some requirements ease the burden on humans, while others simplify the job of computer software. A satisfactory solution requires minimizing human investment, satisfying computer requirements, and compromising between both sets of demands.

## 2.2.1 Minimizing Human Investment

From the human's perspective, information must be represented with minimal effort and cost. There are requirements associated with the two primary roles for humans: producers of information and consumers of information. There are also requirements common to both roles.

### 2.2.1.1 Information Representation Producers

Information representation producers typically provide content from existing sources (e.g., databases). Producers include software developers, web application developers, database developers (of databases that export content), and information maintainers. The goal of these producers is to effectively, quickly, and inexpensively generate information representations that will be useful for consuming applications.

Producers typically represent information about a particular domain. Producers often involve domain experts to create information representations for their domain. Domain experts should be able to represent information using natural human models of information. Efficient processes should support producers' information authoring tasks.

Different content authors should be able to support multiple parallel efforts to represent distributed information. Different people may describe the same concept differently. Existing representations should be extendable, enabling the addition of new content, rather than requiring content authors to reinvent or duplicate existing information representations. Leveraging previous investments in existing content (e.g., generating information representations from existing databases) helps minimize costs. Authors should be able to work with current web development and maintenance tools.

Human understanding of domains evolves, and the associated information representations must evolve and change as well. Information representations should be versioned and configuration managed just like software.

## 2.2.1.2 Information Representation Consumers

Information representation consumers are the humans that develop software that use the information. The goal of these consumers is to efficiently and inexpensively write quality software applications that can parse, interpret, and manipulate information representations

Software applications should be able to link information from various domains. Just as database tables are connected through "joins", information representations can be strung together through "semantic joins".

Traditionally, software engineers have studied a particular domain and then developed software interfaces to handle importing, processing, and exporting that domain's data. Software should be able to use others' data without understanding their internal data model a priori. The software that imports the information should reduce human intervention in searches and queries. Applications should be quick and easy for web application developers to implement.

## 2.2.1.3 Requirements Common to Both Producers and Consumers

Minimizing the cost to humans of implementing a new solution is an important objective. Therefore, the technology adoption requirements should not be oppressive. Acquiring the required skills and knowledge should represent a small barrier to adopting the new technology.

Both producers and consumers need easy intuitive ways to translate to/from a human's mental model and the information representation. Information representation approaches that leverage the current web will reduce the additional investments required for the information technology (IT) software infrastructure. The solution should be evolutionary, not revolutionary, because people have invested in their skills and knowledge. Semantic web solutions need to leverage existing web standards. By reusing existing web concepts for distributing information, the Semantic Web can provide important features without introducing new burdens on producers and consumers of information representations.

## 2.2.2 Satisfying Computer Requirements

Computers require specificity in information representations and need easily parseable formats and serialization techniques. The computer requirements include structured distributed representations to enable applications, and a supporting language.

### 2.2.2.1 Structured Distributed Representations Enable Applications

Computers excel at performing certain classes of formulaic repetitive tasks. Information structure is required to support efficient automated processing of content. For the Semantic Web to function, computers must have access to consistently structured collections of information and sets of inference rules they can use to conduct automated reasoning.

Information representations must be formal enough for software to detect inconsistencies and errors. Just as humans make contradictory statements in natural text, inconsistent statements are bound to occur, and must be identifiable.

Information representations will be distributed on geographically-distributed servers controlled by diverse authors of content. Distributing information over servers supports scalability. The current web communicates and distributes information. Just as its value grew as more sites were linked, the Semantic Web will become more valuable as information representations are connected.

### 2.2.2.2 Supporting Language Requirements

The largest barrier to software is not reasoning, but the fact that most information sources are not talking the same language. Content must be "marked up" according to a language standard for representing machine-processable information. The language can partially support the desired information representation features by defining explicit descriptive tags.

An information representation language supports many of the requirements for the Semantic Web. The language specifies interchangeable statements. As with any language, a variety of design tradeoffs must be considered. A satisfactory language would provide syntax, semantics, expressiveness, and standards.

## Chapter 2 - Semantic Web Introduction

A syntax is a set of rules for the format of a language. A formal syntax supports the markup information required to interchange information. The syntactical convention provides the format standardization required by automated parsers. The syntax should be open and vendor-neutral.

The semantics of information explain the meaning of concepts being represented. The Semantic Web needs a formal means of describing explicit semantic relationships. Standardized grammars containing modeling primitives and specifying relationships between the primitives can describe the semantics. The language should be formal, finite, maintained, and extensible.

Modeling primitives are simple information representation constructs that describe explicit semantics. They capture common knowledge representation idioms and serve as building blocks for defining domain-specific vocabularies. Examples of modeling primitives are concepts for representing classes and properties.

Expressiveness is the richness of a language for making statements. The Semantic Web's language for encoding vocabularies must be expressive enough to represent complex concepts and relationships.

A powerful feature needed to support the Semantic Web vision is inferencing. Inferencing enables the discovery of new facts from existing facts. Information representation must be sufficiently expressive to support inferencing. Expressiveness requirements include completeness, correctness, and efficiency. An issue with inferencing is that it introduces scalability issues because of the complexity of performing reasoning over huge amounts of distributed facts.

Standards document agreements on a common language. The language supporting the Semantic Web should leverage open standards. The existing web is supported by standard languages including HTML, used for formatting documents that are read by browsers that render documents for human viewing. Standardizing the language reduces the burden on tool development and increases the business case for tool developers by expanding their potential market of users.

Section 1 – Semantic Web Overview

## 2.2.3 Compromise

The Semantic Web's language must support producers and consumers through ease of use and expressivity capabilities, while at the same time being formal enough to support efficient software processing (see Figure 2-1).

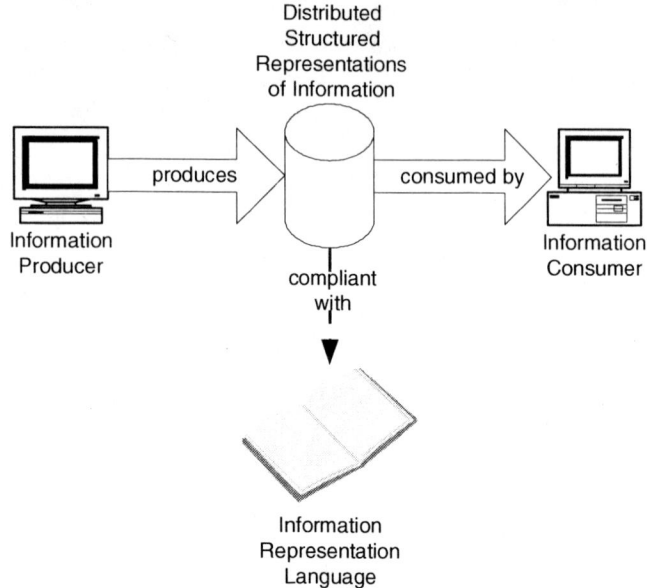

Figure 2-1. Representing Information using a Language

If we allowed humans to dictate their preferred solution, we would likely have most information represented using natural language. Nirvana in the Natural Language Processing world would be for software to be able to read and understand text documents such as the HTML documents currently presented on the web through browsers. However, this challenge is beyond our current state-of-the-art technology.

At the other extreme, information could be represented using formal data structures. Software easily interfaces with database and logic information representations. However, we do not want to require humans to use complex data structures that require extensive training to represent information.

# Chapter 2 - Semantic Web Introduction

The desired solution is a reasonable balance between expressivity and complexity that supports most of the information represented. Instead of using NLP, or requiring complex databases, we ask humans to perform some level of effort to translate their content into markup. However, they must see some return on investment (ROI) value proposition for their markup effort.

As the computer's needs for consistency and the human's needs for expressivity are weighed, tradeoffs must be made. These tradeoffs affect the complexity of information representations and the resulting scalability of applications.

## 2.3 Semantic Web to the Rescue

Semantic Web solutions have been proposed to meet the web information representation requirements described above. The following sections introduce the Semantic Web by providing the history, vision, implementation, use cases, and characteristics of appropriate applications.

Competing concepts for the Semantic Web have been proffered. Sir Tim Berners-Lee has described his concept of the Semantic Web as:

> *"A new form of web content that is meaningful to computers [that] will unleash a revolution of new possibilities."*

The Semantic Web is the next evolutionary generation of the web in which structured information representations provide explicit semantics. As in the current web, information is "marked up" according to language standards, distributed across servers, and is accessible by software that conforms to those language standards. However, the software that interprets, exchanges, and processes the structured information representations will provide new functionality because it will be able to understand and leverage the semantics of the information. The technologies that enable the Semantic Web focus on information representations tied to explicit meaning.

Section 1 – Semantic Web Overview

## 2.3.1 Semantic Web History

The term "Semantic Web" was popularized by Sir Tim Berners-Lee. As the inventor of the current web and in his role as director of the W3C, Berners-Lee's vision and perspective are highly valued and respected. Berners-Lee envisions a web that allows more advanced computer processing than the current web. To support his vision, many researchers have been working to make the Semantic Web a reality. Much of this research has focused on the supporting languages for describing meaning.

The United States Department of Defense (DoD) invested in Semantic Web research through its Defense Advanced Research Products Agency (DARPA) organization. DARPA was instrumental in early research that led to many of the Internet concepts that enable the current web. The primary DARPA contribution to Semantic Web technology has been the DARPA Agent Markup Language (DAML). DAML helped define critical Semantic Web concepts.

The European Union (EU) also saw promise in Semantic Web technology. The EU researchers saw the same potential as U.S. researchers in ontologies – explicit representations of information semantics. One product of EU research was the Ontology Interface Layer (OIL). Eventually, a Joint EU/US Committee on Agent Markup Languages merged many concepts from OIL with DAML to form a language called DAML+OIL.

The W3C initiated a Semantic Web activity to standardize a Semantic Web language. The W3C's Web Ontology Group focused on the standard language elements required to support the explicit semantics of the Semantic Web. Competing recommendations have coalesced into the Web Ontology Language – OWL, which was released in February 2004.

## 2.3.2 Semantic Web Vision

The Semantic Web is a vision for the next evolution of the web. As with many new technologies, the Semantic Web is proffered as the solution for many of the world's IT challenges. The Semantic Web is described as the next generation of the web. Some view the Semantic Web as a vast object-oriented distributed database with machine-understandable schemas.

## Chapter 2 - Semantic Web Introduction

Various communities envision aspects of the Semantic Web that will enable new functionality in their particular domain. For example, the e-commerce community anticipates simpler mechanisms for helping buyers find and purchase products.

The Semantic Web provides a world-wide web of interconnected machine-understandable information. It is envisioned as a single integrated knowledge base of web-sized proportions. Implementing this vision requires the integration of complex technology. However, most Semantic Web technology will be transparent to users. Software will perform new functionality that is enabled "behind the scenes" by the explicit semantics of distributed information marked up with the Semantic Web language.

One goal is to give users near omniscience over vast resources on the web, transforming existing database islands into a single virtual gigantic database of machine-understandable information. The Semantic Web will enable more "intelligent" applications by closing the gap between the humans' mental models and computer data models.

Sir Tim Berners-Lee (see Figure 2-2) published a Semantic Web road map creating his vision for a web of machine-understandable data, represented as web resources, that he called the Semantic Web. Berners-Lee shared his vision of the Semantic Web as part of an XML 2000 conference speech. His vision relies on structured information representations that enable computer understanding.

Figure 2-2. Sir Tim Berners-Lee

His dream involves not only linking documents, but also having software recognize the meaning of information in those documents.

The Semantic Web represents the next generation web, superseding the current HTML and XML-supported web. The current web grew exponentially as people saw the value of publishing HTML documents. As documents were linked together with simple unidirectional hyperlinks and they could be found through search engines, a value proposition emerged for authors of content.

# Section 1 – Semantic Web Overview

Similarly, as people begin to recognize the value of marking up their information using the Semantic Web language, more people will begin to provide their information on the Semantic Web. The Semantic Web involves a new form of web content that is meaningful to computers. It will unleash a revolution of new possibilities by making the Internet more useful by easing the burden on software to manipulate information.

High level features of the Semantic Web include leveraging the current web's infrastructure and providing connected, distributed, and structured knowledge bases that can be accessed and inferenced.

These features provide a variety of benefits to make information representation better, faster, and cheaper. The Semantic Web will enable new applications by providing functionality previously thought to be impossible. There are insufficient resources available to employ the human capital required to satisfy the ever-increasing expectations and demands for information using current web approaches.

New applications will remove expensive humans from "the loop". People will perform tasks faster with Semantic Web technology. For example, finding software will find content/answers, not just identify web pages that might contain the desired data. Users will no longer have to know how to skillfully navigate applications (e.g., finding lowest price of a restaurant menu item). A key goal of the Semantic Web is to reduce the cost of performing tasks.

## 2.3.3 Populating the Semantic Web

Implementing the vision of the Semantic Web will require the production of structured information that complies with representation standards.

There are several steps involved in developing information representations. These steps should include scoping the domain, performing a requirements analysis, defining terms and their relationships, encoding vocabularies and relationships using a Semantic Web language, and publishing the information representations on servers.

As with any IT system development, the most important phase of development is requirements analysis. Specify a list of items required in the information representation as the first step in making information available on the Semantic Web. Most domains have existing documents, IT systems, and domain experts that provide varying levels of domain descriptions. Whenever possible, harvest domain terms and their associated definitions from authoritative data sources.

The vocabulary terms and their relationships should be depicted graphically using languages such as the Unified Modeling Language (UML) to help visualize the model of the domain. Then, editors and other tools can generate the information representations from the design diagrams. Encoded information representations files are published like HTML or XML on distributed web servers. The information representations can be provided as static files, or served up dynamically using software and databases. Once Semantic Web content is available, it can be located, interpreted, and processed by consuming applications that leverage its explicit semantics.

The vocabularies described in the Semantic Web are called ontologies. Chapter 3 provides a full description of ontologies. A significant effort is required to develop ontologies and encode compliant information representations. However, this investment will ultimately yield returns that exceed the results currently produced from investments in current web technology. Also, as the number of standard vocabularies grows, reuse will result in cost reductions.

### 2.3.4 Use Cases

There are a variety of reasons for representing information on the web. Information representation is useless without consumption by software applications. A variety of applications are envisioned for the Semantic Web. Semantic web features described above enable applications that would otherwise be difficult or impossible to develop.

The Semantic Web is exciting because it enables new applications and functionality at both tactical and strategic levels. Tactical level functionality represents the lower-level functions that perform basic operations. Strategic level applications are higher-level functions that compose lower-level tactical features to provide a more complex set of functionality. Normally, end-users will interact with strategic-level applications that are empowered by tactical level functions.

Section 1 – Semantic Web Overview

## 2.3.4.1 Tactical Services

Semantic Web technology enables new low-level functionality. At the lowest level, the Semantic Web provides the capability to describe information and support inferencing of new information. Tactical-level services include describing distributed information, supporting queries, supporting searching and finding, and inferring new information.

The most basic feature of the Semantic Web is to provide a mechanism for structuring distributed information to enable efficient machine processing of the content. Markup language features standardize the structure of information representations. The real power of the Semantic Web will be realized when software can harvest web content from diverse sources, process information, and exchange results with other programs. Software will achieve a shared understanding by exchanging the semantics of the information.

Ultimately, many software applications involve supporting decision-makers by answering questions. Querying applications need to access information, perform inferencing, provide an answer to a question, and explain how it determined the answer. Connecting information through semantic joins helps answer questions by combining multiple sources of information. An example of a query is "which restaurants within 5 miles of my house offer Key lime pie on their menus".

Finding is a specific type of querying. A common activity on the current web is searching for information using keyword matching. The Semantic Web will support more intelligent searches instead of keyword matching. Traditional search engines rely heavily on text strings (syntax) matches to identify candidate documents and provide many responses with no concept of context. Semantic web finders are expected to return answers to questions, much like a database query returns values. Semantic Web-based finders will consider the semantics of the information.

One of the most exciting features of the Semantic Web is the ability to infer additional facts from provided facts. This software feature is enabled by representing information in a Semantic Web language that can be understood well enough to perform inferencing. Inferencing reduces the need to explicitly state all facts and greatly reduces the size and complexity of knowledge bases. The inferencing capability supports more sophisticated query processing.

## 2.3.4.2 Strategic Applications

Strategic applications are composed by leveraging the tactical applications described above. As the number of developed applications rises, design patterns will likely emerge. Strategic applications can be categorized as vertical applications, agent support, or information management.

Vertical applications provide specialized services to a particular domain. Perhaps the largest potential vertical applications will be in the e-commerce world (including business-to-business and business-to-consumer). Vertical applications will support a specific domain and likely will use information representations that describe a model of that domain. For example, a restaurant inventory application is a vertical application that supports restaurant management. A restaurant inventory application could benefit from knowledge (in the form of ontologies) about restaurant items such as supplies and menus.

Agent software refers to a broad class of software code characterized by specialized functions executed fairly autonomously and ideally mobile to different computing infrastructures. Agent support was an important initial motivator for DARPA's research. The intention of the Semantic Web is to enable software agent applications by providing agents with access to structured information with explicit semantics.

Agent software typically needs to find information, interpret information, and use the information to perform some functionality, and communicate a result. Agents also need to generate information that is usable by other agents. Often, agents are expected to be able to understand information, link it to related information, and perform inferencing.

Personal agents could support tasks such as financial management, travel planning, and shopping. An example of personal finance agent functionality would be to monitor stocks within certain screening criteria to alert an investor of a buying opportunity. A personal travel agent might scour descriptions of hotel rooms to help find accommodations close to a meeting location.

Section 1 – Semantic Web Overview

An example of a shopping agent function might be to look at menus, recipes and historical sales to negotiate purchases of food for the restaurant and arrange for e-purchase and delivery.

The United States Air Force is researching the applicability of Semantic Web representations for supporting transportation planning software using agents. Planning constraints represented in the United States (U.S.) Government's Foreign Clearance Guide (FCG) document are being represented using Semantic Web technologies and accessed by software agents to support planners. As agent technology continues to mature, the focus will shift from agent software and architectures to ensuring that usable information is available to agent software.

Information management involves being able to find, access, and use information. For example, an information management system might support restaurant recipes. By migrating intelligence from software into the explicit semantics of the information, generic software can be more intelligent and domain-agile. A goal in information management systems is to provide different functionality without modifying software. This is achieved through domain-agile software that leverages domain-specific ontologies. The Semantic Web will enable intelligent services that offer greater functionality than previously possible. Repositories of information can now be integrated that support "connecting of the dots" by integrating information.

## 2.3.5 Appropriate Applications

There is a temptation to succumb to the hype of any new technology rather than setting realistic expectations. It is important to focus on the set of appropriate applications for the Semantic Web. Semantic Web technology is appropriate for applications that: publish content targeted for both humans and computers; share information with others that may not understand the native information's semantics; and perform inferencing using the explicit semantics and "joins" of the information. Characteristics of appropriate applications include a well understood domain, heterogeneous information sources, and information interchange requirements.

An appropriate application should have a well-understood domain partitionable into object-oriented descriptive elements such as identifiable object classes, properties, and instances. Many domains will contain design patterns that will help to consistently represent the domain. Additionally, some domains have associated IT systems with databases of content that are often the source of data.

There should be authoritative data sources and domain experts to support descriptions of the model of a domain. Semantic web solutions are especially appropriate in situations with distributed, heterogeneous information sources. Semantic web information representations can serve as neutral Data Interchange Formats (DIFs). A DIF provides a single interchange format rather than requiring point to point interfaces for every combination of connected applications.

A picture is worth a thousand words. However, image processing technology is a complex application. Most information representation languages support textual descriptions. The interchange of text is straight-forward and lends itself to current Semantic Web information representations. Images are important and can be associated with textual descriptions through metadata.

## 2.4 Semantic Web Introduction Summary

There are a variety of challenges in representing information on the web. There are increased demands and expectations for making information available. Humans want to express their information in natural ways. However, software requires specific formal representations. A satisfactory solution to web information representation requires minimizing the investment that humans must make, while still satisfying computer demands.

The Semantic Web is an evolution of the current web that provides new information representation features. The Semantic Web will accomplish the vision of Sir Tim Berners-Lee for shareable data on the web that is both human and computer-understandable and will support a variety of applications.

The next chapter describes a key enabler for the Semantic Web – ontologies.

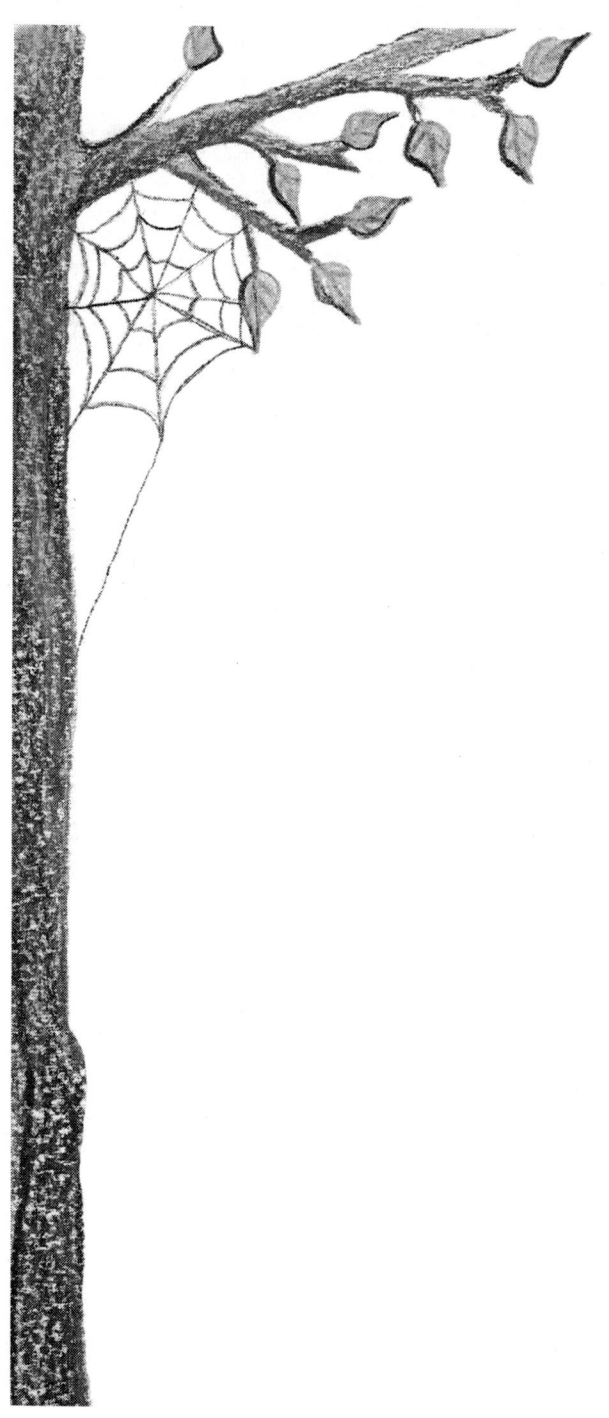

Section 1 – Semantic Web Overview

> *"The problem is not that there are no semantics, the problem is that the semantics is hidden in software components"*, Stefan Decker, quoted by Christopher Welty in *"Towards a Semantics for the Web"*.

# 3 Ontologies – Enablers of the Semantic Web

The Semantic Web requires explicit semantics that support machine processing of information. The concept of ontologies, which originated in the Artificial Intelligence (AI) community, enables the description of explicit semantics. This chapter describes ontology-related material including competing definitions, purposes of ontologies, development issues, description methods, ontology features, and language issues.

## *3.1 Ontology Definitions*

The term "ontology" is extremely overloaded and means something completely different to members of some communities. Historically, the term "ontology" originated in philosophy and metaphysics and referred to studies of the science of being. It dealt with the nature and the organization of reality. Historic ontology definitions described the abstract philosophical notions of what types of things exist. Ontologies provided definitive and exhaustive classifications of objects and their relationships in all spheres of being. Mathematical formalisms and classifications described these historical ontologies.

In defining the use of the term within the context of the Web Ontology Language – OWL, it is useful to consider the computer science community's use of the term, the various types of ontologies, and Thomas Gruber's definition.

### 3.1.1 Computer Science Definition

The computer science community uses the term "ontology" in the context of information sharing to refer to formal descriptions of particular domains. The AI community popularized ontologies for knowledge sharing and reuse. Computer science literature differentiates between terminological components (Tbox) and assertional components (Abox).

Section 1 – Semantic Web Overview

Tbox vocabularies define concepts that have associated Abox facts. The combination of Tbox vocabularies and Abox facts represent a knowledge base (see Figure 3-1).

The distinction between a Tbox and a set of conforming Abox instances is important in defining ontologies and their conforming instances because there is a similar distinction between Semantic Web ontologies and associated individuals.

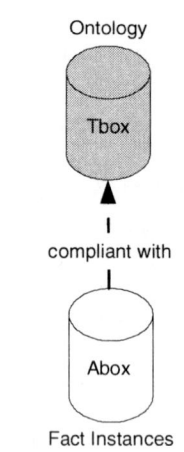

Figure 3-1. Knowledge Base

Computer science ontologies serve a similar function as database schemas by providing machine-processable semantics of information sources through collections of terms and their relationships. The semantics support a shared and common understanding of a domain that can be communicated between people and software. AI researchers often encourage maximizing the amount of knowledge in a system. Using ontologies reflects a fundamental change in emphasis from encoding information in software to encoding the information as data.

### 3.1.2 Types of Ontologies

There are many types of ontologies. AI literature describes major categories of ontology types including domain ontologies, metadata ontologies (e.g., Dublin Core), generic / common sense ontologies, representational ontologies (e.g., frame ontology), and method / task ontologies.

Certain ontology characteristics identify dimensions (e.g., formality, regularity) for describing the spectrum of ontology types. Dr. Deborah McGuiness, an ontology expert at Stanford University, has described a continuum of ontology formalisms. Ontology characteristic dimensions include shallow vs. deep, upper vs. domain, formal vs. informal, and regular vs. irregular. Ontologies also vary in terms of their formalisms, type of domain represented, and expressiveness. Characteristics of ontologies also include the target of the representation (i.e., human, computer) and the ontology's features.

The most common form of ontology is a taxonomy. A taxonomical ontology typically provides a hierarchy of concepts related with specialization ("is-a") relationships. A taxonomy is normally represented as a tree that has a single root node. Taxonomical trees are easier to understand and navigate than more complex information representation schemes. However, they lack the expressiveness needed to describe complex relationships.

### 3.1.3 Gruber Definition

A widely accepted definition of ontologies was established by Thomas Gruber:

> *An ontology is a "formal specification of a conceptualization" T. Gruber in "A Translation Approach to Portable Ontology Specifications", Knowledge Acquisition 5:199-220.*

An ontology specification is a formally described, machine-readable collection of terms and their relationships expressed with a language in a document file. A conceptualization refers to an abstract model of a domain that identifies concepts. Figure 3-2 shows the relationship between a represented domain, conceptualization model, and an ontology specification.

### 3.1.4 OWL-Specific Ontology Definitions

This text describes ontologies in the context of the Web Ontology Language - OWL. The OWL documentation set (see Section 10.1.3) describes the OWL concept of ontologies. According to the OWL documentation, ontologies provide a means to define classes, properties, individuals, and relationships between them.

The ontology definition in this text extends Gruber's definition and focuses on the Tbox (non-instance) specification parts of OWL ontologies. Therefore, the term "ontology" in this text represents:

> *An OWL-encoded web-distributed vocabulary of declarative formalisms describing a model of a domain.*

Section 1 – Semantic Web Overview

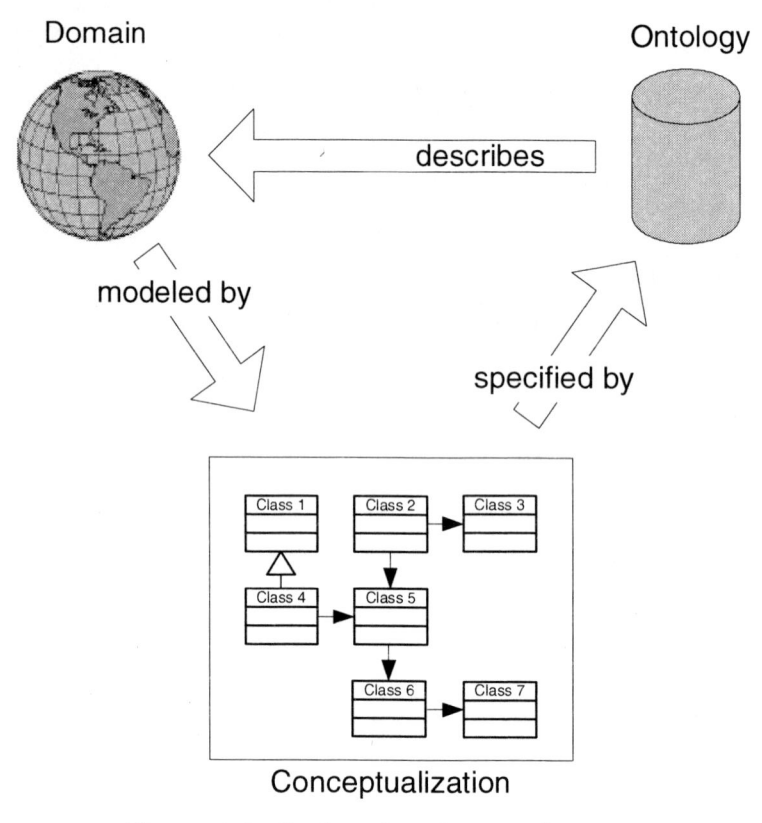

Figure 3-2. Gruber Ontology Definition

Ontologies are *distributed* on *web* servers governed by web standards. They are *vocabularies* that *declare* a set of specific terms with *formal* definitions. The definitions *describe a model of a domain*. Ontologies are *encoded* into files using the Web Ontology Language – OWL.

A domain is a specific subject area or area of knowledge that is typically the focus of a particular community of interest. An ontology defines the terms used to describe and represent (model) the domain. An important distinction must be made between a domain, and a model of a domain. For example, a flight simulator's software encodes a model of the world, not the world itself. Similarly, an ontology enodes a description of a simplified model of a domain, rather than the domain itself.

## 3.2 *Ontology Features*

Ontologies communicate a common understanding of a domain, declare explicit semantics, make expressive statements, and support sharing of information.

### 3.2.1 Common Understanding of a Domain

Various communities of interest provide authoritative descriptions of their domain. For example, a restaurant association might describe the relationships between the various types of menu items. A common understanding helps support consistent treatment (by humans and software agents) of the information associated with the domain.

The intention of ontologies is to reduce misunderstandings by formally describing terminological concepts and their relationships that describe a domain. Domains can be modeled in a variety of ways and at varying levels of resolution. An ontology formally documents one common understanding of the domain.

Ontologies provide a shared and common understanding of a domain communicated between people and heterogeneous and distributed application systems. An ontological representation defines semantics independent of the reader and context.

### 3.2.2 Explicit Semantics

Semantics are the formal descriptions of terms and their relationships that support machine understanding. Traditionally, information semantics have been hidden and hard-coded within software or proprietary database schemas. Explicitly defining semantics reduces ambiguity, resulting in a simpler process for software developers to code applications that understand and integrate information.

Explicit semantics document a domain's concepts with modeling primitives and semantic relationships. Modeling primitives are the building blocks for providing explicit semantics. The semantic relationships exist among and between the modeling primitives to make expressive statements about the domain model.

Section 1 – Semantic Web Overview

Explicit semantics enable software (e.g., web applications, intelligent agents) to understand information, make domain assumptions explicit, reduce interpretation ambiguity, and enable interoperability.

Explicit semantics move toward formalisms just as mathematics provides a concrete mechanism for dealing with numbers. It is difficult to describe the meaning of terms in a manner that is machine-understandable. However, it is fairly straightforward to define simple categories of concepts and to relate concepts to each other.

### 3.2.3 Expressiveness

The expressiveness of an information representation is the extensiveness of the description. Expressive statements are needed to provide a useful domain description. Information representation statements must be sufficiently expressive to enable software interpretation. An expressive language is also needed by humans. An ontology provides markup about content assertions. The language must be expressive enough to represent formal semantics and have known reasoning properties to support efficient inferencing. Statements must support canonical granular representations, but be limited to keep reasoning decidable and scaleable.

### 3.2.4 Sharing Information

Ontologies also support sharing, using, and reusing information. Ontologies support sharing by describing a domain with explicit semantics that support expressing statements. Because OWL-compliant software can interpret ontologies, they can accurately manipulate the information internally and interoperate with other software. They enable semantic mapping between information sources.

A prerequisite to sharing is using the same language and having access to the information. To share information effectively between heterogeneous IT systems, semantics are needed to assist in interpretation. By sharing an ontology, applications should have a shared understanding of conforming information.

## 3.3 Ontology Development Issues

Historically, the emphasis in systems development has been on the software that encodes functional processing. However, data is becoming increasingly important as a sharable resource that enables communication. Developing ontologies requires authoring ontologies, separating ontologies from individuals, and ontological commitment.

Communities of interest are best suited to represent their domains. Often, ontologies spawn from grass-roots efforts within a community of interest. Domain specialists might be professional groups, subject matter experts, or other organizations that share expertise in a particular area. The current web has enabled geographically disparate groups to form virtual communities of interest. Often these groups have their own sublanguage. Although there is nothing wrong with an individual developing their own ontology, the best ontologies result from consensus-based standards development groups. These groups leverage the expertise of their collective domain experts. Their content is best organized and formalized using consistent terminology. Ontologies that describe a particular domain are sometimes referred to as vertical ontologies. Upper ontologies are horizontal ontologies that span multiple domains and describe basic concepts. Vertical ontologies can extend the concepts from upper ontologies that serve as a common mapping point.

It is normally preferable to separate ontologies from associated data about conforming individuals. However, at times it is necessary to include data about individuals in an ontology. Individuals are sometimes required to help define a class, and are therefore inseparable from their ontologies. For example, assume there are two classes: "IceCream" and "Flavor". If "Vanilla" is a member (rather than a subclass) of a "Flavor" class, then it may be needed to define the class "VanillaIceCream". However, the best practice is to define ontologies separately from individual instances whenever possible.

Software applications and agents use ontologies to support their functionality. By examining the ontology, the software can better interpret the related data about individuals. When software uses a particular ontology, it is said to "commit" to that ontology. Ontological commitment using the semantics from the ontology to interpret conforming individuals. Committing to the ontology supports a common interpretation of individuals and resulting reasoning.

Section 1 – Semantic Web Overview

Software developers make certain assumptions when they develop their applications. All data-intensive applications commit to either an implicit or explicit ontology. Processing data without committing to a particular explicit ontology is simply manipulating data. By committing to an explicit ontology, an application is easier to understand, modify, and reuse.

## 3.4 Describing Semantics

Ontology language constructs are required to describe semantics. Ontologies express semantics by defining information representation building blocks, describing relationships between building blocks, and describing relationships within building blocks.

### 3.4.1 Information Representation Building Blocks

Rich modeling primitives are needed to precisely specify defined terms. One method for describing ontologies is with building blocks that represent class constructs, property constructs, and individual constructs (see Figure 3-3).

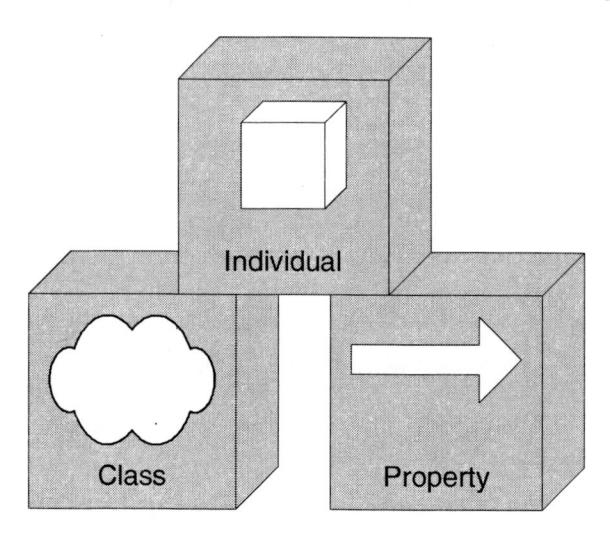

Figure 3-3. Representation Building Blocks

These constructs can describe a model of a domain. Each type of building block requires a computer understandable representation and identifiers for referencing these representations.

#### 3.4.1.1 Class Construct

The ontological class concept is related to the object class concept in object-oriented programming (OOP) and tables from Relational Database Management Systems (RDBMS). Objects in the "real world" can be categorized into groups or sets of objects with similar characteristics.

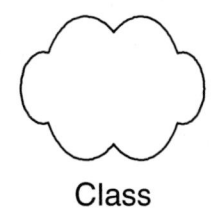

Similarly, individuals can be "binned" into class sets. Classes represent a group of object instances (individuals) with similar properties (implicit or explicit). A class is a conceptual set with some describable commonality. By grouping objects into ontological classes, general statements can include all the class's member objects at once. Examples of classes could include "Food", "Menu Item", "Person", "Pie", and "Restaurant".

#### 3.4.1.2 Property Construct

The ontological property concept associates attribute/value pairs with instances. A property is a binary association that relates an object (instance) to a value. The value might be a simple data value or an object. Examples of properties include "price", "size", and "name".

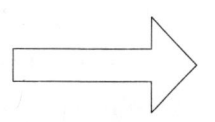

Properties provide attributes for individuals. They are similar to the accessor methods in object-oriented programming (OOP) that provide values from class objects or table columns (fields) from RDBMS. Unlike OOP methods, a property can be associated with multiple unrelated classes, rather than a single class. This leads to reusability of property descriptions.

### 3.4.1.3 Individuals

The ontological concept of individuals represents class object instances in the described domain. The treatment of ontological instances is similar to objects (class instances) in OOP or records from RDBMS. However, unlike objects in OOP, individuals are merely information representations and do not have associated functionality. Individuals can represent either physical things or virtual concepts.

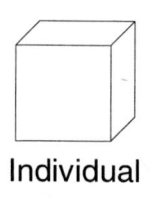

Examples of names of physical individuals include "Mark", "KnightOwlRestaurant", and "MyPieSlice". Examples of names of virtual individuals include "PhoneNumber", "Order456", and "Transaction123". It is often difficult to differentiate between individuals and classes. For example, "KeyLimePie" could be considered an individual instance of the "Pie" class, or a class in its own right with specific pies in a display case as its individuals. Individuals are typically specific "things" that have identity. Physical individuals are often "things" that you might be able to take a picture of if they are in the real world or represent with an icon if they represent a virtual concept. Literal values (e.g., "1", "Mark") can be considered a special case of individuals.

### 3.4.2 Relating Information Representation Constructs

In addition to describing classes, properties, and individuals themselves, we need to be able to describe relationships between them (see Figure 3-4).

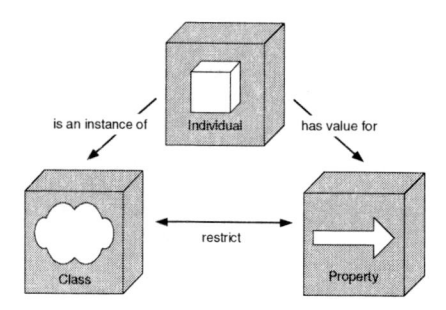

Figure 3-4. Relationships between Building Blocks

The most important inter-concept relationships include "is an instance of" (individual to class), "has value for" (individual to property), and restrictions (between classes and properties).

### 3.4.2.1 Relating Individuals to Classes

Individuals are the member object instances that make up classes. The membership ("is an instance of") relationship between an individual and a class that it belongs to must be explicitly stated. Since classes represent groups of individuals, an ontology must support the identification of a class's members (see Figure 3-5). For example, we might want to specify that "KnightOWLRestaurant" is an instance of the "Restaurant" class or that "Mark" is an instance of the "Person" class.

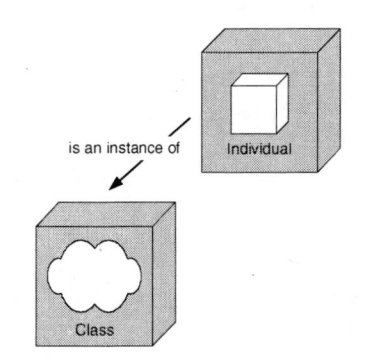

Figure 3-5. Individual/Class Relationship

### 3.4.2.2 Relating Individuals to Properties

Individuals have values described by properties. The "has value for" relationship between an individual and a property allows the specification of values for particular attributes of the individual (see Figure 3-6).

The individual's attribute is described by the property. For example, an individual might have a value of "$2" for the property "price".

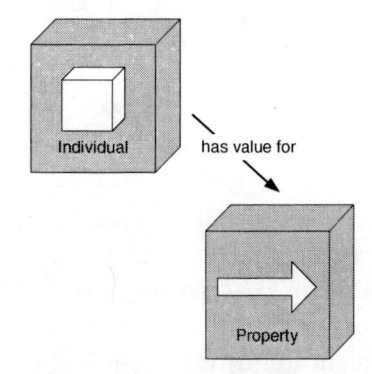

Figure 3-6. Individual/Property Relationship

### 3.4.2.3 Relating Classes to Properties

Whole classes of instances can have associated restrictions regarding their use of properties. Also, a property can be used to help define a class. The restriction relationship constrains the use of the properties with the class's individual members and the contents of a class based on a property's values (see Figure 3-7).

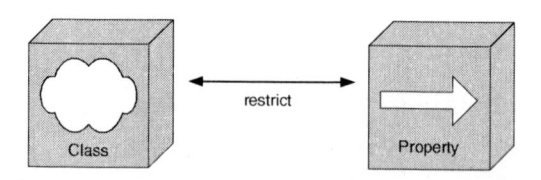

Figure 3-7. Class/Property Relationship

Properties may restrict classes by defining membership in a class. Property restrictions associated with classes may include restricting which classes can have which properties. Classes restrict properties because the use of the property may be constrained to being used with a particular class's individuals. Restrictions may constrain property values to be of a certain class (range) or to only describe particular classes (domain).

### 3.4.3 Semantic Relationships within Building Blocks

We also need a way to describe key semantic relationships within classes, properties, and individuals including synonymy, antonymy, hyponymy, and meronymy.

#### 3.4.3.1 Synonymy Relation

It is often desirable to specify that things are similar. The synonym relation connects concepts with similar meaning (synonyms). A stricter form of synonym is equivalence. Synonymous concepts have similar meaning, while equivalent items have identical values.

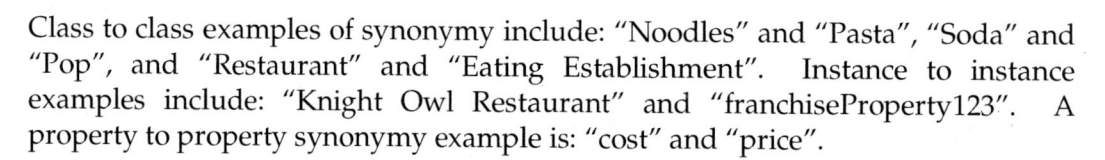

Class to class examples of synonymy include: "Noodles" and "Pasta", "Soda" and "Pop", and "Restaurant" and "Eating Establishment". Instance to instance examples include: "Knight Owl Restaurant" and "franchiseProperty123". A property to property synonymy example is: "cost" and "price".

36

Synonymy helps translate between different perspectives, cultures, and domains. It allows us to merge concepts and link heterogeneous knowledge bases. We often use analogous examples to introduce a concept to someone from another domain.

There is a subtle semantic difference between two items being *the same* and being *the same thing*. Two items can have the same meaning (synonymy) and two names can be used for the same thing (equivalence). Synonymy is a weaker relationship than true equivalence. The name "JoeSmith" might represent the same thing as "Restaurant123Owner".

Synonymous relationships can be specified between classes and other classes, properties and other properties, and individuals and other individuals.

### 3.4.3.2 Antonymy Relation

In contrast to synonymy, we often want to identify opposite concepts. The antonymy relationship identifies opposite concepts. The strictest form of antonymy is disjointness, in which an item cannot be an instance of both of the disjoint items.

Examples of class to class antonymy are "Regular Priced Menu Item" and "Sale Priced Menu Item". The antonymy relationship of oppositeness establishes a contrast or a clear dichotomy of meaning between terms. Antonyms can be specified between classes to other classes, properties to other properties, and individuals and other individuals.

### 3.4.3.3 Hyponymy Relation

The hyponymy relation describes a specialization or generalization relation. It can create taxonomic hierarchies. Taxonomies are methods for describing classification relationships. For example, a taxonomy of menu items can be specified for a restaurant (see Figure 3-8).

Section 1 – Semantic Web Overview

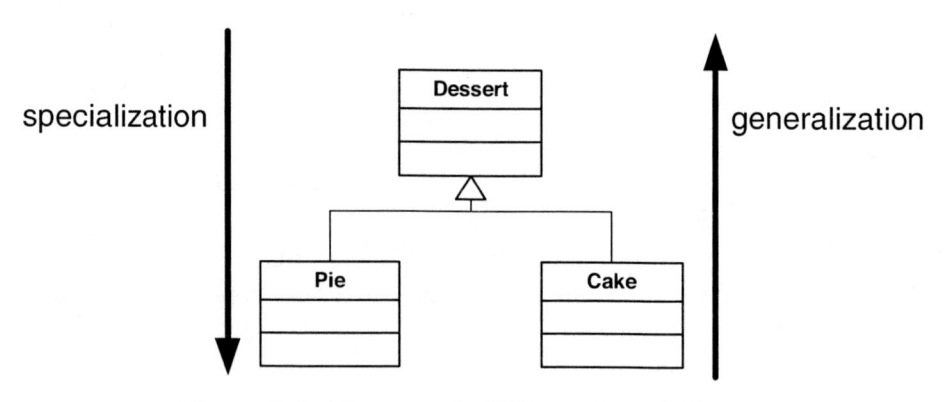

Figure 3-8. Taxonomical Hierarchy of Classes

Hyponymy is used to define "is-a" relationships, also referred to as inheritance, subsumption, generalization, and specialization. To subsume is to consider as part of a more comprehensive concept. The hyponymy relation identifies subordinate or specialization relationships.

---

Class to class example:

Spaghetti "is-a" Pasta
Key Lime Pie "is-a" Pie
New York Style Pizzeria "is-a" Italian Style Restaurant "is-a" Ethnic Restaurant "is-a" Restaurant

Property to property example:

salePrice "is-a" price

---

Hyponymy reuses or extends a concept by defining a generalization or specialization. Object-oriented programming frequently uses the relationship to provide inheritance. Subclass/subproperty relationships are related to object-oriented inheritance. Subclasses of classes can be defined. Hyponymy is a transitive relationship that relates classes to classes and properties to properties.

It is best to use hyponymy for permanent relationships rather than a dynamic role (e.g., Sale Priced Item). Dynamic role relationships are best described with properties.

### 3.4.3.4 Meronymy/Holonymy Relation

Another natural information representation concept is aggregation/composition. We naturally think of the parts that make up objects. The meronymy relationship defines a composition or a part-of relationship by relating parts to wholes. Mereology is the formal theory of part-whole relationships. The inverse (opposite) of the meronymy relationship is holonymy. Holonymy relates wholes to parts (see Figure 3-9).

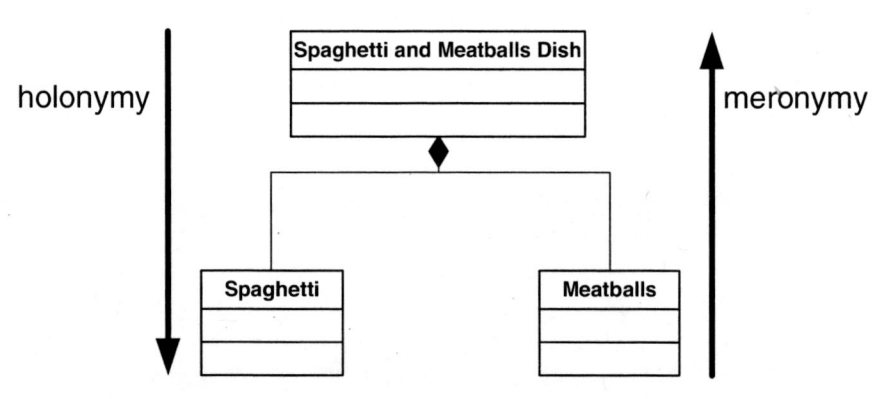

Figure 3-9. Meronymy and Holonymy

Class to class examples:

Meatball "part-of" Spaghetti and Meatballs Dish
Dish Price "part-of" Menu Item
Fork "part-of" Place Setting

Individual to individual examples:

Part 123 "part-of" Subassembly 456
Drink Order 321 "part-of" Restaurant Bill 789

Meronymy defines components and is closely related to ownership. The meronymy relationship is transitive. Meronymy and holonymy relate clases to classes and individuals to individuals.

### 3.4.4 Semantics Summary

The explicit semantics used to describe an ontology include the information representation building blocks (see Table 3-1) and semantic relationships (see Table 3-2).

Table 3-1. Information Representation Building Blocks

| Construct | Description |
|---|---|
| Class | The class construct represents a group or set of individual objects with similar characteristics. |
| Property | The property construct associates attribute/value pairs with individuals or restricts classes. |
| Individual | The individual construct represents a specific object instance of a class. |

Table 3-2. Semantic Relationships

| Functionality | Relationship | Summary Concept |
|---|---|---|
| Relating Building Blocks to each other | Relates individuals to classes | Membership |
| | Relates individuals to properties | Attribute values |
| | Relates classes with properties | Restrictions |
| Describing Relationships | Synonymy | Similarities |
| | Antonymy | Differences |
| | Hyponymy | Specialization |
| | Meronymy | Part/Whole |
| | Holonymy | Whole/Part |

## 3.5  Ontology Languages

Ontologies are represented in formal languages to make them parseable and understandable by software. An ontology is expressed as a set of definitions for a formal vocabulary. One goal of an ontology language is to define semantics in a way that is independent of the reader and the context of the situation. Ontology languages normally must support some level of logic expression. OWL is not the first or only language for describing ontologies.

There are varieties of formal language techniques that can be used to describe ontologies. OWL is based on two of these types of languages that are described in the following sections on frame-based systems and description logics.

### 3.5.1  Frame-Based Systems

Frame-based systems have a long history in the computer science and AI communities. Frames are an easy to use technique where the modeling primitives are classes (i.e., frames) with properties called slots. The values of the frame slots are called fillers. Frame slots are applicable only to classes. The same slot name can be used with other classes (with different range and value restrictions). Frames are similar to object-oriented classes with attributes.

### 3.5.2  Description Logics

Description Logics (DLs) are a mature knowledge representation technique influenced by frame system technologies. DLs have classes (called concepts) and properties (called roles). Sometimes, DLs are referred to as terminological logics or concept languages. DLs represent a class of logic-based knowledge representation formalism that balances expressiveness with decidability.

DL concepts are defined with membership constraints of objects based on their properties. DLs provide formal descriptions of semantic networks. They describe knowledge in terms of concepts and role restrictions used to automatically derive classification taxonomies

DLs use a set of domain-independent primitives to construct object descriptions. They define higher-level terms (e.g., "hasPrice") from epistemological primitives. DL features specify class constructors, property constructors, and axioms that relate classes and properties.

DL languages allow construction of composite descriptions, including restrictions on the binary relationships (usually called roles) connecting objects. DLs have well-defined formal semantics and can be used for performing inferencing.

DLs are very expressive through their use of first-order logic, yet are still decidable and support efficient inferencing. Decidability involves the theoretical issue of whether software can reach a conclusion when processing a description.

## 3.6 Ontologies Summary

Various communities have defined concepts of ontologies. Definitions come from historical use, the computer science / AI community, Thomas Gruber, the OWL documentation, and this text.

The purpose of ontologies is to communicate a specification of a domain, declare explicit semantics, and support information sharing. There are different types of ontologies, with taxonomical styled ontologies being the most common. It is important to differentiate between the terminological (Tbox) and assertional (Abox) portions of an ontology. Software commits to an ontology.

Semantic building blocks are the class, property, and individual constructs. Relationships between these constructs include defining individuals of a class, providing attribute/value pairs for individuals, and restricting properties for certain classes. The necessary semantic relationships include synonymy, antonymy, hyponymy, meronymy, and holonymy. The resulting ontologies are described using ontology languages.

The next chapter introduces the Web Ontology Language – OWL.

> "OWL is an important step for making data on the Web more machine processable and reusable across applications," said Tim Berners-Lee, W3C Director, in a 8/19/2003 W3C press release.

# 4 OWL Introduction

The current web has deficiencies that will be overcome with the Semantic Web. A language is required to describe the ontologies that enable the Semantic Web. The Web Ontology Language – OWL is a language for defining ontologies and associated individual data. Frame-based reasoning systems, Description Logics, and existing web languages influenced OWL's development. OWL was developed to represent computer-parseable information.

This chapter provides an introduction to OWL in terms of its features and the Semantic Web's layered architecture.

## 4.1 OWL Features

Developers of OWL wanted to make the language intuitive for humans and to have sufficient expressive power to describe machine-readable content needed to support Semantic Web applications. OWL satisfies the Semantic Web's requirements of providing minimal investment of human producers and consumers and supporting software requirements for a language with explicit semantics.

The resulting OWL language is based on W3C standards and provides producers with information representation features to define their own ontologies and to extend others' ontologies. It supports expressive statements in a manner that supports scalability. OWL builds on XML and allows users to provide machine-readable semantic annotations for specific communities of interest.

OWL is used to make statements, called assertions, about classes, properties, and individuals. Assertions can be stated in a single ontology, or in a combination of multiple joined ontologies. In addition to explicit assertions, additional facts can be derived or logically entailed as a result of inferencing.

Section 1 – Semantic Web Overview

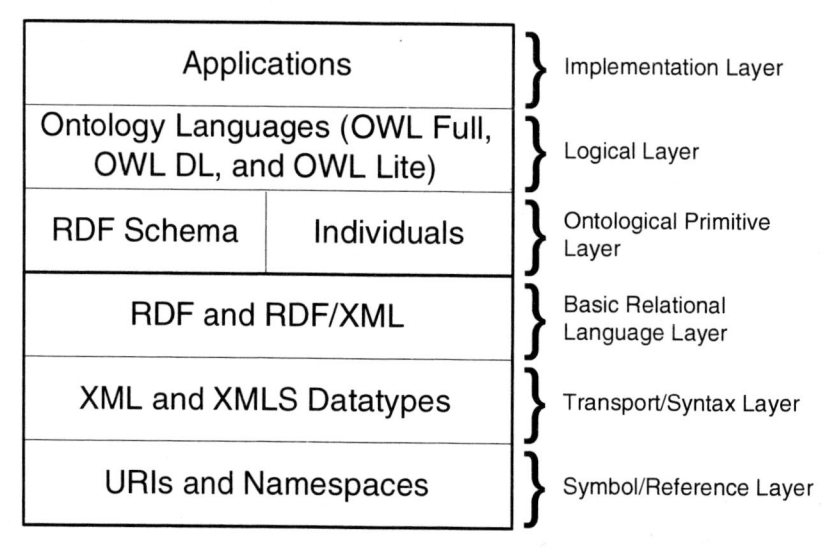

## 4.2  Semantic Web's Layered Architecture

While the current web focuses on supporting humans reading text, its infrastructure provides the opportunity for more sophisticated applications. One objective of OWL's developers was to provide layering of language features. OWL builds on open W3C web standards and can be viewed as part of a layered architecture with each increasingly powerful layer building on the layer below. Tim Berners-Lee defined an initial layered architecture view of the Semantic Web. Various alternative views of the layered architecture have since been developed.

Figure 4-1 presents one layered conceptual view of the Semantic Web. The layers shown are not true layers in the sense of networking models but illustrate rough dependencies. Each layer depends on the layers beneath and uses their features to provide its capability. The figure shows that the top layer, the implementation layer, provides specific applications. In the next layer down, the logical layer, OWL supports formal semantics and reasoning. Below OWL, the Resource Description Framework (RDF) Schema (RDFS) language supports the ontological primitives layer (defines a vocabulary). RDF supports the basic relational language layer through its simple data model and syntax for making statements. RDF is serialized using RDF/XML. XML and XML Schema datatypes support the transport/syntax layer, and Uniform Resource Identifiers (URIs) and namespaces support the symbolic / reference layer.

|  |  |
| --- | --- |
| Applications | Implementation Layer |
| Ontology Languages (OWL Full, OWL DL, and OWL Lite) | Logical Layer |
| RDF Schema / Individuals | Ontological Primitive Layer |
| RDF and RDF/XML | Basic Relational Language Layer |
| XML and XMLS Datatypes | Transport/Syntax Layer |
| URIs and Namespaces | Symbol/Reference Layer |

Figure 4-1. Semantic Web's Layered Architecture

44

## 4.3 Technology Support for the Layers

The diagram above is used in subsequent sections to orient the reader to the relative position of each layer as it is described. The technologies that support these layers are most easily understood from the bottom layer up to the top layer.

The symbol/reference (bottom) layer is used to provide symbols (identifiers) and references to the objects being described in ontologies and instance files. We achieve this through URIs and XML namespaces.

The next layer up is the Transport/Syntax Layer. XML is used to serialize the OWL syntax. XML is a metalanguage for specifying formats (syntax, but not semantics). XML Schema (XMLS) defines standard datatypes. XML uses Unicode for its character encoding, which supports multiple languages.

RDF provides the Semantic Web's basic relational language layer of data representation. It can be used to make statements with attribute/value pairs that describe objects.

RDFS provides the ontological primitive layer. RDFS is used to provide a standard vocabulary for data model items. This standard vocabulary describes RDF classes and properties. RDFS also provides semantics for subclasses and subproperties. Instances are defined using RDF. Property values of instances are specified using RDF syntax.

OWL dialects are ontology languages in the logical layer, used for specifying ontologies (classes, properties, and related restrictions). OWL is part of a series of related layers of standard languages standardized by the W3C.

The implementation layer represents the applications built using information represented with OWL. Applications leverage the OWL ontologies and associated instance data.

Eventually, additional layers may be added to the Semantic Web's layered architecture. These layers may support concepts such as rules and trust.

Understanding OWL requires familiarity with the "alphabet soup" of underlying technologies including XML, XML Schema datatypes, RDF, and RDFS. Section 2 describes these technologies.

Section 1 – Semantic Web Overview

## *4.4 OWL Introduction Summary*

OWL is the web ontology language defined by the W3C. OWL is used for making statements about classes, properties, and individuals. The Semantic Web is built on a layered architecture.

The sections that follow describe the enabling technologies that make up the Semantic Web's architecture layers.

# Section 2

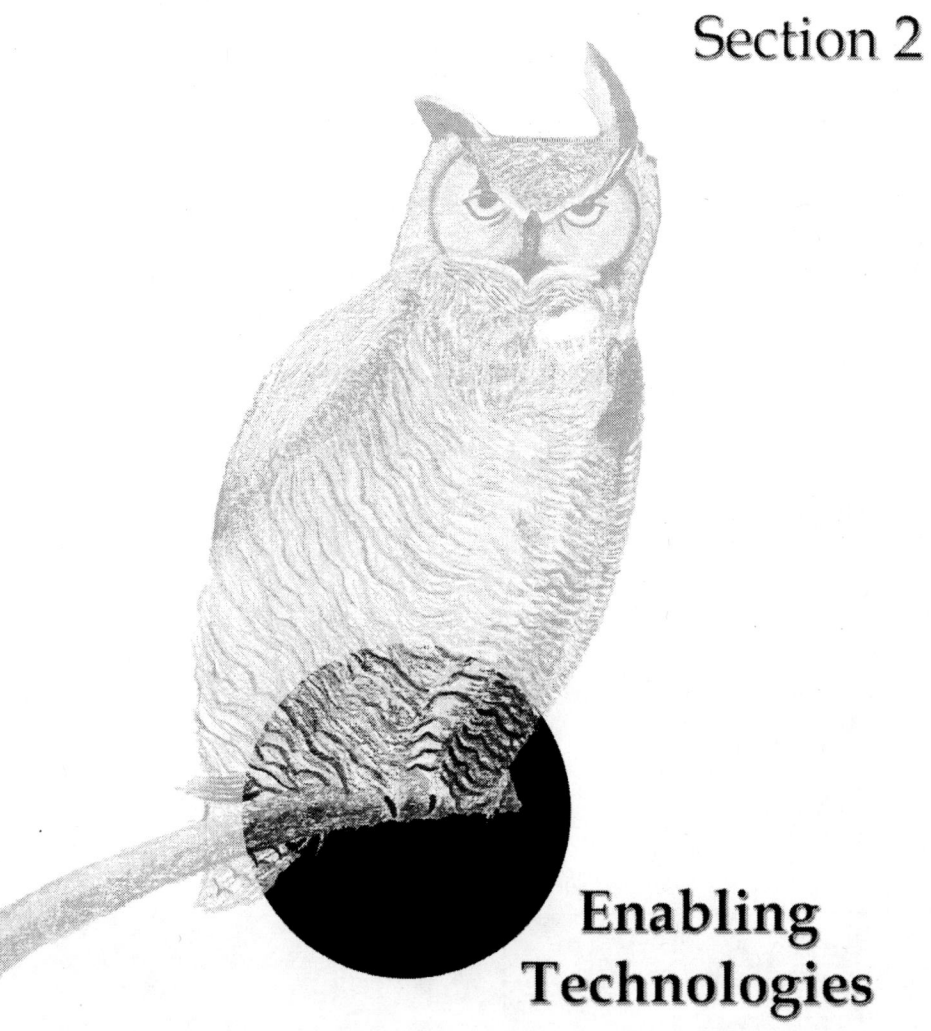

# Enabling Technologies

Section 2 – Enabling Technologies

---

Section 1 reviewed the state of the current web, the promises of the Semantic Web, and the need for ontologies. The Semantic Web's layered architecture was introduced. The current web is possible because content developers comply with a set of open standards that enable interoperability. Similarly, a set of layered open standards enable the Semantic Web.

Section 2 describes technologies that enable the Web Ontology Language – OWL.

Chapter 5 – URIs and Namespaces – describes absolute URIs, URI references, namespaces, and base URIs.

Chapter 6 – XML – provides an overview of the Extensible Markup Language and XML Schema (XMLS) datatypes.

Chapter 7 – RDF – provides an overview of RDF, describes its features, and explains the RDF data model.

Chapter 8 – RDF/XML – provides an overview of RDF/XML, describes the use of XML, and describes how to populate files with RDF/XML statements.

Chapter 9 – RDFS - provides an overview of RDFS, and describes its features, classes, and individuals.

Chapter 10 - OWL Language – introduces the OWL language and its three species.

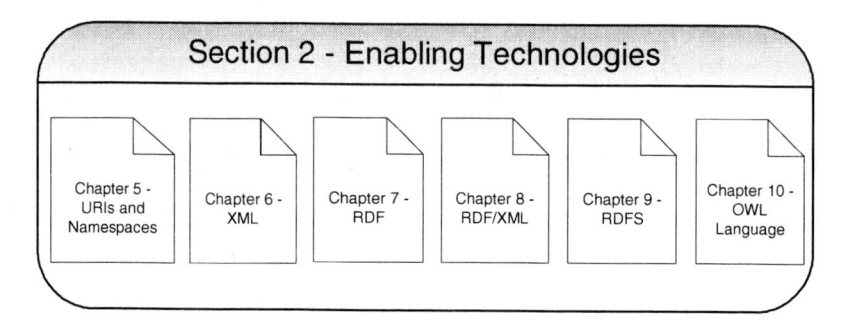

# 5 URIs and Namespaces

> *"Now the Lord God had formed out of the ground all the beasts of the field and all the birds of the air. He brought them to the man to see what he would name them; and whatever the man called each living creature, that was its name. So the man gave names to all the livestock, the birds of the air and all the beasts of the field."* Genesis 2:19-20a. NIV version

A basic tenet of the Semantic Web is the ability for anyone to name and describe anything. Uniform Resource Identifiers (URIs) and XML namespace features are used to reference information representation constructs. The lowest level of the Semantic Web's layered architecture, the symbol/reference layer, supports naming things in ontologies with URIs and namespaces (see Figure 5-1).

| Applications |          |
|---|---|
| Ontology Languages (OWL Full, OWL DL, and OWL Lite) ||
| RDF Schema | Individuals |
| RDF and RDF/XML ||
| XML and XMLS Datatypes ||
| URIs and Namespaces ||

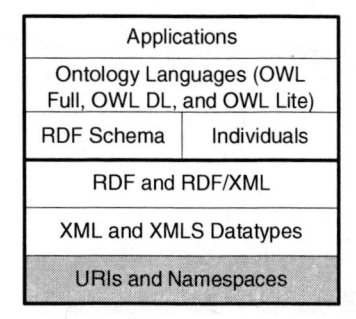

Figure 5-1. Symbol/Reference Layer

This chapter describes the standards that support naming things within RDF and OWL using absolute URIs, URI references, namespaces, and base URIs.

## 5.1 Absolute URIs

URIs enable the web by providing a naming scheme. In order to describe things, we first need a way to reference or identify them. Both the current web and the Semantic Web use URIs for this purpose.

The first exposure most people had to the current web was when someone gave them a Uniform Resource Locator (URL) to type into a browser. What they probably did not realize was that the web address was a URL and that URLs are a type of URI. In the last few years, URIs have become ubiquitous in our society.

A URI is a string of characters (text string) that identifies a resource and conforms to a particular syntax. The named resources can be anything (abstract or physical) that has identity.

Section 2 – Enabling Technologies

The authoritative standard for URIs is RFC2396 (see Table 5-1). RFC2396 differentiates between absolute URIs and relative URIs. An absolute URI is independent of the context of where we find the URI.

Table 5-1. URI Authoritative Description

| | Title: | **Uniform Resource Identifiers (URI): Generic Syntax (RFC2396)** |
|---|---|---|
| | Document URI: | http://www.ietf.org/rfc/rfc2396.txt |
| | Purpose: | Specifies the syntax for URIs |

An absolute URI has a scheme part and a scheme-specific part. The URI scheme defines the name space of the URI. A colon separates the scheme from the scheme-specific part.

---

The syntax of an absolute URI is:

**URIschemeName:scheme-specificPart**

Where **URIschemeName** is the name of the scheme being used and **scheme-specificPart** is the portion of the URI whose interpretation is based on the **URIschemeName** of the URI.

---

Examples of absolute URIs are:

http://www.KnightOwlRestaurant.com
isbn:0595307191
soap://www.visa.com/CreditCardService

---

The URI serves as the foundation of both the current web and the Semantic Web because of its use in identifying resources. The purpose of an absolute URI is to unambiguously specify a name (identifier) to represent something (a resource) in a standard (uniform) way. URIs identify information representation constructs, including classes, properties, and individuals. They provide uniformity, extensibility (an infinite set of names), and simplicity.

## Chapter 5 – URIs and Namespaces

There are different types of URIs, including URLs and Uniform Resource Names (URNs) (see Figure 5-2). The best known type of URI, a URL, identifies a resource with a character string that identifies its primary network access mechanism (acts as a locator). Both URIs and URLs can be independently used and created to identify things. However, they are different in key areas. URIs can name anything and do not have to be resolvable (does not have to have a network location). URLs are limited to identifying resolvable resources with network locations and normally identify document-level resources. A URN is another type of URI. URNs provide globally unique and persistent identifiers.

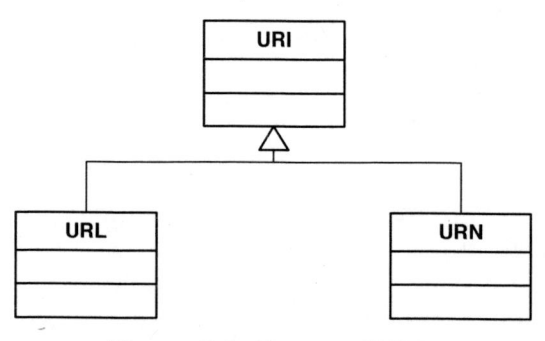

Figure 5-2. Types of URIs

Resources are the things identified by URIs. URIs can point to resources with resolvable network locations as well as things that are not machine-addressable. URIs are treated like logical constants (expressions interpreted as having a single value). Since an absolute URI is simply a name, it can refer to any type of resource imaginable including physical things and virtual things.

The first part of an absolute URI specifies a scheme. A variety of predefined URI schemes are used on the web with corresponding standard prefixes including: "esl", "http", "mid", "tag", and "vvid". URI schemes represent standard ways to interpret the scheme-specific portion of an absolute URI. The Internet Assigned Numbers Authority (IANA) manages some URI schemes. IANA provides central coordinating functions for the Internet.

Most people are familiar with the use of URLs in web browsers to retrieve HTML documents for rendering. While URLs must target network-retrievable resources, URIs in general can point to anything including non-retrievable resources.

# Section 2 – Enabling Technologies

Some people have used the URIs that represent web pages (URLs) to identify the subject of the website. For example, the Dynamics Research Corporation (DRC) website URL is "http://www.drc.com". However, that URI identifies the company's website, not the company. A better absolute URI might be constructed using a unique identifier like the company's federal tax identification number.

It is best to use separate URIs to identify the subject of a website and the website itself. A URI is simply a name, not directions on how to access information about the named resource.

The creation and use of URIs is not controlled. This provides a powerful flexibility. Just as anyone can publish a website, anyone can define a URI. People enjoy naming things (e.g., children, pets, hurricanes). Anyone, including people, organizations, and software can specify a URI. There is no centralized system for defining URIs. Although this independence in authoring URIs is a powerful concept, it can result in duplication. Another challenge is that more than one URI can exist for the same resource.

An important step in developing web sites is typically to design a tree structure of pages and assign URLs to each page. Similarly, it is important to carefully plan the assignment of URIs to resources. Whenever possible, consider using or adapting an existing scheme instead of creating a new scheme from scratch. For a resource associated with something described by your website, consider extending your Domain Name Service (DNS) managed URL that you use for your website to generate URIs. Also, consider placing documents and ontologies at the specified URL.

As with many areas of our lives, the only constant in information representation is change. It is best to anticipate new versions of information by providing explicit and parseable versioning metadata. It helps to think ahead about how your content will evolve and how you will address information compatibility issues. A long term approach for managing URIs should be developed. The best naming approach results in not having to change a URI. One approach to anticipating versioning is to use dates as part of the URI.

---

An example of a URI for a version of an ontology updated on March 12, 2005 is:

"http://www.KnightOwlRestaurant.com/Menus/Menu20050312-ont".

At least for now, given bandwidth and storage constraints in certain Semantic Web applications, the chunk of information provided at a resolvable URI should be kept to the size of a typical web page.

## 5.2 URI References

In practical terms, the use of absolute URIs is often cumbersome. The URI concept extends to provide a more specific reference – called a URI reference (URIref). The URIref mechanism provides relative references to URIs that identify resources or portions of resources.

A URIref is a string of characters (text string) that represents a URI. A URIref may have an optional fragment identifier suffix. If using a fragment identifier suffix, the "#" character is used to separate the fragment identifier from the rest of the URIref. The characters before the "#" indicate a URI, which identifies a resource. The characters after the "#" identify a portion of the resource.

URIrefs are typically relative in contrast to full (absolute) URIs. However, if a fragment follows a full URI, it is considered a URIref because absolute URIs do not have fragments. There are four forms that a URIref can take, depending on whether it is full or relative and whether it has or does not have a fragment (see Table 5-2).

Table 5-2. URIref Forms

|  | With fragment | Without fragment |
|---|---|---|
| Full | Form 1 | Form 2 |
| Relative | Form 3 | Form 4 |

The syntax of Form 1 (full URIref with a fragment) is:
**URIschemeName:scheme-specificPart#fragment**
Where **URIschemeName:scheme-specificPart** is a full (absolute) URI and **fragment** is an optional fragment.

An example of Form 1 is:
http://www.restaurant.org/food-ont#Pizza

## Section 2 – Enabling Technologies

---

The syntax of Form 2 (full URIref without a fragment) is:
**URIschemeName:scheme-specificPart**
Where **URIschemeName:scheme-specificPart** is a full (absolute) URI

An example of Form 2 is:
http://www.restaurant.org/food-ont

---

The syntax of Form 3 (relative URIref with a fragment) is:
**relativeURI#fragment**
Where **relativeURI** is a relative URI and **fragment** is an optional fragment.

An example of Form 3 is:
food-ont#pizza
If occurring in www.restaurant.org, it would be equivalent to:
www.restaurant.org/food-ont#pizza

---

The syntax of Form 4 (relative URIref without a fragment) is:
**relativeURI**
Where **relativeURI** is a relative URI.

An example of Form 4 is:
food-ont
if occurring in www.restaurant.org, it would be equivalent to:
www.restaurant.org/food-ont

---

A URIref is either full or relative. A full URIref (form 1, 2) specifies an absolute (complete) URI with the characters that precede the "#" character (if there is one). A relative URIref (form 3, 4) specifies an absolute URI by using the base URI of the containing document and the characters before the "#" separator (if there is one). The part of the URIref that precedes the "#" fragment identifier (if there is one) can be used to derive an absolute URI if that portion is not already a complete (absolute) URI. The non-fragment portion of the relative URI is converted to its absolute value and then concatenated with the fragment identifier. A relative URIref must be converted into an equivalent full URIref to be useful.

An optional fragment identifier provided with a relative URIref (form 3) is interpreted relative to the base URI. If a fragment identifier is provided with an absolute URI (form 1), the fragment identifies a portion of the resource identified by the absolute URI.

## Chapter 5 – URIs and Namespaces

An absolute URIref is a self-contained, context-free, complete identifier that references a resource. An absolute URIref unambiguously identifies a resource by providing a fully qualified reference. A full URIref is a URIref that results from resolving a relative URIref.

A relative URIref is an abbreviated form of an absolute (full) URIref whose expanded value is dependent on the "xml:base" value. Relative URIs (forms 3, 4) are converted to full (non-relative) (absolute) URIs to be useful to software. Relative URIs are "relative" to a base URI. The base URI is normally the URL of the containing document. A full URIref references a portion of an object, identified with a URI and a fragment identifier (see Figure 5-3).

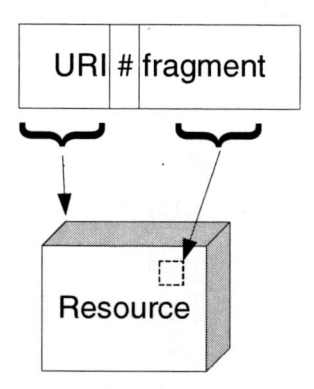

Figure 5-3. URIref Fragments Identify Portions of Resources

In OWL, a common special case of a relative URIref with a fragment is one without a URI part (form 3) (e.g., "#pizza"). The missing URI part is considered equal to the base URI. If a URIref does not have a URI part, it references a fragment in the document that it is in.

In URLs, a fragment identifies a specific place within a document identified by the URL. An object can be referenced from within the document in which it was defined, or outside. The default base URI used to resolve relative URIrefs is the URL of the containing document unless it is modified with an "xml:base" attribute declaration (described below in section 5.4).

## 5.3 XML Namespaces (xmlns)

Life would be simpler if we only needed to worry about unique markup element names within a single file. However, the reality of most applications is that multiple files are involved. To avoid name space collisions, and to resolve ambiguity, XML namespaces are used. A URI, normally associated with a shorthand prefix, creates a unique identifier.

The same XML tags are sometimes defined in multiple distributed files because multiple authors may define the same tag name. The XML namespace construct disambiguates duplicate element names by associating namespaces with URIrefs. The namespace prefix is used to associate the namespace name (prefix) specified with the namespace URIref. Namespaces enable shorthand (alias) references – prefixes to specify qualified names (QNames). A QName is a local XML tag name prefixed with a namespace abbreviation. Table 5-3 specifies the authoritative data source for defining and using namespaces.

Table 5-3. URI Authoritative Description

| | Title: | **Namespaces in XML** |
|---|---|---|
| | Document URI: | http://www.w3.org/TR/1999/REC-xml-names-19990114/ |
| | Purpose: | Specifies the uses of namespaces in XML |

A namespace declaration attribute can appear anywhere in an XML document. However, placing namespace attributes in the "<rdf:RDF>" tag makes their scope clear (the whole RDF element) and easy to locate in the file for human readers. Multiple namespaces can be declared.

---

The syntax for declaring a namespace is:

xmlns:**namespacePrefix**="**nsURIref**"

Where **namespacePrefix** is the local abbreviated reference and
**nsURIref** is the URIref for use in expanding references containing the abbreviation prefix. It is the namespace name.

---

## Chapter 5 – URIs and Namespaces

Namespace URIs typically end with a "#" so that qualified names can reference fragments without repeating the "#". If the ":" and the namespace prefix are omitted, the namespace is assumed to be the default namespace. There can only be one default namespace per file.

---

An example of a namespace declaration is:
<rdf xmlns:rest="http://www.restaurant.org/menuontology#">

In this example, the namespace attribute declares a namespace that associates the prefix "rest" to the namespace URIref :
"http://www.restaurant.org/menuontology#".

The qualified name "rest:pie" would expand to:
"http://www.restaurant.org/menuontology#pie"

An example of a default namespace declaration is:
xmlns="http://www.restaurant.org/menuontology"

The name "#pie" would expand to:
"http://www.restaurant.org/menuontology#pie"

---

### Qualified Names (QNames)

Once namespaces have been declared, they can be used in Qualified Names (QNames). XML namespace QNames are used to abbreviate URIs for element tag names and attribute names, but not for attribute values.

A QName is specified with a namespace prefix, followed by a colon and an XML local name. To resolve a qualified name, the URIref associated with the namespace prefix (the namespace name) is concatenated with the tagName.

---

The syntax for using a namespace (in a qualified name) is:

**namespacePrefix:tagName**

Where **namespacePrefix** is the previously declared abbreviation prefix and **tagName** is a tag name that is expanded to a complete URI reference using the value associated with the abbreviated prefix.

---

57

The prefix must have been previously defined within the current scope in an "xmlns" attribute. An example of a QName is "menu:dessert".

Tags are qualified with a URI associated with a namespace prefix to create unique identifiers. Although a QName appears in a file with a prefix, the value used by consuming software is the associated expanded URI.

All RDF/XML element names and attributes names must be QNames. The exceptions (for backward compatibility) are: "bagID", "about", "resource", "parsetype", and "type". The best practice is to specify these constructs as QNames regardless of the exception.

Shorthand using QNames (prefixing name with namespace) for element and attribute names allows everyone to create their own local tag names without worrying about name space collisions. Namespaces identify a set of element names by using prefixes in the file and declaring the namespace, usually in the header of the document.

The XML namespace does not have to exist as a physical or conceptual entity. There is no requirement for anything to exist at the location specified by a URI in the namespace attribute. However, a helpful practice is to provide a web page at the specified location that describes the referenced item. The best practice is to provide the URL of an associated file (e.g., the file containing the ontology) as the namespace URI.

## 5.4 Specifying an Alternative Base URI (xml:base)

Normally, a relative URIref is resolved based on its containing file's URL. However, an alternative base URI can be declared with the "xml:base" attribute. The alternative "xml:base" is normally specified along with the "xmlns" declarations within an RDF header element. Table 5-4 specifies the authoritative data source for defining and using the "xml:base" attribute.

Chapter 5 – URIs and Namespaces

Table 5-4. Alternative Base URI Authoritative Description

| | Title: | **XML Base** |
|---|---|---|
| | Document URI: | http://www.w3.org/TR/xmlbase |
| | Purpose: | specifies the uses of the "xml:base" attribute in XML |

---

The syntax for specifying the xml:base attribute is:

xml:base="**baseURI**"

Where **baseURI** is the URI to be used to determine a fully expanded URI reference.

---

An example of an xml:base attribute use is:

<somexmltag xml:base="http://www.restaurant.org/menu"/>

---

There are several reasons to specify an alternative "xml:base". The same file might be replicated on various mirror sites, so the URIrefs can be made consistent despite the different URLs of the containing documents. Instances distributed over multiple sites could share a base URI to give the illusion/appearance of a single document. An alternative base URI can also be used to group related items. Since the locations of documents are dynamic, a more stable approach is to reference a base URI.

The default "xml:base" is the containing document's URI. The "xml:base" is normally defined along with namespace declarations. The specification of an "xml:base" affects all other RDF/XML attributes in the file. If you do not specify an "xml:base", changes to the containing document's location (URL) or filename effectively changes the full URIref of the relative URIrefs that identify resources. The "xml:base" declaration can be used to make sure that URIrefs remain valid when a file is renamed.

## *5.5 URIs and Namespace Summary*

Identifiers are a key aspect of the Semantic Web because they name resources. Absolute URIs are fully specified references to resources. URIrefs specify URIs and provide identification of resource components through the optional use of fragments. XML namespaces help prevent symbol name space collisions by annotating an element or resource name with a URI associated with a namespace prefix. The "xml:base" attribute provides an alternative URI for converting relative URIrefs into full URIrefs. These naming related features support referencing resources and portions of resources. URIs and namespaces are referenced within XML statements. The next chapter describes XML's support for the Semantic Web.

# 6 XML

> "XML just clears away some of the syntactical distractions so that we can get down to the big problem: how we arrive at common understandings about knowledge representation. That's the biggie. XML says, 'let's stop arguing about how we're going to represent trees and how we're going to represent attribute/value pairs.' We'll just decide, 'Let's do it [as XML]'."
>
> Jon Bosak, considered by many to be the "father of XML", in an interview with Mark Johnson: http://www.javaworld.com/javaworld/javaone00/j1-00-bosak.html

A consistent, standardized, computer-parseable syntax is needed to underpin a Semantic Web language. XML provides a concrete syntax for OWL. Although OWL does not technically require the use of XML, this book focuses on XML as a common, efficient mechanism for representing OWL constructs.

The transport/syntax layer of the Semantic Web's layered architecture is provided by XML and XML Schema datatypes (see Figure 6-1). XML uses markup to identify document structures.

To share information easily within a data structure, a language is needed to translate the information into a form that can be interchanged. XML syntax is commonly used to serialize information into a well-defined encoding.

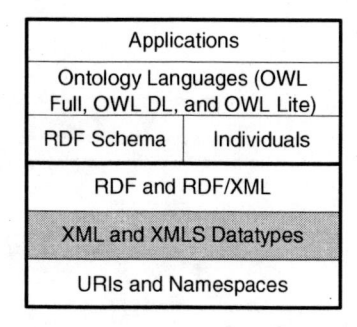

Figure 6-1. Transport/Syntax Layer

| Applications |
| --- |
| Ontology Languages (OWL Full, OWL DL, and OWL Lite) |
| RDF Schema \| Individuals |
| RDF and RDF/XML |
| XML and XMLS Datatypes |
| URIs and Namespaces |

This text highlights key XML features that support OWL. XML supports markup of data with arbitrary structure. XHTML is an example of a language defined using XML. XHTML has a specific purpose involving fixed representation structures for marking up hypertext.

This chapter provides an overview of XML, and describes XML Schema's datatypes.

Section 2 – Enabling Technologies

## *6.1 XML Overview*

XML is a tag-based metalanguage used to define domain-specific grammars. A metalanguage is a language for defining languages. XML is a metalanguage, because it allows authors to generate tags that specify the structure and syntax of documents. It is used for serializing tree-based data structures into a linear text format.

XML is a W3C recommendation (standard) developed as a simplified version of the International Organization for Standardization (ISO) Standard Generalized Markup Language (SGML) standard. XML is used for web data interchange (unlike HTML which is only for format) (see Figure 6-2). For example, XML can represent menu information (see Figure 6-3).

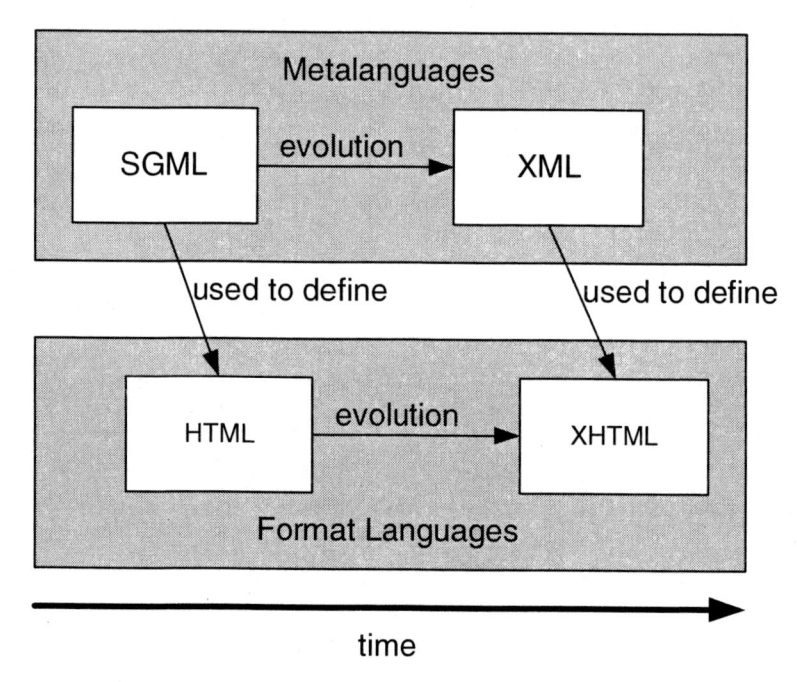

Figure 6-2. Markup Language Evolution

Chapter 6 - XML

Figure 6-3. Sample Menu

The following example shows how some menu items might be interchanged using XML.

```
<menu>
    <menuitem>
        <dishName>Key Lime Pie</dishName>
        <dishPrice>$2.75</dishPrice>
    </menuitem>
    <menuitem>
        <dishName>Apple Pie</dishName>
        <dishPrice>$2.50</dishPrice>
    </menuitem>
</menu>
```

The W3C took responsibility for authoritatively defining XML and related technologies (see Table 6-1). XML has become the de facto standard for interchanging structured data on the web. Its use has been buoyed by Commercial-Off-The-Shelf (COTS) applications, which drive down the costs of developing parsers and data translators.

Section 2 – Enabling Technologies

Table 6-1. XML Authoritative Description

| | | |
|---|---|---|
| | Title: | W3C XML Recommendation - Extensible Markup Language (XML) 1.0 (Third Edition) |
| | Document URI: | http://www.w3.org/TR/REC-xml |
| | Purpose: | This document describes XML as a subset of SGML. |

## 6.1.1 XML Features

OWL language developers selected XML to interchange ontologies because of its features. XML is a widely-supported web standard metalanguage that allows anyone to develop markup languages for any domain and purpose to support data interchange. Markup languages specify the structure and format of documents. They provide a concrete serialization syntax for content to exchange data. Serialization involves creating a linear textual representation of a possibly complex data model.

XML's features include its structured syntax which has been widely adopted and is supported by software. XML adds consistency for data interchange. Its regularity allows software to parse it easily. Although XML's text markup is verbose and ugly, it is human readable. Resulting XML compliant documents enable parsing software to interpret the content, which supports data interchange on the web. XML is a vendor-neutral format supported by Application Programming Interfaces (APIs) and tools. There is a large community of XML-savvy application developers who leverage the commercial tools that are XML-compliant.

## 6.1.2 Syntax and Structure

XML elements, attributes, and content are defined through named markup tags. The tags delimit the element and attribute values. Elements' optional attributes are best used to specify metadata about the element. XML content is normally delimited by a start tag (e.g., <Description>) and an end tag (e.g., "</Description>"). The tagged XML content can be text or other sets of tags with tagged content.

XML provides structure through nested elements. Documents with arbitrary structure can be defined. The nesting of tags in XML documents are serializations of a tree-structured data model. Each labeled node in the tree can include attributes with values and content.

The regular structure of XML documents, designated by tags, supports parsing software. The tags help the software understand the structure and syntax of the document.

### 6.1.3 XML Declaration

The optional (but highly recommended) XML declaration should appear at the beginning of an XML document. It should include version and encoding attributes (e.g., "<?xml version="1.0" encoding="UTF-8"?>"). The example declaration indicates that the file contains XML content compliant with version 1.0 of the W3C's XML Recommendation and uses the UTF-8 encoding form. The best practice is to include the optional tag and use ".xml" as the filename suffix.

### 6.1.4 Elements

Embedded (nested) elements are used to define the tree structure of XML documents. Elements are indicated with tag names that appear in angled brackets. The content associated with the element is terminated with a matching tag that has a "/" before the tag name. Alternatively, self-closing tags identify an XML element with a single tag.

Tag names label the element contents and are often meant to provide meaning for human readers. However, unless an application is written to a priori understand the tags associated with a particular domain, no semantics can be inferred. QNames can be used as element names.

### 6.1.5 XML Element Attributes

XML attributes can occur within a start tag or a self-closing tag (see the example below of XML syntax). The attribute name and value occur after the tag name. Attributes provide information about the elements and are best used for metadata (e.g., units) rather than element content.

Section 2 – Enabling Technologies

---

The syntax of an XML attribute within a self-closing tag is:

<someXMLtag attributeName="attributeValue" />

Where **attributeName** is the name of the attribute and **attributeValue** is the value of the attribute.

---

An example of an XML element with an attribute and content is:

<menu:dishPrice currency="USD">2.5</menu:dishPrice>

---

A common use of XML attributes is to identify a language variant of an element's contents.

### 6.1.5.1 Specifying the Language of the Content (xml:lang)

A specific predefined XML attribute, "xml:lang", is used for specifying the language of an element's content. The attribute can be specified at various levels of the XML document's structure and applies to content within that portion of the document. The use of "xml:lang" is specified in the documents listed in Table 6-2.

Table 6-2. Authoritative "xml:lang" Support Documents

| | | |
|---|---|---|
| | Title: | **Tags for the Identification of Languages** |
| | Document URI: | http://www.ietf.org/rfc/rfc1766.txt |
| | Purpose: | Describes a language tag for indicating the language of an information object. |
| | Title: | **Code for the representation of names of languages (ISO 639)** |
| | Document URI: | (available for purchase at www.iso.org) |
| | Purpose: | Defines the interpretation of two letter language tags. |

# Chapter 6 - XML

> The syntax of an xml:lang attribute is:
>
> xml:lang="**languageIdentifier**"
>
> Where **languageIdentifier** identifies the language. Omitting the **languageIdentifier** indicates that no language is specified.

> An example of using the xml:lang attribute is:
>
> &lt;menu:meatDishType xml:lang="en"&gt;chicken&lt;/menu:meatDishType &gt;
> &lt;menu:meatDishType xml:lang="es"&gt;pollo&lt;/menu:meatDishType &gt;

Multilingual documentation of OWL ontologies is supported at the syntactic level through use of the "xml:lang" language tagging facility. The values of the "xml:lang" attribute are normally two letter language code abbreviations specified by ISO standard 639, (e.g., "en" for English, "es" for Spanish) and extended with dialects (e.g., "en-US").

### 6.1.5.2 XML Syntax Approaches

Various methods can be used to represent information in XML. A preferred method for XML in support of OWL is to use an element-centric rather than attribute-centric approach.

> An example of an XML tag that uses element values for an item is:
>
> &lt;menuitem&gt;
>     &lt;dishName&gt;keyLimePie&lt;/dishName&gt;
>     &lt;dishPrice&gt;$2.75&lt;/dishPrice &gt;
> &lt;/menuitem &gt;

In contrast, attribute-centric syntax provides values in attributes.

> An example of an XML tag that uses element attributes to provide the values for an item is:
>
> &lt;menuitem dishName="keyLimePie" dishPrice="$2.75"/&gt;

67

# Section 2 – Enabling Technologies

While less compact, element-centric forms are preferred because their content is parseable and can easily be subdivided into lower levels of the XML tree structure. Attributes should be used for metadata. Most syntax specifications and examples in this text will only indicate element-centric syntax forms. However, attribute-centric approaches are usually equally valid.

### 6.1.5.3 XML Entities

XML provides a shorthand mechanism that can be used for abbreviating references to URIs. XML entities are used for string substitution by parsers. XML entities are useful in OWL documents for abbreviating URIref prefixes in attribute values since namespace prefixes cannot be used in attribute values.

---

The syntax for an XML ENTITY declaration is:

<!ENTITY **entityName** "**fullURI**">

where **entityName** is the shorthand name to be used in the XML document and **fullURI** is a URI that will be substituted for the **entityName** by the XML parser.

---

Declare XML entities at the beginning of the XML document in the "DOCTYPE" XML declaration.

---

An example of declaring an XML entity within a DOCTYPE declaration is:

```
<!DOCTYPE rdf:RDF [
<!ENTITY owl "http://www.w3.org/2002/07/owl #">
]>
```

---

XML entities are referenced by prefixing them with a "&" symbol and suffixing them with a ";" symbol.

---

An example of using an XML entity is:

`<rdfs:subClassOf rdf:resource="&owl;Thing"/>`

which, if in conjunction with the previous example is interpreted by the parser as http://www.w3.org/2002/07/owl#Thing

---

A resource can be referenced using its full URI, or a shorthand (abbreviated reference). The shorthand can be a QName for a tag name (e.g., "menu:Dish"). However, since QNames cannot be used as attribute values, an XML entity reference (e.g., "&menu;Dish") can be used as the shorthand in an attribute value.

## 6.2 XML Schema Datatypes

XML Schema (XMLS) is an important companion standard to XML. XMLS provides important features for documenting the structure of XML documents in XML instead of DTDs. XMLS also defines datatype features. OWL adopted the XMLS datatypes.

The XMLS specification has three parts, two of which are of specific interest to users of OWL (see Table 6-3). However, the most important part of the XML documentation from an OWL perspective is part 2, which describes datatypes.

Table 6-3. XML Schema Authoritative Description

| | Title: | **W3C XMLS Recommendation - Primer** |
|---|---|---|
| | Document URI: | http://www.w3.org/XML/Schema#dev |
| | Purpose: | Provides an introduction to XMLS concepts. |
| | Title: | **W3C XMLS Recommendation – Part 2 (Datatypes)** |
| | Document URI: | http://www.w3.org/TR/xmlschema-2/ |
| | Purpose: | Part 2 describes a number of built-in datatypes as well as the means for defining data types using the XML Schema Definition (XSD) Schema Definition Language. |

Table 6-4 shows the recommended namespace URI associated with XMLS.

Section 2 – Enabling Technologies

Table 6-4. XML Schema Namespace

| Recommended Namespace Prefix: | xsd |
| Namespace Name: | http://www.w3.org/2001/XMLSchema |

In plain XML, DTDs only provide character string data, referred to as parsed character data ("PCDATA"). XMLS adds datatype support for OWL with built-in primitive and derived datatypes. The literal domain is categorized into predefined datatypes provided by part 2 of the XMLS specification. XMLS defines primitive datatypes (e.g., string, decimal, float) and complex derived types (e.g., integer sub-ranges).

Datatypes are conceptual groups (e.g., integers) represented by names used to describe the groups and their members. Datatypes represent types of literal values (e.g., integers). They restrict values and associate representations with values. OWL does not use the following datatypes from XMLS: "duration", "QName", "NOTATION", "NMTOKENS", "ID", "IDREF", "ENTITY", "IDREFS", and "ENTITIES".

### 6.2.1 User Defined Datatypes

OWL leverages XML Schema's method for defining new datatypes.

---

For example, a numSlices datatype can be defined as an integer range from 1 to 8 using a restriction on the core positive integer type from XML Schema datatypes.

```
<xsd:schema xmlns:xsd="http://www.w3.org/2001/XMLSchema">
    <xsd:simpleType name="numSlices">
        <xsd:restriction base="&xsd;positiveInteger">
            <xsd:maxExclusive value="8"/>
        </xsd:restriction>
    </xsd:simpleType>
</xsd:schema>
```

---

### 6.2.2 Built-in OWL Datatypes

Table 6-5 lists the built-in XMLS simple datatypes recommended for use with OWL. Figure 6-4 presents a graphical view (based on the graphical view in the XML documentation) of the XMLS datatypes used in OWL.

Table 6-5. XML Schema Datatypes used in OWL

| Datatype category | Datatype |
|---|---|
| Strings | xsd:string |
| | xsd:normalizedString |
| | xsd:token |
| | xsd:language |
| | xsd:NMTOKEN |
| | xsd:Name |
| | xsd:NCName |
| Boolean | xsd:boolean |
| Numerical | xsd:decimal |
| | xsd:float |
| | xsd:double |
| Decimal-derived | xsd:integer |
| | xsd:nonNegativeInteger |
| | xsd:positiveInteger |
| | xsd:nonPositiveInteger |
| | xsd:negativeInteger |
| | xsd:long |
| | xsd:int |
| | xsd:short |
| | xsd:byte |
| | xsd:unsignedLong |
| | xsd:unsignedInt |
| | xsd:unsignedShort |
| | xsd:unsignedByte |
| Binary | xsd:hexBinary |
| | xsd:base64Binary |
| Date/Time-related | xsd:dateTime |
| | xsd:time |
| | xsd:date |
| | xsd:gYearMonth |
| | xsd:gYear |
| | xsd:gMonthDay |
| | xsd:gDay |
| | xsd:gMonth |
| Resource | xsd:anyURI |

## 6.3  XML Summary

XML is a standard metalanguage used to define custom tag sets. It is used to define interchange formats for exchanging information on the web. The Semantic Web uses OWL as the serialization syntax for information representations. XMLS provides standard datatype definitions that are used in the Semantic Web.

Section 2 – Enabling Technologies

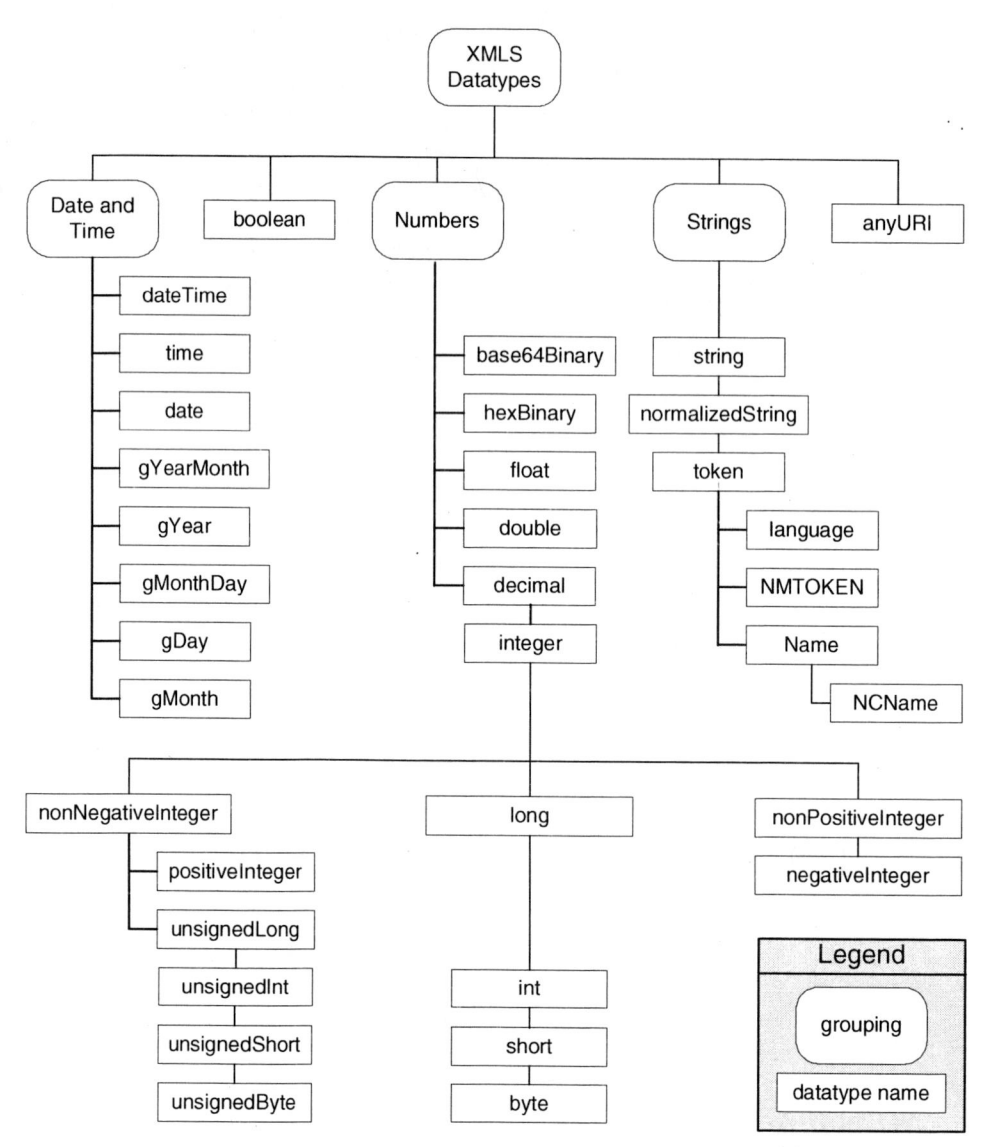

Figure 6-4. XML Schema Datatypes used in OWL (graphical view)

## 6.4 Why XML is not Enough

While XML provides features for representing and interchanging information, it is insufficient for supporting Semantic Web requirements. The primary reasons that XML cannot support the Semantic Web directly are that XML defines syntax, not semantics, and XML descriptions are ambiguous to a computer.

XML is a data formatting language that only provides a grammar (syntax). XML tag names provide few hints to support importing software. XML tags are no better than natural language for providing meaning. XML tag names are simply strings that may be meaningful to humans but are meaningless to software. While XML tag names may suggest meaning to a human reader, they have no meaning by themselves to parsing software. A tag name (e.g., "<apple>") may be ascribed with semantics by a human reader. However, to software, it is simply a character string with no relation to another XML tag (e.g., "<orange>"). The meaning of the tags must be agreed to a priori to support interoperability. XML languages often require voluminous companion documentation to explain the meaning of tags.

XML does not represent the semantics, the meaning of a concept. Software must understand how to interpret XML tags to perform more meaningful applications. However, there is no straightforward way to describe semantics in traditional XML. XML formats can be specified in DTDs and XML Schemas, but these specifications do not describe the relationship between resources.

XML adds structure to data on the current web. However, it is too focused on syntax and exhibits ambiguity that make it insufficient to support the Semantic Web by itself. A common problem with using XML is that there are too many ways to describe the same thing. Semantic Web developers leverage XML's features in different ways. They can define their own tag names, nesting structures, identifiers, and representation styles.

While XML provides a number of useful features, there are serious problems with using XML by itself to support the Semantic Web. RDF overcomes many of these challenges, which is the subject of the next chapter.

Section 2 – Enabling Technologies

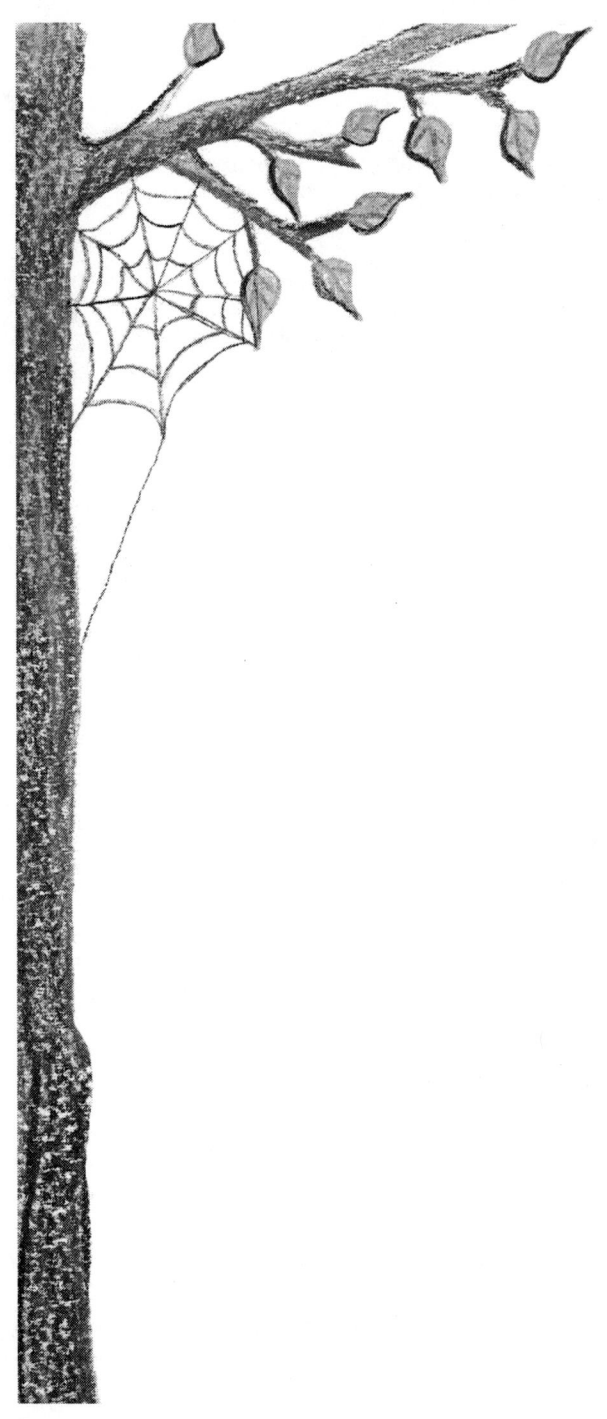

# 7 RDF

> *The most fundamental benefit of RDF compared to other meta-data approaches is that using RDF, you can say anything about anything. Anyone can make RDF statements about any identifiable resource. Using RDF, the problems of extending meta-data and combining meta-data of different formats, from different schemas disappear, as RDF does not use closed documents.", in Mikael Nilsson's "The Semantic Web: How RDF will change learning technology standards", http://www.cetis.ac.uk/content/20010927172953*

RDF is an approved W3C recommendation for asserting values of properties associated with web resources. RDF and RDF/XML form the basic relational language layer of the Semantic Web architecture and build on XML and XML Schema datatypes (see Figure 7-1). If we tried to standardize the way XML supports the Semantic Web, we would likely wind up reinventing RDF and RDFS.

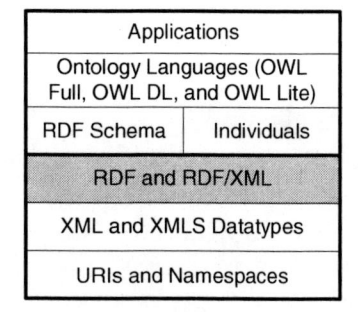

| Applications |  |
| --- | --- |
| Ontology Languages (OWL Full, OWL DL, and OWL Lite) ||
| RDF Schema | Individuals |
| RDF and RDF/XML ||
| XML and XMLS Datatypes ||
| URIs and Namespaces ||

Figure 7-1. Basic Relational Language Layer

RDF is used to specify OWL instances. It is the most important value-added layer of the Semantic Web's architecture. Entire books are available that describe RDF. This text will focus on the essential RDF features needed to enable OWL representations, especially the XML serialization of the RDF data model.

This chapter provides an overview of RDF and describes RDF including its features and data model.

Section 2 – Enabling Technologies

## 7.1 RDF Overview

As the name describes, RDF is a framework for describing resources. RDF is a standard mechanism for making simple statements about resources. As the following sections will explain, a resource can be anything that is named with a URIref. The statements about the resources provide "descriptions" of the resources through attribute/value pairs. Making statements (assertions) about resources is the basis of information representation.

RDF is a new, yet relatively mature technology. The current version of RDF was developed in a collaborative manner by the W3C's RDF Core Working Group and documented in a series of W3C publications. RDF concepts were influenced by metadata and knowledge representation principles.

### 7.1.1 Metadata

Initially, RDF was designed to encode metadata. Many texts describe RDF as a standard way to represent metadata. If RDF only supported the description of web pages, it would be simpler to understand common types of properties associations such as title, author, and creation date.

"Metadata" is an overused term with multiple interpretations. This has resulted in confusion regarding RDF's support for OWL. There are different types of metadata. The classic example of document-level metadata is the Dublin Core specification. Another use for the term metadata involves tagging that describes the data being passed. XML element tag names are an example of this type of metadata. In this text, the term "metadata" refers to data that describes document-level data in the Dublin Core style.

### 7.1.2 RDF Purpose

The purpose of RDF is to provide a general-purpose standard framework for making statements about resources and their attributes. The goals of the RDF authors included developing a standard mechanism describing the semantics of data so that it could be interchanged easily. RDF can be used for publishing database contents on the web.

## 7.1.3 RDF Specification

The RDF specification has several parts, as described in Table 7-1. Chapter 8 describes the XML serialization of RDF with RDF/XML. Chapter 9 describes the RDF Vocabulary Description Language as part of the discussion on RDF Schema (RDFS).

Table 7-1. RDF Authoritative Description

| | Title: | **RDF Concepts and Abstract Syntax** |
|---|---|---|
| | Document URI: | http://www.w3c.org/TR/rdf-concepts/ |
| | Purpose: | Describes fundamental concepts and provides an abstract syntax on which RDF is based, and which serves to link its concrete syntax to its formal semantics. |
| | Title: | **RDF Semantics** |
| | Document URI: | http://www.w3c.org/TR/rdf-mt/ |
| | Purpose: | Provides precise semantics, and corresponding complete systems of inference rules for RDF and RDFS. |
| | Title: | **RDF Primer** |
| | Document URI: | http://www.w3c.org/TR/rdf-primer/ |
| | Purpose: | Provides basic knowledge required to effectively use RDF and contains numerous useful examples. |
| | Title: | **RDF Test Cases** |
| | Document URI: | http://www.w3c.org/TR/rdf-testcases/ |
| | Purpose: | Describes the RDF Test Cases that can be used to ensure certain RDF features operate correctly in software implementations. |

## 7.2 RDF Features

RDF provides a standard way to make statements about resources with properties (attribute/value pairs). RDF represents statements in sets of triples, similar to the subject, verb, and object of a sentence. These machine-processable descriptions are uniform, formal, and standard without being inflexible or constraining.

Although RDF only makes simple statements, it is a very powerful basis for describing information. RDF's approach to information representation supports data sharing and simplifies the job of importing software.

Unlike typical XML vocabularies developed to only support a particular Community of Interest (COI), RDF statements are generic and can describe any domain. By distributing the responsibility for representing information, various communities of interest can develop their own representations.

RDF statements can be distributed on servers similar to HTML content. As more RDF statements are shared on the web, and become accessible to more consuming applications, the value of the information grows. Distributed sets of statements can be combined to create a large "virtual" knowledgebase.

RDF statements can be exchanged by heterogeneous applications and interpreted in a common way without losing meaning. Interoperability involves sharing information between applications not specifically designed to interface with each other.

RDF descriptions enable new capabilities. By having standard representations and being able to share information, new capabilities become available. By understanding the explicit semantics described in these representations, inferencing can be performed and queries answered.

## 7.3 RDF Data Model

The RDF documentation defines a simple syntax-independent data model. The data model includes resources, literals, and statements. It defines properties as a special type of resource and typed literals as a type of literal. The data model is used to make statements about resources. The statements are attribute/value pairs formed by named properties with associated values.

The RDF documentation also describes a graphical representation method for visualizing the RDF data model with graphs. While RDF graphs are useful for visualizing statements, they are not used directly in OWL's RDF/XML syntax.

The following sections provide more detailed descriptions of the concepts defined by the data model.

### 7.3.1 Resources

Resources are the key building block in RDF. Resources are typically associated with nouns (i.e., people, places, things). An RDF resource is anything with an associated URIref. Since anything can have a URIref, anything can be a resource. RDF resources are always named by URIrefs.

---

Examples of URIrefs that identify RDF resources are:

www.restaurant.org/RestOwner
#JoeSmith
location123

---

Resources described by RDF include physical and virtual things. Virtual things may or may not be directly network accessible. Examples of physical resources identified by URIrefs include books, menus, and food. Examples of virtual resources with associated URIrefs include web pages, pictures, services, collections of other resources, and people.

**Properties**

A property is a specific type of resource that serves as a predicate in statements to describe another resource. Properties describe attributes of resources and relationships between resources. Properties describe a binary relationship between a subject resource and a value.

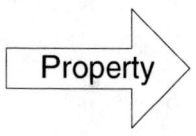

Properties are similar to methods in OOP. However, unlike OOP methods that exist only in association with classes, RDF properties are first class objects with URI names. Since properties are resources, they can themselves be described by properties. Examples of properties include "owner", "price", and "name".

Section 2 – Enabling Technologies

Since RDF properties are binary relationships, intermediate resources are often used to describe a more complex relationship.

### 7.3.2 Literals

RDF literals are text strings with optional language identifiers and optional datatype identifiers. A literal with a datatype specifier is called a typed literal. A literal without a datatype specifier is called a plain literal. Literals are one type of property value in an RDF statement. RDF literals are an atomic datatype, like XML's only native datatype.

Data Value

```
Examples of plain literals are:
"$3.45"
"Knight Owl Restaurant"
"123 Main Street"
"123" (interpreted as characters, not a number)
"<price>3.25</price>" (interpreted as an XML string rather than RDF markup)
```

```
Examples of typed literals are:
xsd:time^^06:00:00
xsd:integer^^6
```

### 7.3.3 Statements

RDF is used to make simple statements about resources. Anyone can say anything about anything (including possibly contradictory statements) with RDF statements.

RDF statements provide a subject resource, a predicate (named property), and an object (literal data value or resource value of the property for the subject resource). The subject of an RDF statement is an RDF resource that is being described. The predicate is a specific property. The object value of the property is either a resource or a literal (see Figure 7-2).

Chapter 7 - RDF

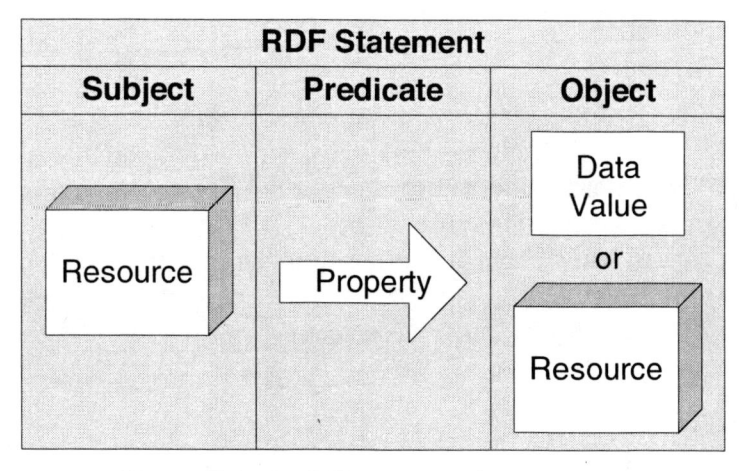

Figure 7-2. RDF Statement Components

Because statements have three parts, they are referred to as a triple in some RDF and OWL documents. Table 7-2 represents the two forms of RDF statements.

Table 7-2. RDF Statement Forms

| Form | Statement type | Subject | Predicate | Object |
|---|---|---|---|---|
| 1 | Literal valued statement | Resource | Property | Literal data value |
| 2 | Resource valued statement | Resource | Property | Resource |

Table 7-3 shows examples of RDF statement contents.

Table 7-3. Examples of RDF Statements

| Subject | Predicate | Object/Value |
|---|---|---|
| KeyLimePie | price | $2.75 |
| Person345 | favoritePie | KeyLimePie |
| Restaurant123 | closingTime | 8 p.m. |

Section 2 – Enabling Technologies

## 7.4 RDF Summary

As the name implies, RDF provides a framework for describing resources. RDF is based on a data model that includes resources, properties, statements, and literals. One way to view this data model is presented in UML notation in Figure 7-3. RDF is used to express simple statements about subject resources, using named properties, and their values. This is a foundational support technology in OWL.

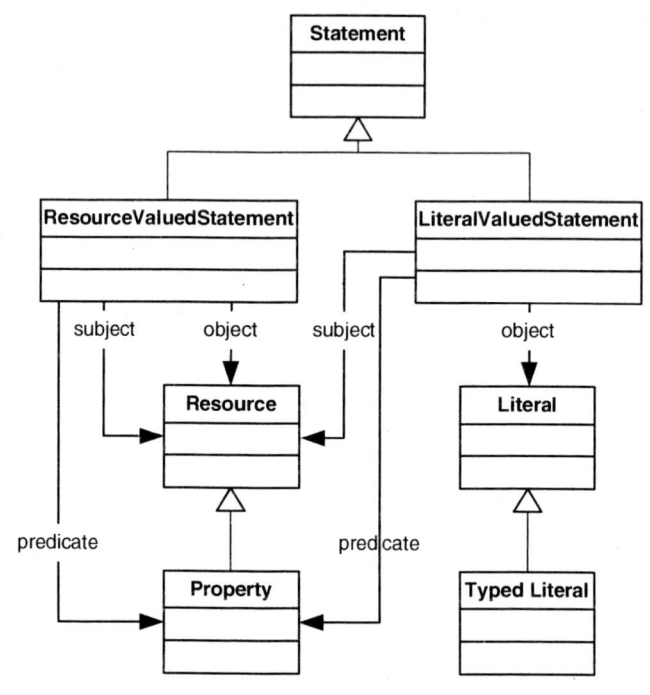

Figure 7-3. RDF Model View

## 7.5 Why RDF is not Enough

RDF provides a content data model for representing the basic elements for making statements. However, a neutral serialization format is needed that can be used to interchange the contents of the RDF data model. Also, RDF is used for making simple statements about resources. More complex semantic expressions are needed to describe an ontology. The next chapter describes the XML serialization syntax for the RDF data model – RDF/XML.

# 8 RDF/XML

> *"You will usually have a need to store RDF in a file or transfer the data somewhere else. There is a common XML format for storing RDF. This format is called RDF/XML. There are several other ways of storing RDF data, but this format is the most common. Some people confusingly refer to this format just as RDF. Actually, the model... is RDF, whereas the syntax is properly called RDF/XML." from XULPlanet's Mozilla SDK Documentation, on-line: http://www.xulplanet.com/tutorials/mozsdk/rdfsyntax.php*

RDF/XML is the standard XML syntax used to serialize the RDF data model. A collection of RDF statements can be represented in a variety of formats. However, XML is the preferable representation scheme because of software support. By using XML, RDF/XML satisfies requirements for character sets, tagging, XML namespaces, and URI technologies. RDF/XML supports the basic relational language layer (see Figure 8-1).

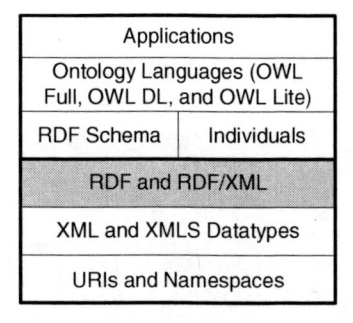

| Applications |
|---|
| Ontology Languages (OWL Full, OWL DL, and OWL Lite) |
| RDF Schema \| Individuals |
| RDF and RDF/XML |
| XML and XMLS Datatypes |
| URIs and Namespaces |

Figure 8-1. Basic Relational Language Layer

This chapter provides an overview of RDF/XML, describes RDF syntax features, and describes how the RDF data model is serialized with RDF/XML.

## *8.1 RDF/XML Overview*

XML provides a concrete syntax for RDF. RDF/XML is a standard linear notation for serializing the RDF model and exchanging RDF statements. RDF/XML specifies both a full serialization syntax and an abbreviated syntax for expressing the RDF data model. It uses XML namespaces, URIs, properties, and values. RDF/XML is used to string together statements of attribute/value pairs associated with resources.

Section 2 – Enabling Technologies

## 8.1.1 Relation to XML

RDF uses RDF/XML, an XML syntax for serializing the RDF statement into a linear syntax. From an XML data engineering perspective, RDF/XML is a standard approach for describing resources in XML.

By consistently following certain guidelines, and by using a standard set of XML tags, the XML ambiguity weakness described above is overcome. RDF/XML is used for making assertions that leverage XML format to represent and transport information. RDF separates the framework and the specific syntax (RDF/XML).

## 8.1.2 RDF/XML Specifications

Table 8-1 describes the W3C's RDF/XML specification.

Table 8-1. RDF/XML Authoritative Description

| Title: | **RDF/XML Syntax Specification (Revised)** |
|---|---|
| Document URI: | http://www.w3.org/TR/rdf-syntax-grammar/ |
| Purpose: | Defines an XML syntax for RDF called RDF/XML |

RDF/XML has an associated mime type. A mime type is an indication to software on how to interpret a file. Table 8-2 presents the recommended namespace prefix, namespace URI, and the mime type associated with RDF/XML.

Table 8-2. RDF Namespace and Mime Type

| Recommended Namespace Prefix: | rdf |
|---|---|
| Namespace Name: | http://www.w3.org/1999/02/22-rdf-syntax-ns# |
| Mime type: | application/rdf+xml |

Chapter 8 – RDF/XML

## 8.2 RDF Syntax Features (Using XML)

RDF/XML is a standardized syntax for encoding RDF statements to make them machine processable. As an XML markup language for representing RDF, RDF/XML benefits from XML features. XML has a large installed base of compliant tools and skilled software professionals. Using XML to serialize RDF leverages investments in tools and people. RDF also benefits from XML's tagging, namespaces, and the ability to use COTS parsers and APIs.

## 8.3 RDF/XML Documents

An RDF/XML file contains a header and a series of RDF statement assertions. The statements are provided as "rdf:Description" XML elements.

### 8.3.1 File Header (rdf:RDF)

RDF/XML files typically contain header information that include an XML declaration, RDF element, and namespace declaration.

XML documents begin with the XML declaration described above in section 6.1.3. RDF content can be within an XML file or in a standalone document that contains only RDF constructs.

The "rdf:RDF" element indicates that its contents should be interpreted as RDF. All RDF content should be contained within the "rdf:RDF" element. The best practice is to only have one "rdf:RDF" element per file.

---

An example of the start tag of an RDF header is:

<rdf:RDF xmlns:rdf="http://www.w3.org/1999/02/22-rdf-syntax-ns#">

---

RDF files typically contain namespace declarations in their headers. The XML namespace declarations are provided as "xmlns" attributes of the "rdf:RDF" start-tag. Section 5.3 described the namespace syntax.

## 8.3.2 Resource Names

RDF resources are named in XML with case sensitive symbol names. The best practice is to name most resources using the camel case (CamelCase) convention. With lower CamelCase, the first letter is lower case. Uppercase letters differentiate parts of the name. Examples of resource names in lower CamelCase are "firstCourse", "menuDish", and "ownedBy". URIrefs provide identifiers for RDF resources that can serve as statement subjects, predicates, and objects.

## 8.3.3 RDF/XML Statements (rdf:Description)

RDF/XML provides features for serializing RDF statements. The XML element "rdf:Description" is used to serialize an RDF statement. The tag name "Description" is used because an RDF statement is a description about a subject resource.

Within an "rdf:Description", property/value pairs are provided as XML elements (representing properties) with the values specified in the element content or as attribute values. The subject resource is identified as an attribute of the "rdf:Description" element. The description describes a resource identified in an "rdf:ID" or "rdf:about" attribute. For a new resource, the URI is defined with the "rdf:ID" attribute.

Alternatively, a description statement can be provided as the content for a predicate (same as giving it an "rdf:ID" and then referencing the URIref in a resource attribute). The best practice is to provide it with an "ID" identifier, so that it can be reused as a value of other statements without replicating its content. Alternating subject and predicates is called striping.

Rather than provide an "rdf:Description" element for each statement, multiple property/value pairs can be identified within the same "rdf:Description" element. Specifying RDF/XML statements includes identifying subject resources, specifying properties, and providing property values.

The subject resource of a statement can be new or existing. The value of the property can be a literal, an existing individual resource, a resource that represents a container, or a resource representing a collection (see Figure 8-2).

Chapter 8 – RDF/XML

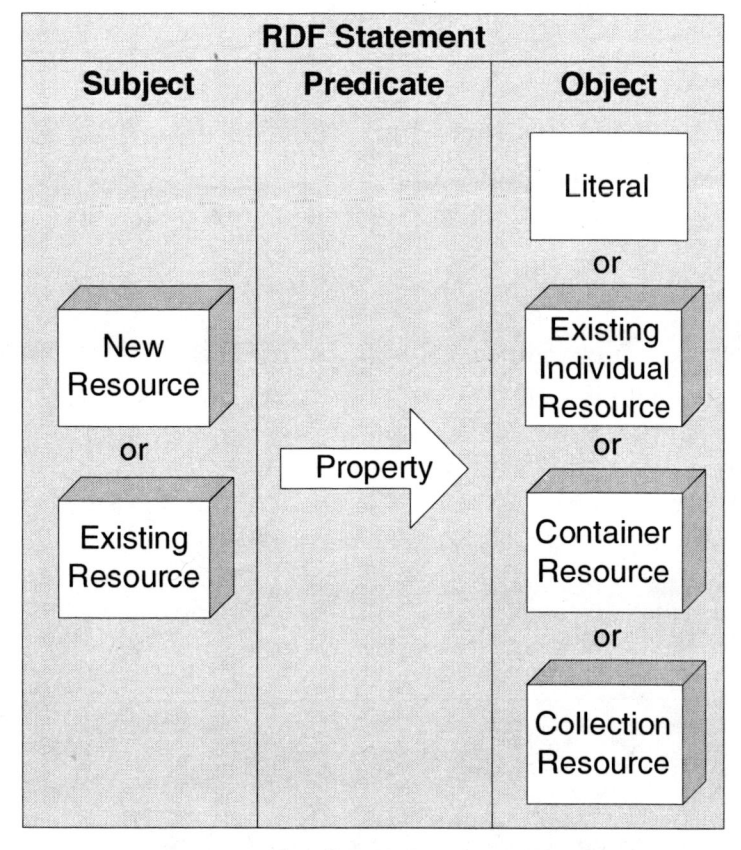

Figure 8-2. RDF/XML Statement Options

Table 8-3 presents the permutations of these items, which can be viewed as 8 forms. Additionally, the "striping" syntax can be used to make other statements ("rdf:Description" elements) the value of RDF statement properties.

Table 8-3. Statement Forms

| Subject | Object Value Type | | | |
|---|---|---|---|---|
| | Literal | Existing Resource | Container Resource | Collection Resource |
| New Resource | Form 1 | Form 2 | Form 3 | Form 4 |
| Existing Resource | Form 5 | Form 6 | Form 7 | Form 8 |

Section 2 – Enabling Technologies

The following sections describe the RDF/XML syntax for these various forms.

## 8.3.4 Describing the Subject of an RDF Statement

There are two sets of forms for describing the subject of an RDF statement. Forms 1-4 are used for defining new resources, while Forms 5-8 are used for describing existing resources.

### 8.3.4.1 Creating a New Subject Resource (rdf:ID)

A new resource is identified in RDF by using the "rdf:ID" attribute in an "rdf:Description" element to create a referencable identifier (forms 1-4). The "rdf:ID" attribute value identifies the new resource being described with a URIref. The full URI that results from resolving the URIref is the name of the resource.

Some resources (e.g., web sites) will already exist and have associated URIs. However, most RDF documents introduce new resources.

> The syntax for creating a new resource is:
>
> <rdf:Description rdf:ID="**resourceURIref**"/>
>
> where **resourceURIref** is the URI reference of the new resource being described.

> An example of creating an RDF resource using rdf:ID (Form 1) is:
>
> <rdf:Description rdf:ID= "Person345"/>

The full URI for the newly minted resource is determined by concatenating the base URI of the containing document, "#", and the value of the "rdf:ID" attribute. The "rdf:ID" attribute is related to XML and HTML's ID attribute.

Once an identifier is established, it can be referenced by its relative URIref in an "rdf:about" attribute. A URIref should only be "created" once. The "rdf:ID" attribute is used to define a name that is unique within the defining file.

## 8.3.4.2 Describing an Existing Subject Resource (rdf:about)

If a resource already exists, we can describe it using the "rdf:about" attribute (forms 5-8). The "rdf:about" attribute is used to reference an existing resource.

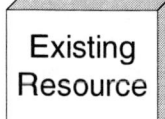

---

The typical syntax for describing an existing resource is:

```
<rdf:Description rdf:about="resourceURIref">
      <property>propertyValue</property>
</rdf:Description>
```

where **resourceURIref** is the **URI reference** of the existing resource being described, **property** is a property describing the resource, and **properyValue** is the value of the property for the resource.

---

Note: since the resource URIref is the value of an XML attribute, it should not be a QName (have a namespace prefix).

---

An example of describing an existing RDF resource with a literal object value (Form 5) (created in example above) using rdf:about is:

```
<rdf:Description rdf:about="#Person345">
      <profile:favoritePie>Key Lime Pie</profile:favoritePie>
</rdf:Description>
```

---

The "rdf:about" attribute extends the description of an existing resource in an "rdf:Description" element. The property element contents describe the subject resource. The value of the "rdf:about" attribute is a URIref. A resource can be a web resource (like a web page or email address) or a reference to an object (e.g., "employee8403" or "myHouse"). The "rdf:about" attribute is used to extend the definition of resources that are created in another part of the ontology or in a totally different ontology.

### 8.3.5 Describing a Statement's Property

All RDF/XML statements have a predicate portion described with a property. RDF/XML predicates are specified with URIrefs. As shown in examples above, properties are specified as XML elements within the "rdf:Description" element. Name properties following the lower CamelCase convention.

### 8.3.6 Describing a Statement Value

The subject resource may have multiple properties. Regardless of whether the subject resource is existing or new, it normally has properties with values. The value of a property in an RDF/XML statement is either a literal, a singular existing resource, a container resource, or a collection resource.

#### 8.3.6.1 Providing a Literal Value as a Property Value

Literals are basic building blocks for supporting RDF/XML statements (forms 1, 5). Literals can be the object of an RDF/XML statement, but not the subject. Previous examples have shown property values.

##### 8.3.6.1.1 Plain Literal Parse Type (rdf:parseType="Literal")

A plain literal is an untyped string combined with an optional language identifier. The rdf:parseType="Literal" attribute instructs parsers to treat the element's contents as a literal string instead of as additional RDF/XML content regardless of what is inside the property element. Parsers read plain literal contents without parsing them. This technique is used to encode well-formed XML tagged content as a property's value.

# Chapter 8 – RDF/XML

> The typical syntax of a plain literal for an existing subject resource is:
>
> ```
> <rdf:Description rdf:about="resourceURIref">
>         <propertyName rdf:parseType="Literal">
>                 xmlContent
>         </propertyName>
> </rdf:Description>
> ```
>
> where **resourceURIref** is the existing resource being described and **propertyName** is the name of the property and **xmlContent** is the literal value for the property.

> An example of specifying a plain literal is:
>
> ```
> <rdf:Description rdf:about="http://www.KnightOwlRestaruant/dessertMenu">
>         <HTMLmenuTitle rdf:parseType="Literal">
>                 <t>Knight Owl Restaurant</t><t>Dessert Menu</t><p/>
>         </HTMLmenuTitle>
> </rdf:Description>
> ```

A literal enables embedding XML within an RDF/XML file. Tagged content (e.g., XML including XHTML) cannot normally be provided as the value of a property without confusing a parser. The parseType attribute signals that the tagged content should not be parsed as anything but a string value.

### 8.3.6.1.2 Typed Literals (rdf:datatype)

RDF typed literals are character string values associated with particular datatypes. Rather than simply providing a literal as a property value, the value's datatype can be specified using the "rdf:datatype" attribute. The attribute's value is normally a reference to an XMLS datatype.

The datatype describes how to interpret the associated literal, which should be consistent with the specified datatype. Datatypes can be considered classes, with typed literals as their instances.

Section 2 – Enabling Technologies

---

The typical syntax of a typed literal is:

&lt;propertyName rdf:datatype="**datatypeURIref**"&gt;**literalValue**&lt;/propertyName&gt;

where **datatypeURIref** is the URIref of a datatype and **literalValue** is a literal string.

The typical syntax for the rdf:datatype attribute value is:
http://www.w3.org/2001/XMLSchema#**datatypeReference**

where **datatypeReference** is the name of an XML Schema datatype

---

An optional language identifier can also be specified.

---

An example of using a typed literal is:

```
<rdf:Description rdf:about="http://www.KnightOwlRestaurant.com">
     <closingTime rdf:datatype="&xsd;time">22:00:00</closingTime>
</rdf:Description>
```

---

Typed literal values are specified as the content of property elements that have an "rdf:datatype" attribute with a value of a datatype URI. The datatype associated with the typed literal should be one of the XMLS datatypes described in Section 6.2.2.

RDF leverages XMLS datatypes by referencing them with a URIref. By standardizing on datatypes identified in XMLS, interoperability is improved. If applications on the Semantic Web encounter unknown datatypes, they will not be able to validate the legality of the value. If the "rdf:datatype" attribute is omitted, the value of the property is interpreted as a plain (string) literal.

#### 8.3.6.1.3   RDF Types (rdf:type)

The "rdf:type" property supports the class concept. The resource identified by the property value represents a set whose members include the described individual. An individual can belong to multiple class sets. An individual member of a set has all the characteristics of the set.

## Chapter 8 – RDF/XML

---

The typical syntax of the type property is:

```
<description rdf:ID="resourceID">
    <rdf:type rdf:resource="ClassName"/>
</description>
```

where **resourceID** is the identifier of the resource and **ClassName** is the name of the class.

---

An example of specifying the type (class) of a new resource is:

```
<rdf:Description rdf:ID="spaghettiDish">
    <rdf:type rdf:resource="http://www.restaurant.org/menus/Dish"/>
</rdf:Description>
```

An example of specifying the class of an existing resource is:

```
<rdf:Description rdf:about="#JoeSmith">
    <rdf:type rdf:resource="#RestaurantOwner"/>
</rdf:Description>
```

---

The "rdf:type" property supports the instance-of relationships between resources and classes. The "rdf:type" property can be used with resources and its value must be a class. The syntax for specifying the "rdf:type" property can be abbreviated using the typed node (typedNode) syntax.

### Typed Node (typedNode) Element Syntax

RDF provides a shorthand notation for declaring a resource (individual) to be a member of a particular class (type). The type (class) QName is used as the tag name instead of using an "rdf:Description" element containing an explicit type declaration. Additional types membership can still be declared.

With the abbreviated typedNode syntax, the "rdf:type" property and its value are deleted and the class's QName is used as the element name instead of the rdf:Description element (see Figure 8-3).

Section 2 – Enabling Technologies

```
Regular    <rdf:Description rdf:ID="someURIref">
Syntax            <rdf:type rdf:resource="classURIref"/>
           </rdf:Description>
```

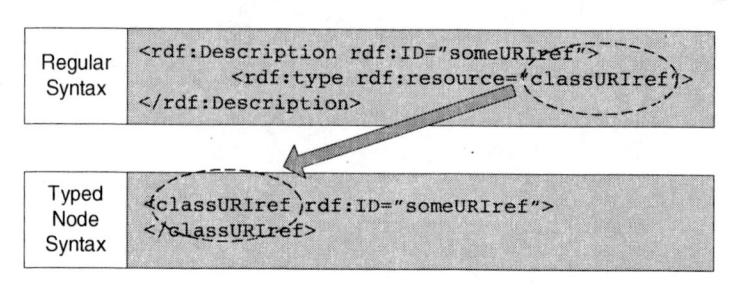

```
Typed      <classURIref rdf:ID="someURIref">
Node       </classURIref>
Syntax
```

Figure 8-3. TypedNode Syntax Abbreviation

The resulting semantics are the same as explicitly specifying the type property. The "rdf:Description" element attributes can be assigned to a typed element.

---

The syntax for specifying a typed node of the form:

&lt;rdf:Description rdf:ID="**resourceIdentifier**"&gt;
    &lt;rdf:type rdf:about="**typeName**"/&gt;
&lt;/rdf:Description&gt;

can be abbreviated as

&lt;**typeName** rdf:ID="**resourceIdentifier**"/&gt;

where **resourceIdentifier** is the identifier of the resource whose type(s) are being specificied and **typeName** is a type that describes the resource.

---

Since an individual may belong to multiple classes, there may be multiple "rdf:type" statements. If the resource is a member of an additional class, a traditional type property is added, but cannot leverage the shortened syntax.

---

An example of describing objects belonging to multiple classes is:

&lt;rdf:Description rdf:ID="Rice"&gt;
    &lt;rdf:type rdf:about="http://www.restaurant.org /food#Starch"/&gt;
    &lt;rdf:type rdf:about="http://www.restaurant.org /menu#SideDish"/&gt;
&lt;/rdf:Description&gt;

One of the type properties can be abbreviated using the typed node element syntax as:

&lt;food:Starch rdf:ID="Rice"&gt;
    &lt;rdf:type rdf:about="http://www.restaurant.org/food#SideDish"/&gt;
&lt;/food:Starch&gt;

# Chapter 8 – RDF/XML

The typedNode syntax makes class instantiations much more obvious for the human reader but makes no semantic difference to interpreting software.

### 8.3.6.2 Existing Individual Resource Property Value (rdf:resource)

Again, resources represent anything that is described with RDF. If a reference to a resource already exists, we can use its URIref as the value of a property using the "rdf:resource" attribute (forms 2, 6). The "rdf:resource" attribute provides a reference to the existing resource.

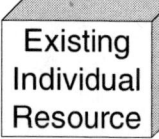

*Existing Individual Resource*

---

The typical syntax for providing an existing resource as the value for a property is:

<rdf:Description rdf:about="**describedResource**">
    <**propertyName** rdf:resource="**resourcePropertyValue**"/>
</rdf:Description>

where **describedResource** is the URIref of the resource being described, **propertyName** is the property being provided, and **resourcePropertyValue** is the URIref of the resource value for the property.

---

An example of referencing an existing RDF resource using rdf:resource is:

<rdf:Description rdf:about="#Pizzaria312">
    <associatedRestaurant rdf:resource="#Pizzaria314"/>
</rdf:Description>

---

The resource specified in the "rdf:about" attribute is called the referent.

### 8.3.6.3 RDF Container Resource Property Value

Normally, a property value is a single item. However, at times a group of things need to be specified as the property value of a new resource (form 3) or an existing resource (form 7). RDF provides a container mechanism to encapsulate data in order to allow a property value to refer to the single container as a resource.

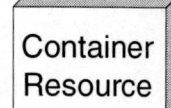

*Container Resource*

## Section 2 – Enabling Technologies

Since RDF syntax only allows a single item to be a property value, a container resource can be defined that serves as a single property value. Therefore, regardless of how many things you have in your container, you only have one resource in a statement (the container). RDF containers group things called members. Container members can be resources or literals.

Pre-defined RDF types and properties describe containers. RDF defines three types of containers: bags, sequences, and alternatives. The three container types have identical semantics internal to RDF (and OWL), but they are defined separately to encourage consistent usage by developers.

The "rdf:type" property is used to specify the type of a container. The value of the "rdf:type" property must be one of the pre-defined resources ("rdf:Bag", "rdf:Seq", or "rdf:Alt") associated with the RDF container types.

An alternative to using containers is to provide multiple property values associated with the subject resource. However, this approach results in a slightly different meaning (semantics).

### 8.3.6.3.1 Container Properties

Container types have intended meanings to encourage consistent treatment. However, there are no formal built-in rules for interpreting container types. Specifying RDF containers is different from defining a programming language data structure. It is more like defining an enumerated list. The rules for RDF containers are unlike what we are used to in the physical world. For example, a resource can occur in a container multiple times and a container can occur as an element within itself. RDF provides container membership properties to describe the members of container resources. They are used to access the contents (members) of a container. The two types of container membership properties are numbered properties (i.e., "rdf:_$n$") and the list property (i.e., "rdf:li").

#### 8.3.6.3.1.1 Numbered Properties (rdf:_$n$)

The names of numbered properties are based on the index number of the members. The properties are used to access a particular member of a container with the number of the item in the container. For example, "rdf:_3" accesses the third item in the container.

# Chapter 8 – RDF/XML

The numbered membership properties are used to state that a resource is a member of a container. The value of the reference number must be a positive integer with no leading zeroes.

---

The typical syntax of a numbered property is:

<rdf:_n rdf:resource="**memberURIref**"/>

where n is the index number of the container's element being set and **memberURIref** is the URIref of the resource being assigned to the nth spot in the container.

---

An example of using RDF numbered properties is:

<rdf:_1 rdf:resource="http://food.org#applePie"/>

---

The "rdf:_n" properties can be used with any resource and its value must be a resource.

### 8.3.6.3.1.2 List Item Convenience Property (rdf:li)

The contents of RDF containers are referenced separately with numbered properties (e.g., "rdf:_1", "rdf:_2"). However, RDF provides a "convenience element" to avoid explicitly numbering each of the items. The equivalent numbered properties are automatically generated (see Figure 8-4 for an example with four items).

The "rdf:li" property is provided by RDF for use with containers to specify an item in a group. RDF parsers automatically substitute each "rdf:li" with the proper corresponding numbered property (e.g., "rdf:_1"). The property name "li" is consistent with HTML's "list item".

---

The typical syntax of a list item is:

<rdf:li rdf:resource="**listItemURI**"/>

where **listItemURI** is the URIref of an item in the list.

---

97

## Section 2 – Enabling Technologies

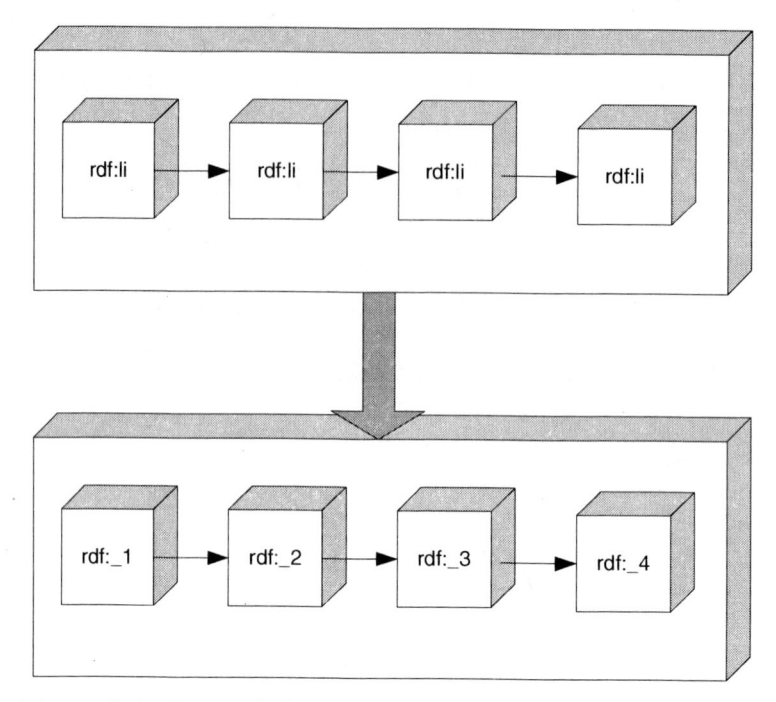

Figure 8-4. Example li to Numbered Property Translations

An example of an rdf:li declaration is:

`<rdf:li rdf:resource="http://www.restaurant.org/dessert/cherryPie"/>`

RDF containers are useful constructs. However, one limitation is that they are open-ended. There can be statements elsewhere that describe additional members. There is no way to "close" a container, specifying that no additional items can be added. The numbered properties can be used with any resource and their values must be resources.

# Chapter 8 – RDF/XML

**8.3.6.3.2 Unordered Container (rdf:Bag)**

Unordered containers are defined using the "rdf:Bag" class. Instances of the "rdf:Bag" class may contain resources and/or literals.

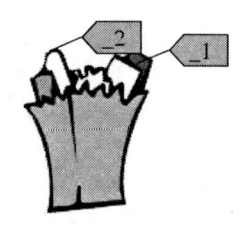

---

The typical syntax for specifying the contents of a bag container is:

```
<rdf:Bag>
        <rdf:li rdf:resource="resourceURIi"/>
</rdf:Bag>
```

where **resourceURIi** is the URIref of the ith member.

---

An example of using the Bag container to represent the sentence
"The pies available on tonight's menu are cherry, apple, and Key lime"
can be written in RDF/XML as:

```
<rdf:Description rdf:about="http://www.KnightOwlRestaurant.com/menu/070304">
        <desserts:pies>
                <rdf:Bag>
                        <rdf:li rdf:resource="&kor;cherry"/>
                        <rdf:li rdf:resource="&kor;apple"/>
                        <rdf:li rdf:resource="&kor;keylime"/>
                </rdf:Bag>
        </desserts:pies>
</rdf:Description>
```

---

An instance of the "rdf:Bag" type is an unordered container that can have duplicate members. The order of the contents of the unordered containers is not considered during production or consumption. Bags are good for generalized containers where order does not matter.

A bag can be the value of a property. A bag identifies an unordered container to human readers. No formal semantics are associated with the "rdf:Bag" type.

## 8.3.6.3.3 Ordered Container (rdf:Seq)

The "rdf:Seq" class is a container class used for representing ordered lists of resources or literals (sequences) (see Figure 8-4). The container can be used as the value of a property. A sequence is a resource of type "rdf:Seq" (an instance of the "rdf:Seq" class).

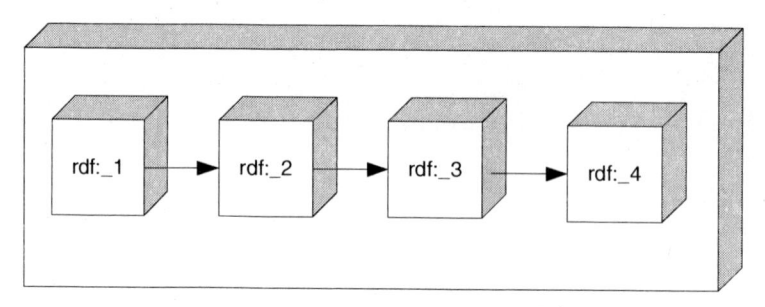

Figure 8-4. Example Ordered Container

---

The typical syntax of an ordered (sequential) container is:

```
<rdf:Seq>
        <rdf:li rdf:resource="resourceURIi"/>
</rdf:Seq>
```

where **resourceURIi** is the URIref of the ith element in a sequential container.

---

An example of describing successive courses as part of a meal could be represented as:

```
<rdf:Seq>
        <rdf:li rdf:resource="http://restaurant.com/menu/course/appetizer"/>
        <rdf:li rdf:resource="http://restaurant.com/menu/course/fish"/>
        <rdf:li rdf:resource="http://restaurant.com/menu/course/meat"/>
        <rdf:li rdf:resource="http://restaurant.com/menu/course/dessert"/>
</rdf:Seq>
```

---

The "rdf:Seq" class is used to instantiate ordered lists (sequences). The "rdf:Seq" class has no formal semantic differences from "rdf:Bag" and "rdf:Alt" but it has an intended standard use. Sequences can have duplicate values.

### 8.3.6.3.4  Container of Alternatives (rdf:Alt)

The "rdf:Alt" class is a container class used for representing lists of alternative resources or literals where any one item is a valid selection. The first item in the list is the default value, so an "rdf:Alt" container should have at least one item.

---

The typical syntax of an alternatives container is:

```
<rdf:Alt>
    <rdf:li rdf:resource="resourceURIi"/>
</rdf:Alt>
```

where **resourceURIi** is the ith URIref of the alternative container members, and **resourceURI1** is the default value.

---

An example of an alternatives container is:

```
<rdf:Alt>
    <rdf:li rdf:resource="#frenchFried"/>
    <rdf:li rdf:resource="#baked"/>
    <rdf:li rdf:resource="#mashed"/>
</rdf:Alt>
```

---

The alternatives container is useful for representing equally valid values for a property. An application can use any of the container's value as a valid representative choice. Software processing an alternatives container will select one of the members of the container. A common use of the "rdf:Alt" container is to provide multiple language variants for an item using the "xml:lang" attribute.

In an alternatives container, the first member has special meaning. This member is referenced by the "rdf:_1" property. It is the preferred alternative from the container. Since the first member has special meaning, an alternatives container should always have at least one member.

Section 2 – Enabling Technologies

### 8.3.6.3.5 RDF Container Summary

Table 8-4 contrasts the different types of containers.

Table 8-4. Container Summary Table

| Container Type | Notes |
|---|---|
| Bag ("rdf:Bag") | Order of contained items is not significant |
| Sequence ("rdf:Seq") | Order of contained items is significant |
| Alternatives ("rdf:Alt") | A minimum of 1 item must exist in the container and the $1^{st}$ item in the container is the default value |

### 8.3.6.4 RDF Collections (rdf:parseType="Collection")

RDF collections are an alternative to RDF containers. They are fixed finite lists of items. Unlike expandable containers, RDF collections are closed sets. A closed set collection may be specified as a value to a property with the rdf:parseType="Collection" attribute (forms 4,8). Lists of items represent RDF collections.

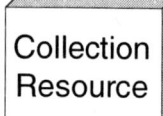

RDF collection lists are supported by the predefined "rdf:List" class. The "rdf:List" class members are referenced by the predefined properties "rdf:first" and "rdf:rest". The predefined resource "rdf:nil" is used to mark the end of an RDF collection list.

RDF collections are identified as the values of a property with an "rdf:parseType" attribute value of "Collection" in the property element. The "Collection" parse type specifies a list structure. The list has a fixed finite set of items.

---

The typical syntax of a property with a collection as its value is:

```
<propName rdf:parseType="Collection">
       collectedContents
</propName>
```

where **collectedContents** are the contents of the collection and **propName** is the name of the property.

# Chapter 8 – RDF/XML

> An example of an RDF collection would be an exhaustive list of pies available on a restaurant menu:
>
> ```
> <rdf:Description rdf:about="http://www.knightowlrestaurant.com/pieList">
>         <menu:hasPies rdf:parseType="Collection">
>                 <rdf:Description rdf:about="http:// www.knightowlrestaurant.com /cherryPie"/>
>                 <rdf:Description rdf:about="http:// www.knightowlrestaurant.com /applePie"/>
>                 <rdf:Description rdf:about="http:// www.knightowlrestaurant.com /keyLimePie"/>
>         </menu:hasPies>
> </rdf:Description>
> ```

### Closure

Unlike containers, when an RDF collection is specified, its complete list of members is provided. No additional members can be specified. RDF collections are closed (can have no members other than those specified in the original declaration of the container).

RDF collections contain a finite list of items. An element with an "rdf:parseType" of "Collection" has its contents interpreted as a closed list. A collection is represented as a list (a resource with an "rdf:type" property value of "rdf:List"). RDF list access properties support list traversal and manipulation. These properties are similar to the Lisp programming language's primary functions for list manipulation (i.e., "car", "cdr").

### 8.3.6.4.1  Specifying an RDF List Structure (rdf:List)

The "rdf:List" is a predefined class for representing a list of items. The list is described using the "rdf:first" and "rdf:rest" properties.

> The typical syntax of an rdf:List is:
>
> ```
> <rdf:List>
>         <rdf:first rdf:resource="rdfResourceDescription"/>
>
>             <rdf:rest rdf:resource="&rdf;nil"/>
>                         or
>             <rdf:rest>
>                         another List structure
>             </rdf:rest>
>
> </rdf:List>
>
> where rdfResourceDescription is the first item in the list
> ```

103

## Section 2 – Enabling Technologies

---

An example of an rdf:List specification is:

```
<rdf:List>
        <rdf:first rdf:resource="#CherryPie"/>
        <rdf:rest>
                <rdf:List>
                        <rdf:first rdf:resource ="#ApplePie"/>
                        <rdf:rest>
                                <rdf:List>
                                        <rdf:first rdf:resource ="#KeyLimePie"/>
                                        <rdf:rest rdf:resource="&rdf;nil"/>
                                </rdf:List>
                        </rdf:rest>
                </rdf:List>
        </rdf:rest>
</rdf:List>
```

---

Two properties are used to access portions of a list: "rdf:first" and "rdf:rest". The "rdf:List" class is similar to a linked list. It is accessed similar to a Lisp list construct with references to the first instance in a list and the rest of the list (see Figure 8-5 for one way to visualize the example of the list structure's use).

### 8.3.6.4.2    Referencing the First Item of a List (rdf:first)

The "rdf:first" property indicates the first item of a list.

---

The typical syntax of an rdf:first property is:

   <rdf:first rdf:resource="**firstResourceDescription**"/>

where **firstResourceDescription** is the individual member at the beginning of a list.

---

Chapter 8 – RDF/XML

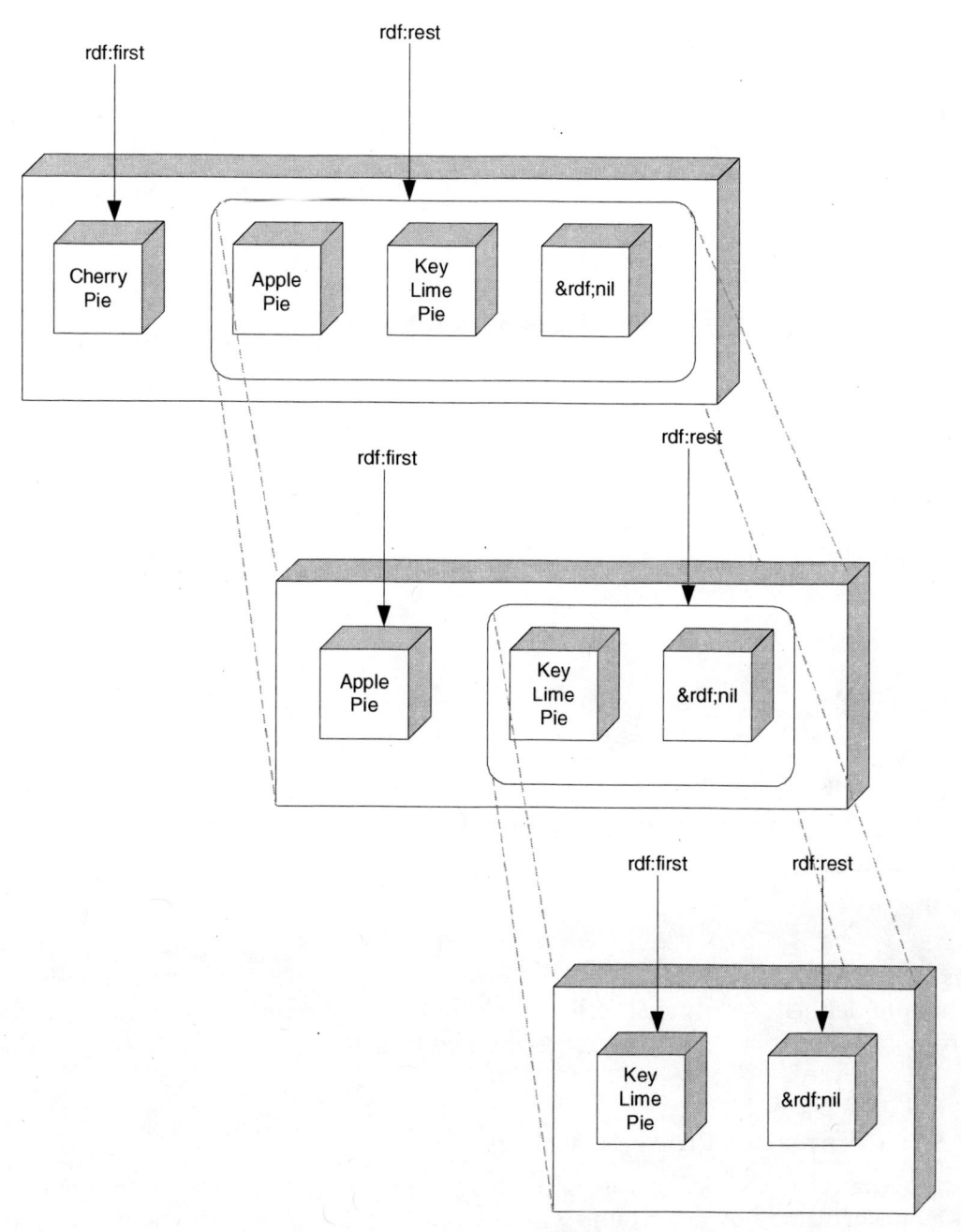

Figure 8-5. Example List Structures

## Section 2 – Enabling Technologies

---

> An example of using an rdf:first property is:
>
> `<rdf:first rdf:resource="#CherryPie"/>`

The "rdf:first" property can be used with any "rdf:List" and its value must be a resource.

### 8.3.6.4.3 Referencing the Remaining List (rdf:rest)

The "rdf:rest" property indicates the portion of the list (sublist) other than the first item in the list. If the "rdf:rest" property's value for a list is "&rdf;nil", the end of the list is referenced (there are no more elements in the list).

> The typical syntax of the rdf:rest property is:
>
> ```
> <rdf:rest rdf:resource="&rdf;nil"/>
>                  or
> <rdf:rest>
>         <rdf:List>
>                 ListStructure
>         </rdf:List>
> </rdf:rest>
> ```
>
> where **ListStructure** is a list structure with an rdf:rest and rdf:rest.

The "rdf:rest" property can be used with any "rdf:List" and its value must be an "rdf:List".

### 8.3.6.4.4 Empty List (&rdf;nil)

The pre-defined empty list called "&rdf;nil" is a predefined instance of the "rdf:List" class. The "&rdf;nil" list terminates lists.

## 8.3.7 Compound Property Values

An alternative to providing a single resource value or a literal value is to provide a compound value. A compound value has multiple value parts, with one part typically identified as the primary value of the property.

# Chapter 8 – RDF/XML

### 8.3.7.1.1 Resource Parse Type (rdf:parseType="Resource")

A compound value is identified by associating an "rdf:parseType" attribute with the property. The value of the attribute is set to "Resource" to identify the value of the property as a compound value.

### 8.3.7.1.2 Qualified Property Value (rdf:value)

The "rdf:value" property identifies the primary value within a compound property value, and is called the qualified property value. Additional properties within the compound value may describe the qualified property value. The qualified value can be either a literal or a resource identified by its URIref in the "rdf:resource" attribute value.

---

The typical syntax of RDF values is:

<rdf:value>**value**</rdf:value>

where **value** is the primary value of the element.

---

An example of specifying a compound property value is:

```
<rdf:Description rdf:about="http://www.KnightOwlRestaurant.com/Menu/Dessert#applePie">
        <price rdf:parseType="Resource">
                <rdf:value>2.5</rdf:value>
                <menu:currency>USD</menu:currency>
        </price>
</rdf:Description>
```

---

RDF properties only represent binary relations. A qualified property value is a way to support higher arity relations. A higher arity relation is a relation between more than two resources. Another way to represent structured information in RDF is to describe an extra intermediate resource with properties.

The "rdf:value" element does not have to be used to identify the primary value. RDF does not treat the "rdf:value" property differently. However, it is available as a convenience property.

Section 2 – Enabling Technologies

## 8.3.8 Striped Syntax

The value of an "rdf:Description" element can be another "rdf:Description" element, resulting in alternating property/value descriptions chained together. The alternating sequence of subject resource property specifications is referred to as striping. An "rdf:Description" element without an "rdf:ID" or "rdf:about" attribute creates a blank (anonymous) node when read by an RDF parser.

---

The typical syntax of a striped syntax set of statements is:

```
<rdf:Description>
        <property1>
                DescriptionElement
        </property1>
<rdf:Description>
```

where **DescriptionElement** is another RDF description element

---

An example of striped syntax used to describe the chained statements that a resource ((KnightOwlRestaurant) has a website property value that has a webmaster (Jorge Garcia)

```
<rdf:Description rdf:about="#KnightOwlRestaurant">
        <website>
                <rdf:Description rdf:about "http://wwww.knightowlrestaurant.com">
                        <webmaster>Jorge Garcia</webmaster >
                </rdf:Description>
        </website>
</rdf:Description>
```

---

Although this variety of syntax may be easier for some to read, it can make the resulting file more difficult to edit and may be more difficult to generate from an automated tool. Therefore, the use of the striped syntax to encode OWL information representations is discouraged.

## 8.3.9 RDF Description Summary

RDF/XML files contain sets of RDF/XML statements. The subject of a statement can be either a new or an existing resource. Properties specify the predicate. The value of the statement can be a literal, single resource, container, or collection. Compound values can also be provided. The alternating of properties and other statements is called striped syntax. Although the RDF/XML syntax may seem tedious, database applications will generate the statements in many situations.

## *8.4 RDF/XML Summary*

RDF/XML provides a structured method for serializing RDF content into XML files using standard constructs. RDF/XML provides a mechanism for interchanging RDF content.

RDF content is serialized by making description statements about resources using XML. The RDF resources are described with XML elements and values represented as properties and property values. Table 8-5 presents a summary of the RDF/XML constructs.

Table 8-5. RDF/XML Summary Table

| Category | Construct | Purpose |
|---|---|---|
| Resource identification | rdf:ID attribute | Establishes reference identifier |
|  | rdf:about attribute | References an identifier subject |
|  | rdf:resource attribute | References an identifier object |
|  | rdf:value attribute | Identifies primary value in a compound value |
|  | rdf:type property | Specifies class membership |
| RDF lists | rdf:_n property | Indexed accessor |
|  | rdf:li property | Convenience access function |
| Container | rdf:Bag class | Unordered container |
|  | rdf:Seq class | Sequentially ordered container |
|  | rdf:Alt class | Container of alternatives |
| Collection | rdf:List class | List of items |
|  | rdf:first property | First item in a list |
|  | rdf:rest property | Sublist of all but first item |
|  | &rdf;nil resource | Empty list to terminate a list |

Section 2 – Enabling Technologies

## 8.5 *Why RDF/XML is not Enough*

Although RDF/XML introduces some standardization to descriptions, more complex semantic relationships (e.g., classes) need to be described with a standard consistent vocabulary. RDF also lacks concepts for enumeration and datatypes (other than typed literals).

The next chapter describes RDFS which adds object-oriented features to RDF.

# 9 RDFS

> *"RDF's vocabulary description language, RDF Schema, is a semantic extension of RDF. It provides mechanisms for describing groups of related resources and the relationships between these resources. RDF Schema vocabulary descriptions are written in RDF", from RDF Vocabulary Description Language 1.0: RDF Schema, W3C Recommendation 10 February 2004, on-line: http://www.w3.org/TR/rdf-schema/*

RDF Schema (RDFS) is part of the ontological primitive layer of the Semantic Web architecture, and builds on RDF (Figure 9-1). RDF provides an abstract data model for making statements about resources. RDF/XML is used to serialize those statements into a concrete syntax. RDFS adds features and provides a standardized vocabulary for describing concepts (a meta-vocabulary).

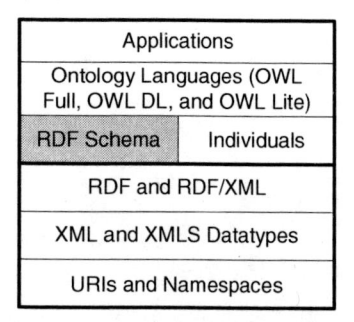

| Applications |  |
|---|---|
| Ontology Languages (OWL Full, OWL DL, and OWL Lite) ||
| RDF Schema | Individuals |
| RDF and RDF/XML ||
| XML and XMLS Datatypes ||
| URIs and Namespaces ||

Figure 9-1. RDFS Portion of the Ontological Primitive Layer

This chapter provides an overview of RDFS and its features, along with an introduction of classes, individuals, and properties.

## 9.1 RDFS Overview

RDFS is a domain-neutral lightweight schema language that provides basic structures such as classes and properties. These ontological structures are formally defined. RDFS builds on the RDF foundation to provide additional descriptive features and a language for describing the expanded vocabulary.

RDFS was developed by the W3C's RDF Model and Syntax Working Group and later refined by the RDF Core Working Group. Table 9-1 identifies the resulting authoritative description of RDFS.

Section 2 – Enabling Technologies

Table 9-1. RDFS Authoritative Description

| Title: | **RDF Vocabulary Description Language 1.0: RDF Schema** |
|---|---|
| Document URI: | http://www.w3.org/TR/rdf-schema/ |
| Purpose: | Defines a vocabulary for using RDF to define RDF vocabularies. |

Table 9-2 identifies the namespace prefix and URI associated with RDFS.

Table 9-2. RDFS Namespace

| Recommended Namespace Prefix: | rdfs |
|---|---|
| Namespace Name: | http://www.w3.org/2000/01/rdf-schema# |

## 9.2 RDFS Features

RDFS adds descriptive features to RDF's basic constructs by defining additional modeling primitives. It enriches RDF by giving semantics to specific resources. RDFS extends RDF's type system to define a formal class concept. RDFS concepts also support restricting property and class use. RDFS concepts extend RDF's support for making simple statements.

RDFS is a vocabulary description language. It provides features for encoding domain-specific vocabularies by adding constructs to RDF while continuing to use the RDF/XML syntax. These vocabularies help applications understand how to interpret RDF statements.

An RDFS vocabulary is a collection of class and property descriptions. RDFS supports making statements that draw on multiple vocabularies. RDF Schema describes domain-specific vocabularies using a collection of RDF resources that define characteristics of other resources.

Independent communities manage these vocabularies in a decentralized fashion. Communities of interest can use RDFS to specify domain-specific collections of descriptions that form extensible vocabularies with explicit semantics.

## 9.3 RDFS Classes

RDFS extends the RDF type concept to provide formal mechanisms for describing classes which represent concepts. RDFS predefines several core classes.

### 9.3.1 RDFS Class Concept

A common knowledge representation requirement is to describe concepts or "kinds of things". RDFS classes are sets used to describe concepts as categories of resources, typically for a particular domain. Classes have associated resources that are instances of the class. Resources can belong to multiple classes.

A class can be considered a template used to instantiate objects (individuals). A class's set of member instances is called the class extension. Two different classes could have the same class extension.

RDFS classes are similar to OOP language classes. However, they are more similar to entities in data models because they do not have associated behaviors. Also, properties are distinct from classes. The same property (similar to an OOP attribute) is useable with multiple RDFS classes.

RDFS classes are also similar to RDBMS tables. In RDF, a class is identified with a resource name in an "rdf:type" property (described previously in Section 8.3.6.1.3). The resource that represents the class should not be confused with the resources that are members of the class (its instances).

### 9.3.2 Predefined RDFS Classes

RDFS formalizes the concepts of resources, classes, and properties by predefining specific RDF resources. Those resources are used to define domain-specific vocabularies. RDFS documentation defines the meaning of these special resources. RDFS pre-defines a number of classes to support a formal vocabulary grounded in the RDF object model and expressed with the RDF/XML syntax.

Section 2 – Enabling Technologies

### 9.3.2.1 Defining RDFS Classes

In RDF, the "rdf:type" property establishes class membership. The "rdfs:Class" type is used to define a class in RDFS. RDFS typically uses the typed node syntax to describe RDFS classes as instances of the "rdfs:Class" type. The fact that classes in RDFS are resources that are members of the "rdfs:Class" class can be confusing at first. Classes are resources whose type is "rdfs:Class". Classes are specified using the "rdfs:Class" class, the "rdf:type" property, and the "rdfs:subClassOf" property.

Although RDFS can be used to define classes for your information representations, OWL extends the class concept and OWL classes are the recommended method for defining domain specific classes. Section 3 describes OWL class specifications. URIrefs name classes because classes are themselves resources. RDFS classes are named with a URIref. The class name URIrefs are assigned with "rdf:ID" attributes in RDF statements.

In RDFS, a class is any resource having an "rdf:type" property whose value is the RDFS-defined resource "rdfs:Class". The long form of specifying an RDFS class is to use an "rdf:Description" element to describe the resource representing the class and "type" the resource as an "rdfs:Class" type (i.e., "rdf:type" = "rdfs:Class"). The short form is to use the typedNode syntax to define the class in an "rdfs:Class" element.

RDFS defines classes and properties for the concepts identified in the RDF data model. RDF classes are defined using the predefined "rdf:type" property (see section 8.3.6.1.5). Files that reference the RDFS namespace obtain the use of these classes. These classes provide the vocabulary that enables people to specify ontologies.

The key to understanding the simplicity of RDFS and the associated XML syntax is that RDFS uses RDF to define itself. RDFS pre-defines classes as part of the RDF schema vocabulary for resources, properties, classes, datatypes, literals, XML literals, containers, membership properties, and list members.

## 9.3.2.2 RDFS Resources (rdfs:Resource)

RDF expressions describe resources. RDFS defines a built-in class called "rdfs:Resource". The "rdfs:Resource" class represents the most general class (root class) of things. All RDF resources are automatically instances of this class. The "rdfs:Resource" class is a root class, meaning that all other classes are subclasses of this class.

## 9.3.2.3 RDF Properties (rdf:Property)

RDFS specifies that the "rdf:Property" class is a predefined part of the RDFS vocabulary for defining properties. The "rdf:Property" class represents RDF resources that define properties. Since properties are an RDF concept, the "rdf:" prefix is used with the "Property" class to represent the RDF namespace. Therefore, all user-defined properties are instances of the "rdf:Property" class.

## 9.3.2.4 RDFS Classes (rdfs:Class)

RDFS defines a resource ("rdfs:Class") that is used for defining classes. Resources that have a type of "rdfs:Class" are considered RDFS classes. The "rdfs:Class" resource is defined as an "rdfs:Class", so "rdfs:Class" is a class. Instances of the "rdfs:Class" class are classes.

## 9.3.2.5 RDFS Literals (rdfs:Literal)

The predefined "rdfs:Literal" class represents the set of atomic plain and typed literal values (e.g., simple textual strings) and is used to represent datatypes. The "rdfs:Literal" class can be used to specify that a property's values (range) must be string literals.

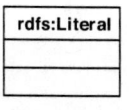

The "rdfs:Literal" class describes literal values such as strings and integers. The "rdfs:Literal" class is considered an OWL datatype. The URIref for the "rdfs:Literal" datatype is "http://www.w3.org/2000/01/rdf-schema#Literal". Data values and string literals are instances of the "rdfs:Literal" class. The "rdfs:Literal" class is implicitly part of all ontologies.

115

Section 2 – Enabling Technologies

### 9.3.2.6 XML Literals (rdf:XMLLiteral)

The predefined class "rdf:XMLLiteral" is a subclass of the "rdfs:Literal" class. It represents XML text strings within RDF statements. The "rdf:XMLLiteral" is a datatype and is the only datatype predefined in RDF. Like "rdf:Property", "rdf:XMLLiteral" is an RDF concept described as part of the RDFS vocabulary.

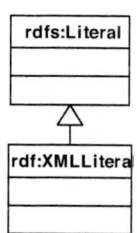

The "rdf:XMLLiteral" datatypes can also include language identifiers. RDF uses a subset of XMLS datatypes for numbers, dates, etc. The names of datatypes are URIrefs. The "rdf:XMLLiteral" class is considered a datatype whose URIref is "http://www.w3.org/1999/02/22-rdf-syntax-ns#XMLLiteral".

### 9.3.2.7 RDFS Datatype Class (rdfs:Datatype)

Datatypes (e.g., integer) define subsets of literal values that have associated semantics for their interpretation. The predefined class "rdfs:Datatype" is used to represent datatypes. Datatypes are considered instances of the "rdfs:Datatype" class. All datatype classes (instances of "rdfs:Datatype") are automatically subclasses of the "rdfs:Literal" class. URIrefs (e.g., "&xsd;integer") are used to reference datatypes that are assumed to conform to RDF datatype concepts.

Datatypes are identified as such by making them instances of the "rdfs:Datatype" class. For example, "&xsd;nonNegativeInteger" is an instance of the datatype class and a subclass of "rdfs:Literal". The "rdfs:Datatype" class should not be confused with the "rdf:datatype" attribute on properties.

RDFS groups datatypes into supported datatypes and unsupported datatypes. Defining new instances of the "rdfs:Datatype" class (defining a new datatype) is a legal, but discouraged practice.

RDFS datatypes provide a mechanism for referring to XMLS datatypes. In addition to the XML Schema datatypes listed in Section 6.2.2, OWL datatypes include "rdfs:Literal" as a datatype.

### 9.3.2.8 RDFS Predefined Class Summary

Table 9-3 presents a summary of the RDFS predefined classes.

Table 9-3. RDFS Predefined Classes

| Predefined Class | Description |
| --- | --- |
| rdfs:Resource | Root class of all resources |
| rdf:Property | Class of all properties |
| rdfs:Class | Class of all classes |
| rdfs:Literal | Class of all literal values |
| rdf:XMLLiteral | XML strings within RDF statements |
| rdfs:Datatype | Identifies datatypes |

## 9.4 Individuals

Instances of user-defined classes are called individuals. Individual resources belong to classes. In RDF, individuals are associated with classes using the "rdf:type" property. Individuals can be created and assigned to one or more classes. Chapter 15 describes individuals in detail.

## 9.5 Properties

RDFS provides features for describing properties (a concept introduced in RDF). RDFS descriptions of properties include restrictions. Properties are instances of the "rdf:Property" class described above.

RDFS provides features for specific constraints on properties. The types of constraints that can be specified include limiting the values that a property can have and limiting which properties a resource can have. RDFS provides a vocabulary for core properties, clarification properties, container descriptions, and documentation properties.

## 9.5.1 Vocabulary for RDF Core Properties

RDFS provides core properties that relate individuals to classes ("rdf:type"), classes to classes ("rdfs:subClassOf"), properties to properties ("rdfs:subPropertyOf"), and properties to classes ("rdfs:domain" and "rdfs:range"). RDFS properties are defined as instances of the pre-defined "rdf:Property" class.

### 9.5.1.1 RDF Type (rdf:type) Property

The "rdf:type" property is a core property used to associate an individual with a particular class. In RDFS compliant representations, the value of an "rdf:type" property should be a class (instance of "rdfs:Class").

### 9.5.1.2 Specializing Classes (rdfs:subClassOf)

Classes can be organized into generalization/specialization hierarchies. Subclasses support the ontology representation requirement for hyponymy.

The predefined RDFS "rdfs:subClassOf" property is used to define specialization relationships between classes and to assemble class hierarchies. The subclass relation is similar to a subset relation between classes. A class can be a subclass of multiple superclasses. A superclass is identified by the "rdfs:subClassOf" property on a subclass. Both the subclass and superclass must be of type "rdfs:Class". Any individual that is an instance of the subclass is considered an instance of the superclass.

> The typical syntax for defining a subclass is:
>
> ```
> <rdfs:Class rdf:ID="classURIref">
>     <rdfs:subClassOf rdf:resource="superClassURIref"/>
> </rdfs:Class>
> ```
>
> where **classURIref** is the URIref of the subclass and **superClassURIref** is the URIref of the superclass.

# Chapter 9 - RDFS

For example, we can state that spaghettiDish is a specialization (subclass) of pastaDish:

```
<rdfs:Class rdf:ID="spaghettiDish">
    <rdfs:subClassOf rdf:resource="#pastaDish"/>
</rdfs:Class>
```

Every class is automatically a subclass of the "rdfs:Resource" class because every class's member instances are also members of the "rdfs:Resource" class. Also, a subclass "inherits" the superclass's property restrictions.

The "rdfs:subClassOf" property is transitive. That means that if a class C is a subclass of a class B, and class B is a subclass of a class A, then class C can also be considered a subclass of class A (see Figure 9-2). A class can be a subclass of multiple superclasses. An instance of a subclass has properties associated with both the subclass and superclass.

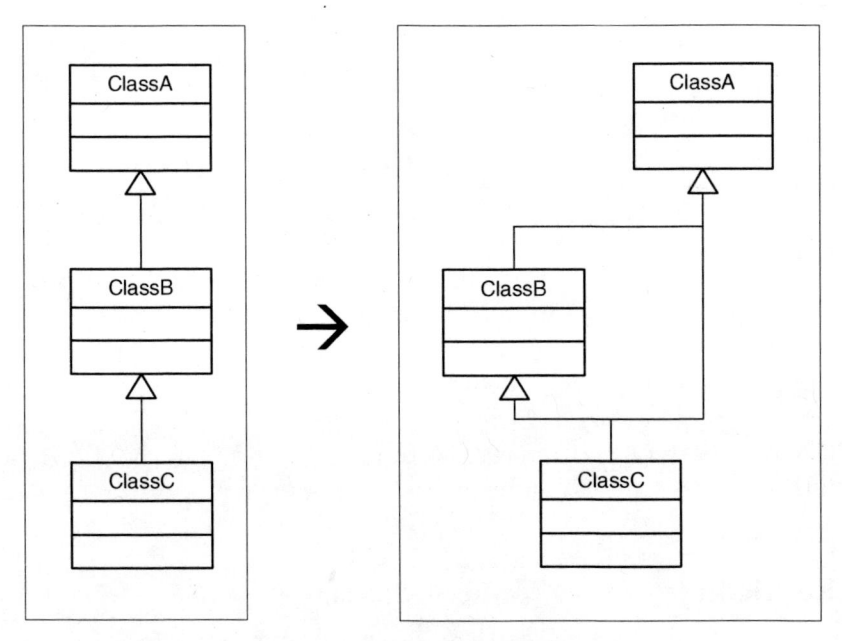

Figure 9-2. Subclass Transitivity

The "rdfs:subClassOf" property can be used with any "rdfs:Class" and its value must be an instance of "rdfs:Class".

119

## 9.5.1.3 Specializing Properties (rdfs:subPropertyOf)

Just as a classes can be specialized with subclass relationships, properties can be specialized with subproperties. The "rdfs:subPropertyOf" property is used to specify a specialization relationship between properties. The described property is a subproperty of the indicated superproperty.

---

The typical syntax for defining a subPropertyOf property is:

```
<rdf:Property rdf:ID="subpropertyURIref">
        <rdfs:subPropertyOf rdf:resource="superpropertyURIref"/>
</rdf:Property>
```

where **subpropertyURIref** is the URIref of the subproperty and **superPropertyURIref** is the URIref of the superproperty.

---

An example of specifying a subPropertyOf is:

```
<rdf:Property rdf:ID="faxNumber">
        <rdfs:subPropertyOf rdf:resource="#phoneNumber"/>
</rdf:Property>
```

---

A property can be the subproperty of multiple properties. All the resources related by the subproperty relationship are also related by its superproperty. If a property is a subproperty of another property, its values for a subject resource are also true for its superproperty. Therefore, a query searching at a superproperty level can consider subproperty information.

The "rdfs:subPropertyOf" property is transitive and can be used with any "rdf:Property" and its value must be an instance of "rdf:Property".

## 9.5.1.4 Restricting Property Values (rdfs:range)

The values of properties can be restricted to belonging to particular classes or data ranges using the "rdfs:range" property (see Figure 9-3).

# Chapter 9 - RDFS

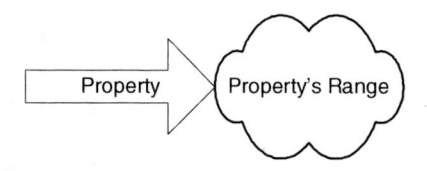

Figure 9-3. Range Restriction

There are two types of range property values: classes and datatypes. The "rdfs:range" property is used to associate a property's values to either the class extension specified by a class description or data values specified by a datatype.

---

A range restriction is typically specified using the following syntax:

`<rdfs:range rdf:resource="`**classname**`"/>`

where **classname** is the name of the class that the property value must belong to.

---

Datatypes can also serve as ranges. Typed literals specify property values conforming to the datatype range.

---

The following example shows how a property's range can be specified:

```
<rdf:Property rdf:ID="ownedBy">
    <rdfs:range rdf:resource="#Person"/>
</rdf:Property>
```

---

This example shows a valid use of a property that has a range restriction:

```
<Person rdf:ID="Person123">
    <personName>Rory Peebles</personName>
</Person>

<Restaurant rdf:ID="JoesPizzaria">
    <restaurantName>Joe's Pizzaria</restaurantName>
    <ownedBy rdf:resource="#Person123"/>
</Restaurant>
```

The example above demonstrates why global property restrictions should be used with care. There may be cases where someone wants to specify that a company is the owner of a restaurant.

A recommended approach if a global property restriction is truly desired, is to make the property name very specific. For example, instead of using the property name "ownedBy", the ontology developer could use a name such as "restaurantOwnerIndividual".

The range specifies which individual or data values can be objects of the property. Range restrictions should not be separate URIs. If every time a user wishes to limit a property of range integer or real number to an interval, they will need to refer to a separate URI. This will cause scalability and usability difficulties.

**Multiple Ranges**

Multiple range restrictions can be specified. The effect of multiple range properties is to limit the property value to being a member of all (intersection) of the specified classes. More precisely, a property can have zero, one, or more range property restrictions (see Table 9-4).

Table 9-4. Multiple Range Cases

| Case | Implication |
| --- | --- |
| 0 (unconstrained) | Says nothing about the values of property |
| 1 | the values of the property are instances of class specified |
| >1 | the values of the property are resources that are instances of all of the classes specified as the ranges |

You can infer that an individual is a member of a class if it is the value of a property that has a range restriction. For example, from the example above, we could infer that "#Person123" is a "Person" from the "Restaurant" description alone because the range of the "ownedBy" property was constrained to the "Person" class.

Even if you specify the range of a particular property to be a certain datatype, you still need to provide an "rdf:datatype" attribute for the property value.

# Chapter 9 - RDFS

The "rdfs:range" property can be used with any "rdf:Property" and its value must be an instance of "rdfs:Class".

## 9.5.1.5 Restricting Property Subjects (rdfs:domain)

The subject of a statement's property can be restricted to instances of a particular class using the "rdfs:domain" property. The "rdfs:domain" property limits the use of a property to a specified intersection of subject classes (see Figure 9-4).

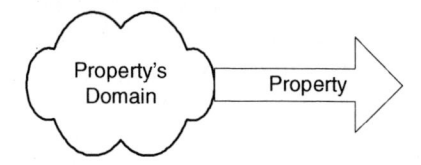

Figure 9-4. Domain Restriction

---

A domain restriction is specified within a property specification with the following syntax:

`<rdfs:domain rdf:resource="`**className**`"/>`

where **className** is the name of the class that can have the property being described.

---

This example shows the specification of a domain property:

```
<rdf:Property rdf:ID="ownedBy">
        <rdfs:domain rdf:resource="#Restaurant"/>
</rdf:Property>
```

In this example, only members of the Restaurant class can use the ownedBy property.

---

This example shows a valid set of assertions because the "ownedBy" property is being associated with an instance of a "Restaurant".

```
<Restaurant rdf:ID="JoesPizzaria">
        <restaurantName>Joe's Pizzaria</restaurantName>
        <ownedBy rdf:resource="#Person123"/>
</Restaurant>
```

123

Section 2 – Enabling Technologies

The "rdfs:domain" property specifies the class extension that can use the property being constrained. The constraint restricts the set of resources that can have the described property. If a property's domain is restricted (with an "rdfs:domain" property) and a statement about an individual contains the constrained property, then the individual can be inferred to be a member of the class identified by the "rdfs:domain" property. The "rdfs:domain" restriction has a global scope (it applies to all uses of the property).

**Multiple Domains**

Multiple "rdfs:domain" restrictions can be specified. When multiple domain restrictions are specified, the property's domain is limited to individuals that belong to all the identified classes (the intersection of the specified domain classes). Table 9-5 shows a summary of the implication of potential cases of domains.

Table 9-5. Multiple Domain Cases

| Case | Implication |
| --- | --- |
| 0 | If there are no domain restrictions, the property is applicable to any resource. |
| 1 | If a single domain class is identified in the domain restriction or property, the property can only be used with the instances of the specified class. |
| >1 | Intersection of all classes (instances of all of the specified classes) |

The "rdfs:domain" property can be used with any "rdf:Property" and its value must be an instance of "rdfs:Class".

### 9.5.1.6 RDFS Core Properties Summary

Table 9-6 presents a summary of the RDFS core properties.

Table 9-6. RDFS Core Properties

| Core Property | Description |
| --- | --- |
| rdf:type | Identifies the class of an individual |
| rdfs:subClassOf | Creates a specialization of a class |
| rdfs:subPropertyOf | Creates a specialization of a property |
| rdfs:range | Limits the values of a property |
| rdfs:domain | Limits the individuals that can have a property |

## 9.5.2 RDFS Clarification Properties

RDFS defines clarification properties for referencing related resources and identifying a resource's source. Clarification properties are non-core properties that provide additional information about a resource.

### 9.5.2.1 Referencing Related Resources (rdfs:seeAlso)

The "rdfs:seeAlso" property identifies a resource that provides additional information about the subject resource.

---

The typical syntax of the seeAlso property is:

<rdfs:seeAlso rdf:resource="**referencedURIref**"/>

where **referencedURIref** is the URIref of a related referenced resource.

---

An example of using the seeAlso property is:

```
<menu:Pie rdf:ID="chocolatePie">
     <rdfs:seeAlso rdf:resource="#frenchSilkPie"/>
</ menu:Pie>
```

---

The "rdfs:seeAlso" property identifies an alternative description of the resource being described. It is a reference to a related resource. The "rdfs:seeAlso" property has weak semantics, but is a pre-defined property that is useful in some circumstances.

The "rdfs:seeAlso" property can be used with any "rdfs:Resource" and its value must be an instance of "rdfs:Resource".

### 9.5.2.2 Identifying a Resource's Source (rdfs:isDefinedBy)

Sometimes there is no obvious relationship between the URIref of a resource and the namespace where it was defined. The "rdfs:isDefinedBy" property is a subproperty of "rdfs:seeAlso" that relates a resource to another authoritative resource that defines it.

Section 2 – Enabling Technologies

---

> The typical syntax for the isDefinedBy property is:
>
> <rdfs:isDefinedBy rdf:resource="**definingURIref**"/>
>
> where **definingURIref** is the URIref that defines the resource being described.

> An example of using the isDefinedBy property is:
>
> <rdfs:isDefinedBy rdf:resource="http://www.restaurant.org/dish"/>

Sometimes, the URIref of a resource does not identify the source of its definition. You cannot assure that the URI portion of a resource URI reference indicates the schema of the resource. The "rdfs:isDefinedBy" property can identify the defining RDF vocabulary for a resource. The "rdfs:isDefinedBy" property can be used with any "rdfs:Resource" and its value must be an instance of "rdfs:Resource".

### 9.5.3  RDFS Container Classes and Properties

RDFS provides classes and properties to support containers.  Containers encapsulate things into groups that can be referenced as a whole.

#### 9.5.3.1  RDFS Containers (rdfs:Container)

The RDF container concept is supported by the pre-defined class "rdfs:Container". It helps manage the description of container types. The "rdfs:Container" class is the superclass of the three previously described RDF container classes: "rdf:Bag", "rdf:Seq", and "rdf:Alt". These predefined classes are subclasses of the "rdfs:Container" class (see Figure 9-5).

| rdfs:Container |
|---|
|  |
|  |

126

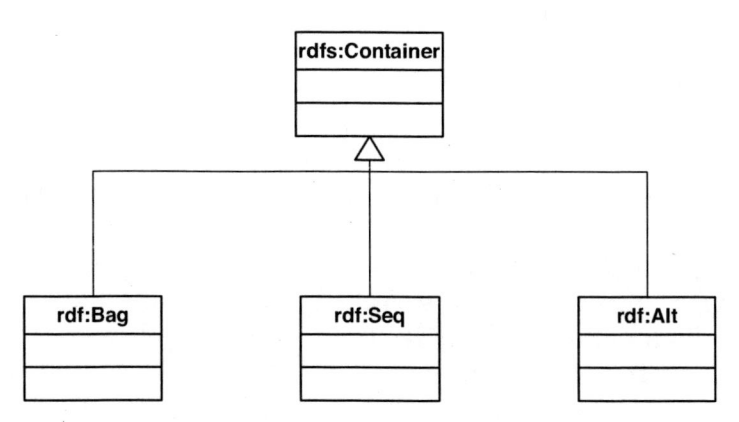

Figure 9-5. Container Class and its Subclasses

### 9.5.3.2 Container Membership Properties (rdfs:ContainerMembershipProperty)

A predefined class called "rdfs:ContainerMembershipProperty" is used to instantiate individual subproperties for accessing members of containers. The individual properties are named "rdf:_1", "rdf:_2", etc.

The container membership properties are specific types of the "rdfs:member" property.

### 9.5.3.3 Member Property (rdfs:member)

The super property of all the container membership properties is the "rdfs:member" property. RDFS defines the "rdfs:member" property as a generalization of all the "rdf:_$n$" container membership properties.

Section 2 – Enabling Technologies

## 9.5.4 RDFS Documentation Properties

As part of the tradeoff between supporting both human and computer requirements for knowledge representation, it is often helpful to provide human-friendly names/labels and descriptions of resources.

RDFS defines two documentation properties ("rdfs:label" and "rdfs:comment") for associating human-readable labels and descriptions with resources. The values of the documentation properties can be leveraged by user interface software to provide more user-friendly text to humans. Multiple values can be provided with "xml:lang" attributes to support internationalization. The best practice is to always label and comment classes and properties. The properties "rdfs:label" and "rdfs:comment" properties are described in the following sections.

### 9.5.4.1 Labeling Resources (rdfs:label)

The "rdfs:label" property provides a human-readable version of a resource's name. The label is normally a short textual string that is especially useful in a user interface (e.g., drop down list box). Since everything in RDFS (i.e., classes, properties, instances) is a resource, anything can have an associated label. A report might use a resource's label to help describe the output value on the report. Labels are properties on resources that must be literals (see Figure 9-6).

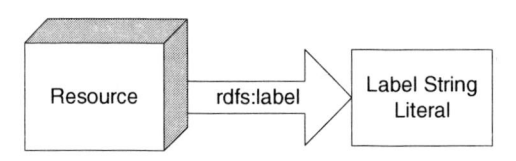

Figure 9-6. Label Property

---

The typical syntax for a label is:

<rdfs:label>**labelString**</rdfs:label>

where **labelString** is the string of text representing the label.

---

## Chapter 9 - RDFS

> For example, if we wanted to label the "KLP" resource as "Key Lime Pie", we could specify:
>
> ```
> <menu:Dessert rdf:ID="KLP">
>         <rdfs:label>Key Lime Pie</rdfs:label>
> </menu:Dessert>
> ```

The best practice is to label everything so that user interfaces can provide textual results that are meaningful to people. Multiple labels may be provided to support different languages by using "xml:lang" attributes. Unlike most properties, the label property does not contribute to logical interpretations of the language. It is only helpful for communicating with humans. The "rdfs:label" property can be used with any "rdfs:Resource" and its value must be an instance of "rdfs:Literal".

### 9.5.4.2 Commenting Resources (rdfs:comment)

The "rdfs:comment" property (see Figure 9-7) is used to describe a resource with free-form human-readable text. Like the "rdfs:label" property, the targeted consumer of the text is a human reader looking directly at the source ontology or the user interface of a tool that reads the value. It is a property on a resource whose value (range) must be a plain literal (string).

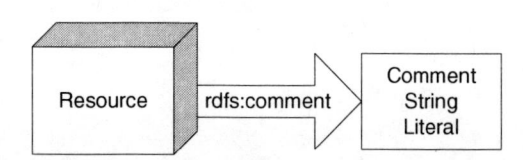

Figure 9-7. RDFS Comment Property

## Section 2 – Enabling Technologies

---

> The typical syntax for a comment is:
>
> &lt;rdfs:comment&gt;**commentString**&lt;/rdfs:comment&gt;
>
> where **commentString** is the string of text representing the comment.

> The following example shows how a human readable string of text can be associated with a resource:
>
> ```
> <menu:Dessert rdf:ID="KLP">
>     <rdfs:label>Key Lime Pie</rdfs:label>
>     <rdfs:comment>Key Lime Pie is a dessert food normally made with sweetened condensed milk, lime juice, and a graham cracker crust</rdfs:comment>
> </menu:Dessert>
> ```

The comment property is useful for tools such as queries that present description information to a human in a viewer. The best practice is to use "rdfs:comment" rather than "&lt;!-- XML comment --&gt;" to preserve information post-parsing.

The "rdfs:comment" property is a form of in-line documentation used to define a human-readable description of a resource. A comment provides more information than a short label and helps clarify meaning. The "xml:lang" attribute can be used to provide multiple language versions of a comment. The difference between "rdfs:label" and "rdfs:comment" is that "rdfs:label" provides a short name, while "rdfs:comment" provides a lengthier description.

The "rdfs:comment" property can be used with any "rdfs:Resource" and its value must be an instance of "rdfs:Resource".

## 9.6 RDFS Summary

RDFS provides many of the features required in a Semantic Web language by extending RDF with additional semantic features. RDFS supports specification of limited ontologies through standardized classes and properties.

```
The following combined example shows the use of the most widely used RDFS language features:

<rdfs:Class rdf:ID="Pie">
      <rdfs:label>dessert</rdfs:label>
      <rdfs:comment>This class represents Key lime pies</rdfs:comment>
      <rdfs:subClassOf rdf:resource="#Dessert"/>
      <rdfs:subClassOf rdf:resource="#FoodItem"/>
</rdfs:Class>

<rdf:Property rdf:ID="primaryIngredient">
      <rdfs:subPropertyOf rdf:resource="#ingredient"/>
      <rdfs:range rdf:resource="&rdfs;Literal"/>
</rdf:Property>

<rdf:Property rdf:ID="Ingredient">
      <rdfs:domain rdf:resource="#FoodItem"/>
</rdf:Property>

<Pie rdf:ID="KLP">
      <primaryIngredient>condensed milk</primaryIngredient>
</Pie>

<rdfs:Datatype rdf:about="http://www.restaurant.org#calories">
      <rdfs:subClassOf rdf:resource="&xsd;integer"/>
</rdfs:Datatype>
```

Key RDFS contributions are the added formal semantic concepts of: classes, properties, individuals, generalizations (i.e., "rdfs:subClassOf", "rdfs:subPropertyOf"), and global Property restrictions (i.e., "rdfs:domain", "rdfs:range").

Section 2 – Enabling Technologies

Table 9-7 summarizes the RDFS language property constructs and provides their domains and ranges.

Table 9-7. RDFS Property Summary Table

| Category | Construct | Domain | Range |
|---|---|---|---|
| Core Properties | rdf:type | &rdfs;Resource | &rdfs;Class |
| | rdfs:subClassOf | &rdfs;Class | &rdfs;Class |
| | rdfs:subPropertyOf | &rdf;Property | &rdf;Property |
| Constraint Properties | rdfs:range | &rdf;Property | &rdfs;Class |
| | rdfs:domain | &rdf;Property | &rdfs;Class |
| Clarification Properties | rdfs:seeAlso | &rdfs;Resource | &rdfs;Resource |
| | rdfs:isDefinedBy | &rdfs;Resource | &rdfs;Resource |
| Documentation Properties | rdfs:label | &rdfs;Resource | &rdfs;Literal |
| | rdfs:comment | &rdfs;Resource | &rdfs;Literal |

## 9.7 Why RDFS is not Enough

RDFS adds ontological primitives that are critical for describing data for the Semantic Web. It provides several features for supporting ontology specifications. However, there are several features still needed to support the requirements of ontology languages. As requirements for the Semantic Web have emerged, it has become clear that a richer vocabulary description language is required.

Property restrictions are useful for specifying class membership. However, RDFS has few mechanisms for restricting properties. For example, RDFS places no restrictions on property cardinality.

RDFS provides few descriptors that support inferencing. Additional rules are needed for reasoners to infer new facts. For example, you cannot infer membership in one class because it is not in another class complement, or that an object belongs to a particular class because it contains a certain type of value.

RDFS does not provide sufficient expressiveness to provide the ontology descriptions required to support the Semantic Web. To provide more expressiveness and to support inferencing, more advanced semantic concepts are required. These concepts are provided by OWL, which is introduced in the following chapter.

# 10 OWL Language

> "*OWL permits the definition of sophisticated ontologies, a fundamental requirement in the integration of heterogeneous information content. OWL ontologies will also be important for the characterization of interoperable services for knowledge-intensive processing on the Web.*" Professor Nigel Shadbolt (Director), Professor David De Roure (Head of Grid and Pervasive Computing), and Dr Nicholas Gibbins, AKT IRC, University of Southampton, quoted on-line: http://www.w3.org/2004/01/sws-testimonial

The logical layer of the Semantic Web's layered architecture builds on RDF and RDFS. OWL supports more expressive descriptions of semantic relationships than RDFS. This chapter provides an overview of OWL and introduces the three species of OWL.

## 10.1 OWL Overview

The Web Ontology Language – OWL was developed to satisfy the requirements for a language to support the Semantic Web. OWL provides the logical layer in the Semantic Web's architecture and builds on RDF(S) features (see Figure 10-1). It adds additional language features for describing ontologies.

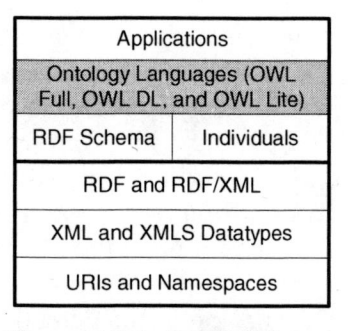

| Applications |  |
| --- | --- |
| Ontology Languages (OWL Full, OWL DL, and OWL Lite) ||
| RDF Schema | Individuals |
| RDF and RDF/XML ||
| XML and XMLS Datatypes ||
| URIs and Namespaces ||

Figure 10-1. Logical Layer

### 10.1.1 OWL Definition

OWL is the W3C's recommended ontology language for representing information in the Semantic Web. It is typically used to define an ontology for a particular domain. An OWL ontology is a set of axioms describing classes, properties, and the relationships between them. RDF/XML is used for marking up conforming instance data.

Section 2 – Enabling Technologies

## 10.1.2 OWL History

OWL has evolved from the DARPA Agent Markup Language (DAML) and Ontology Inference Layer (OIL) languages into the W3C recommendation. The DAML+OIL language was developed from DAML and OIL and served as the starting point for W3C Semantic Web initiatives.

DAML was developed as a result of a Defense Advanced Research Projects Agency (DARPA) program. DARPA is a research organization in the United States Department of Defense (DoD) that has made significant contributions to information technology. DARPA is credited with the development of much of the Internet's infrastructure through its ARPANET research.

DARPA initiated a research effort in August of 2000 to develop an agent markup language called the DARPA Agent Markup Language (DAML). The intention of DAML was to support interoperability between DoD IT systems. Dr. James Hendler (see Figure 10-2) initially led the research. Upon completing his tenure at DARPA, Dr. Hendler returned to the University of Maryland where he continues to lead innovative Semantic Web research efforts. Responsibility for the DARPA program passed first to Murray Burke, and then to Dr. Mark Greaves.

Figure 10-2. Dr. James Hendler

DARPA cleverly included the W3C's host organization – the Massachusetts Institute of Technology (MIT) as part of the DARPA team. This helped ease the eventual evolution of DAML+OIL into OWL by including leaders in the web community including Sir Tim Berners-Lee and Dan Connolly.

In parallel with the DARPA initiative, European Union (EU) researchers were developing the Ontology Interface Layer (OIL). A Joint EU/US Committee on Agent Markup Languages merged DAML with OIL in March 2001, resulting in the DAML+OIL language.

DAML+OIL was developed in response to the need for a language that can define ontologies that enable communication of agents. DAML+OIL was designed as a "thin layer" on top of RDFS, providing only a small number of additional features. DAML+OIL served as the starting point for the W3C Web Ontology Working Group.

The W3C chartered the Web Ontology (WebOnt) Working Group led by Dr. Hendler and Dr. Guus Schreiber as part of their Semantic Web Activity to develop a language to add an ontology support layer on top of XML and RDF(S). The intention of the language was to describe expressive semantics. The charter required a formal semantics to precisely define the meaning of expressions in the language and valid inferences that could be made from those expressions.

The language was required to use the XML syntax and XML datatypes and be compatible wherever possible, and provide maximum compatibility with XML and RDF concepts. The working group successfully shepherded the Web Ontology Language – OWL through the W3C standardization process. The W3C adopted OWL as an official recommendation on February 10, 2004.

## 10.1.3 OWL Specification

Table 10-1 identifies the six W3C recommendations that document OWL. The OWL Overview, OWL Guide, and OWL Reference should be read (in that order) by anyone developing ontologies and complaint instance data files. The OWL Semantics and Abstract Syntax document is difficult for mere mortals to understand, but is very important as the normative (official) definition of the language. The Test Cases document is important for anyone developing OWL-compliant software. The OWL Use Cases and Requirements document provides background on anticipated OWL uses and the objectives of its developers.

Section 2 – Enabling Technologies

Although this text endeavors to fully describe OWL, readers should familiarize themselves with the normative documents and use them as the authoritative source of information.

Table 10-1. OWL Authoritative Description

| | Title: | **OWL Overview** |
|---|---|---|
| | Document URI: | http://www.w3.org/TR/owl-features/ |
| | Purpose: | Provides an OWL introduction |
| | Title: | **OWL Guide** |
| | Document URI: | http://www.w3.org/TR/owl-guide/ |
| | Purpose: | Demonstrates the use of OWL with examples |
| | Title: | **OWL Reference** |
| | Document URI: | http://www.w3.org/TR/owl-ref/ |
| | Purpose: | Structured informal introduction to OWL constructs (modeling primitives) |
| | Title: | **OWL Semantics and Abstract Syntax** |
| | Document URI: | http://www.w3.org/TR/owl-semantics/ |
| | Purpose: | Provides the normative definition of OWL. |
| | Title: | **OWL Test Cases** |
| | Document URI: | http://www.w3.org/TR/owl-test/ |
| | Purpose: | Provides test cases for OWL |
| | Title: | **OWL Use Cases and Requirements** |
| | Document URI: | http://www.w3.org/TR/webont-req/ |
| | Purpose: | Specifies usage scenarios, goals and requirements |

Table 10-2 identifies the OWL namespace.

Table 10-2. OWL Namespace and Mime Type

| Recommended Namespace Prefix: | owl |
| --- | --- |
| Namespace Name: | http://www.w3.org/2002/07/owl# |
| Mime type: | application/rdf+xml |

### 10.1.4 OWL Features

The purpose of OWL is to provide a standard language for Semantic Web information representations. The OWL language provides even more features than RDFS for defining classes, properties, and the relationships between them, so that conforming instance information is easily understood by consuming software applications.

OWL provides a variety of language features to support the Semantic Web by adding standard constructs to RDFS. OWL's richer expressions enable better inferencing. As domain-specific ontologies are developed in OWL, conforming instance data will represent information. The ontological representations enable domain-agile tools and reasoning that in turn support new functionality. Using OWL transitions effort from coding complex software to representing information.

## 10.2 OWL Species

The OWL documentation describes three dialects (or species) of the Web Ontology Language – OWL. The intention of the language variants is to support different groups of users that need varying levels of expressional capability. The language variants are OWL Full, OWL DL, and OWL Lite.

### 10.2.1 OWL Full

OWL Full refers to the complete OWL language. OWL Full is not a sublanguage, it is the complete set of OWL language constructs. It is a superset of RDF. OWL Full places no restrictions on an RDF file. RDF statements are mixable with the OWL Full constructs. At one extreme, an OWL document could have no OWL definitions, just RDF, and still be considered legal OWL Full. Some users will want OWL Full's full expressiveness. However, they will have to deal with challenges in performing reasoning.

### 10.2.2 OWL DL

A more computationally efficient alternative to OWL Full is the OWL DL sublanguage. The primary purpose of the OWL DL sublanguage is to provide a Description Language (DL) dialect that supports reasoning applications. The OWL DL sublanguage of OWL has restrictions on how some of the OWL language constructs are used. OWL DL uses the OWL Full constructs, but the use of some of the constructs is restricted.

There is an existing community of DL users that can leverage OWL DL. Over the years, developers have created reasoning systems that support ontologies that are constrained by certain restrictions. These restrictions are required for OWL DL to be decidable.

OWL DL supports a compromise between expressivity and decidable reasoning. The restrictions on OWL DL are the same restrictions that make reasoning systems decidable and are meant to support reasoning system requirements. Decidability means that computations will finish in a finite amount of time. Computationally complete representation conclusions can be computed.

### 10.2.3 OWL Lite

OWL Lite is another sublanguage of OWL that supports efficient reasoning. It is even simpler than OWL DL because it supports only a subset of OWL Full constructs, some of which are restricted (as in OWL DL).

OWL Lite provides a minimal set of features for users that want to benefit from ontologies without a significant investment in encoding complex semantic relationships. OWL Lite provides sufficient support for people that want to upgrade their existing database, XML, or RDF(S) information representations into OWL-compliant ontological information representations.

The primary reason for providing the simplified version of OWL is to ease the burden on tool developers. OWL Lite compliant tools have fewer constructs to support than OWL DL and OWL Full compliant tools. OWL Lite and OWL DL can be viewed as extensions of a restricted view of RDF.

### 10.2.4 OWL Species Summary

Table 10-3 summarizes the three species of OWL.

Table 10-3. OWL Species Summary

| Species | Summary | Subset of Constructs | Restrictions on Use |
|---|---|---|---|
| OWL Full | Superset of RDF | | |
| OWL DL | Same constructs as OWL Full but restrictions on use | | X |
| OWL Lite | Subset of OWL Full constructs and same restrictions as OWL DL | X | X |

Section 2 – Enabling Technologies

Figure 10-3 shows one way to view the relationship between species.

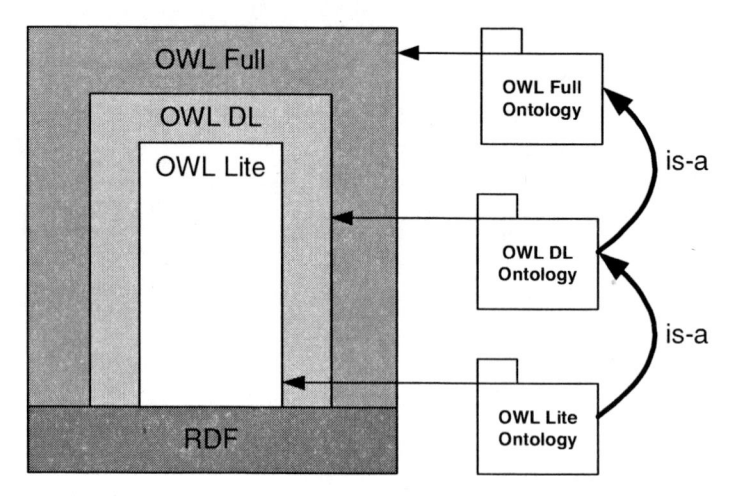

Figure 10-3. Species Relationships

## 10.3 OWL Language Summary

The Web Ontology Language – OWL is a new language supporting the Semantic Web. OWL is described in a series of documents provided by the W3C. The complete language - OWL Full has two sublanguages: OWL DL and OWL Lite. Because OWL Lite is simpler, it is described first in Section 3, along with the concept of individuals. Then, OWL DL and OWL Full are described in Section 4.

# Section 3

**OWL
Lite**

# Section 3 – OWL Lite

Section 3 describes the subset of OWL referred to as OWL Lite. OWL Lite provides the basic features of OWL needed to provide most of the desired benefits of the Semantic Web. By eliminating a few rarely used OWL Full constructs and simplifying some concepts, OWL Lite is simpler for tool developers to support. It is anticipated that many tools will support OWL Lite initially, and then upgrade their features to support OWL Full.

Chapter 11 - Encoding an OWL Ontology – describes how OWL files are organized.

Chapter 12 - Defining Basic OWL Lite Classes and Properties - describes the definition of simple classes and describes the predefined OWL classes.

Chapter 13 - Describing OWL Lite Property Characteristics - describes the definition of global property restrictions relating properties, defining inference shortcuts, and defining local property restrictions.

Chapter 14 - Deriving OWL Lite Classes – describes class descriptions, subclasses, class equivalency, and defining classes with intersections.

Chapter 15 – Describing Individuals – describes how to determine whether something is an individual, the unique names assumption in OWL, instantiating individuals, relating individuals, and automatically generating individual descriptions.

Chapter 16 - OWL Lite Summary – summarizes the OWL Lite language constructs.

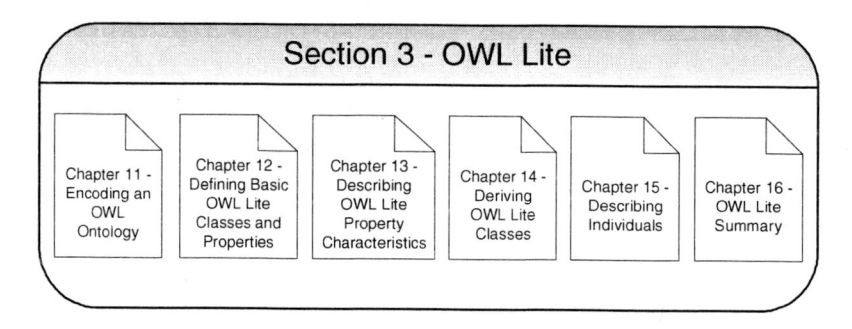

# 11 Encoding an OWL Ontology

Ontology encodings are typically represented in web documents that can be referenced using a URI. The encoding of an OWL ontology should follow object-oriented requirements analysis, knowledge acquisition, knowledge engineering, and design phases. Specify ontology requirements in a document to develop common expectations for the domain description. Collect information about the domain from authoritative sources. Describe a structured interpretation of acquired knowledge in a knowledge engineering document that references the authoritative data sources. Graphical design languages such as UML are helpful for visualizing class and property relationships derived from the knowledge engineering document.

Ontologies are encoded into files using one of the OWL dialects. They are used by applications (see Figure 11-1). The files use RDF/XML syntax, contain datatype information, and most importantly – describe classes and properties. OWL knowledge bases are typically encoded into sets of physical files for ontologies, instance data, and datatypes.

| Applications |  |
|---|---|
| Ontology Languages (OWL Full, OWL DL, and OWL Lite) ||
| RDF Schema | Individuals |
| RDF and RDF/XML ||
| XML and XMLS Datatypes ||
| URIs and Namespaces ||

Figure 11-1. Ontology Language Layer

The following sections describe encoding OWL ontologies including OWL Ontology File Structures, and the Header, Body, and Footer portions of an OWL ontology file.

## 11.1 OWL Ontology File Structure

Figure 11-2 presents an example of the relationship between an ontology file and the namespaces and related files for a particular implementation. Related files often include leveraged ontologies and instance files. These files can be distributed in various ways on the web. This example demonstrates a situation where an organization standardizes their ontologies that extend another organization's ontologies. Individuals are specified in an RDF instance file that conforms to the ontology.

## Section 3 – OWL Lite

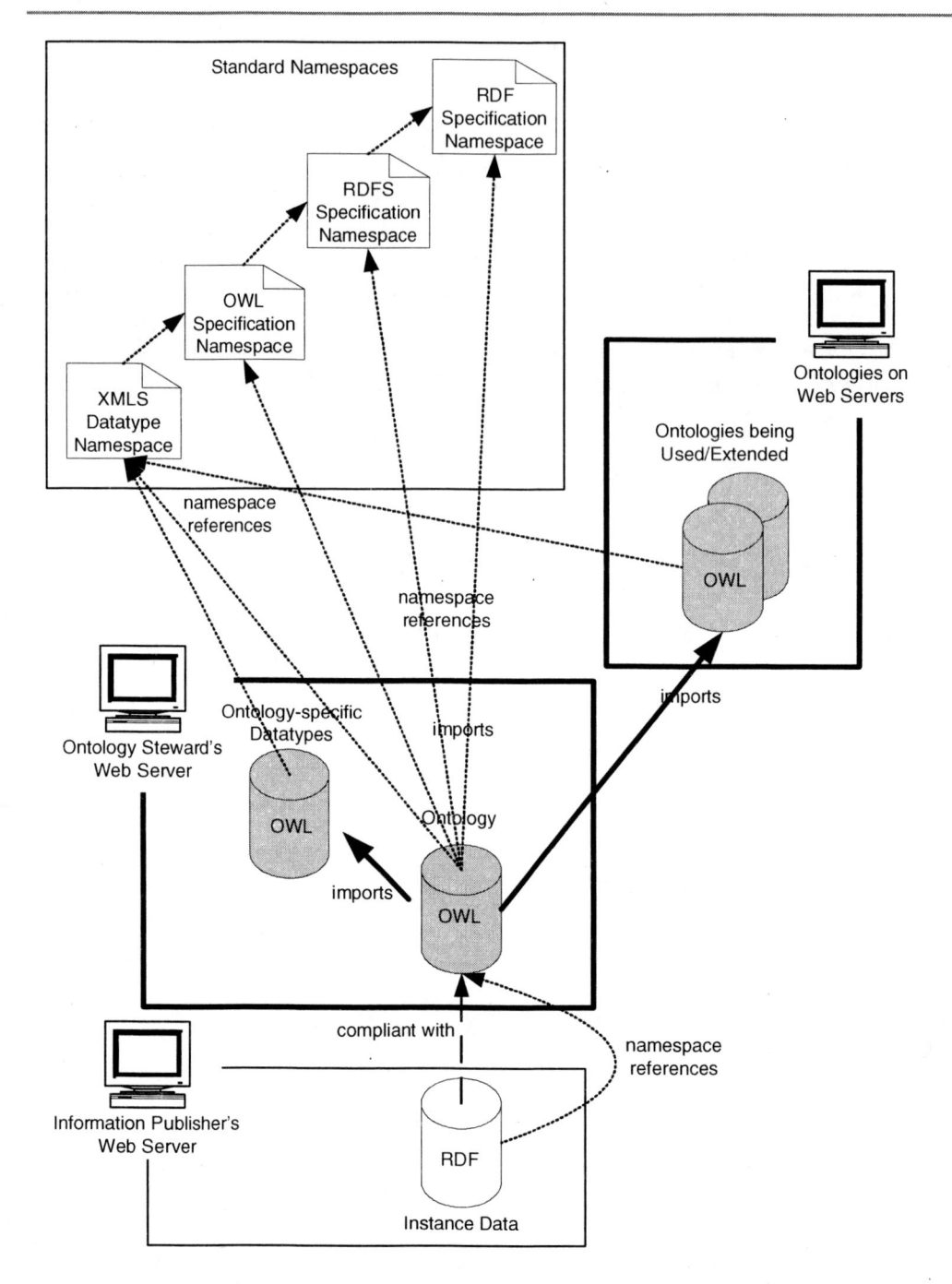

Figure 11-2. Imports and Namespace Dependency Relationships

Chapter 11 – Encoding an OWL Ontology

Ontologies are encoded into web documents. RDF instance data references ontologies. Ontology files reference other ontologies in order to extend or reuse them. Ontologies also reference datatypes that build on top of XML Schema datatypes. Ontologies reference standard namespaces.

Ontologies and instances are best described as separate files with optional distinguishing text in their URIs (e.g., "http://www.restaurant.com/menu-ont"). Filenames should use ".owl" for their extension if an extension is necessary.

An OWL Lite ontology web document typically includes the "owl:Ontology" element, class definitions, and property definitions. OWL ontologies are coded into one or more physical files following a prescribed format. The format of the file, represented in Figure 11-3, typically includes a header, body, and footer.

## *11.2 OWL Header*

An OWL ontology file begins with a header section. The purpose of the header is to specify the RDF start tag (including namespace attributes) and the ontology element including versioning and imports information.

### 11.2.1 XML Declaration and RDF Start Tag

OWL ontologies are represented in RDF/XML. Therefore, it is recommended practice to begin the file with an XML declaration that specifies the version of XML being used and the encoding (e.g., <?xml version="1.0" encoding="UTF-8"?>). This provides hints to some tools such as web browsers.

The use of "rdf:" as the RDF namespace prefix is recommended and assumed. The RDF start tag serves as an enveloping element. An ontology begins with an RDF start tag. Only one start tag should appear within an ontology file. The RDF start tag should include namespace declarations.

---

The typical syntax of the XML declaration and RDF start tag is:

<?xml version="1.0" encoding="UTF-8"?>
<rdf:RDF **namespaceDeclarations**>

where **namespaceDeclarations** are the namespace declarations described in the next section.

---

145

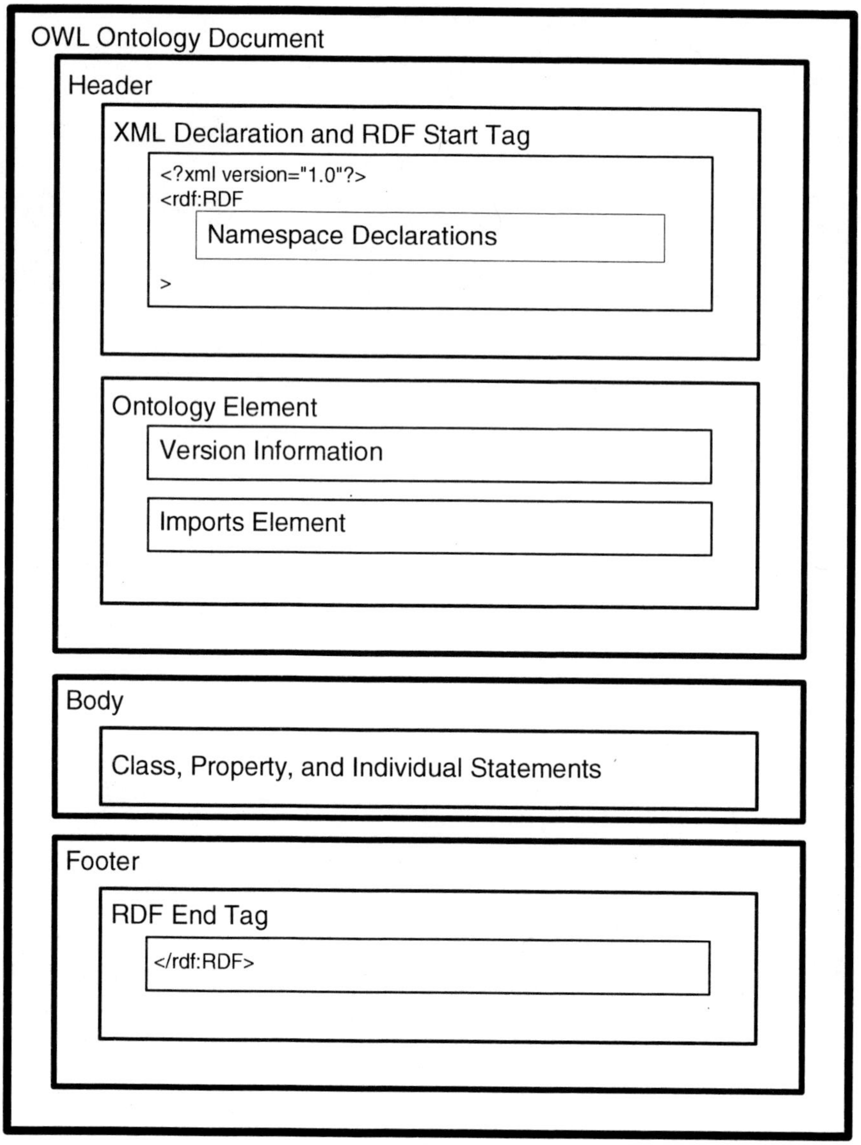

Section 3 – OWL Lite

```
OWL Ontology Document
  Header
    XML Declaration and RDF Start Tag
      <?xml version="1.0"?>
      <rdf:RDF
          Namespace Declarations
      >
    Ontology Element
      Version Information
      Imports Element
  Body
    Class, Property, and Individual Statements
  Footer
    RDF End Tag
      </rdf:RDF>
```

Figure 11-3. Ontology File Structure

## 11.2.2 Namespaces for OWL Ontology Files

Section 5.3 described namespaces in general. OWL ontology namespaces are identified as attributes to the "<rdf:RDF>" start tag. The ontology's namespace declarations identify the abbreviated references that are in the ontology file. The namespaces help unambiguously identify tags and makes the ontology file more readable for humans. Namespaces can only be used in XML tag names and attribute names, not in attribute values.

There are typically three types of namespaces in OWL ontology headers:
- Standard namespace references,
- Namespaces associated with imports statements, and
- A namespace identifying the ontology currently being described.

Standard namespace references specify namespaces that are part of the OWL standard: XMLS, RDF, RDFS, and OWL. Namespaces associated with imported ontologies only setup shorthand abbreviations to reference URIs. An "imports" statement (described later) is still needed to actually use the contents of another ontology. The ontology being described is referenced using namespace definitions and/or "xml:base" attributes.

As long as you follow XML namespace rules, the order of namespace declarations does not affect their interpretation. However, by defining namespaces in the order of layers from bottom to top, the dependencies are easier for humans to follow. A recommended order for stating namespaces is:
- XML schema, (for datatypes)
- RDF,
- RDFS,
- OWL,
- reused ontologies,
- extended ontologies, and
- current/default namespaces.

The XML Schema Datatypes namespace is defined to support datatypes. The recommended prefix for specifying the fixed XML Schema Datatypes file is "xsd:".

# Section 3 – OWL Lite

> The following RDF start tag attribute identifies the namespace abbreviation for the XML Schema specification:
>
> xmlns:xsd="http://www.w3.org/2001/XMLSchema#"

The recommended prefix for specifying the RDF specification is "rdf:".

> The following RDF start tag attribute identifies the namespace abbreviation for the RDF specification:
>
> xmlns:rdf="http://www.w3.org/1999/02/22-rdf-syntax-ns#"

The RDF Schema namespace is referenced to use tags such as "rdfs:subClassOf". The recommended prefix for specifying the fixed RDF Schema specification is "rdfs:".

> The following RDF start tag attribute identifies the namespace abbreviation for the RDFS specification:
>
> xmlns:rdfs="http://www.w3.org/2000/01/rdf-schema#"

The recommended prefix for specifying the fixed OWL specification is "owl:".

> The following RDF start tag attribute identifies the namespace abbreviation for the OWL specification:
>
> xmlns:owl="http://www.w3.org/2002/07/owl#"

Concepts in external ontologies that are used or extended by the ontology being defined need to be referenced. The prefixes associated with imported ontologies should reflect their names for human readability.

> The following RDF start tag attribute identifies the namespace abbreviation for an imported ontology:
>
> xmlns:pasta="http://www.food.org/pastaDishes#"

The ontology's namespace is also specified. The ontology is either the document containing the specification or another document referenced using an "xml:base" attribute.

> The following RDF start tag attribute identifies the namespace abbreviation for the current document:
>
> xmlns="http://www.food.org/food-ex#"

URIrefs are normally relative to the current document (the default base URI). However, the "xml:base" declaration affects this.

## XML Base

Ontologies often include an "xml:base" specification (described in Section 5.4). The base URI can be assigned using the "xml:base" attribute. RDF URIrefs will be expanded using the "xml:base" URI. Always include an "xml:base" in OWL ontology files or use fully resolved URIs in "rdf:about" attribute values.

## Namespaces

The recommended prefixes specified in Table 11-1 should be used. Although you could use different prefixes, it is not recommended.

Table 11-1. Recommended Namespace Abbreviations

| Namespace | Prefix | URI |
| --- | --- | --- |
| XML Schema Datatypes | xsd | http://www.w3.org/2001/XMLSchema# |
| RDF | rdf | http://www.w3.org/1999/02/22-rdf-syntax-ns# |
| RDFS | rdfs | http://www.w3.org/2000/01/rdf-schema# |
| OWL | owl | http://www.w3.org/2002/07/owl# |

Throughout this text, the recommended prefixes are assumed to be associated with the URIs identified in Table 11-1 using XML namespaces and entity declarations.

Section 3 – OWL Lite

---

> The following example shows a complete RDF start tag with namespace attributes and an xml:base attribute:
>
> ```
> <rdf:RDF
>         xmlns:xsd ="http://www.w3.org/2001/XMLSchema#"
>         xmlns:rdf ="http://www.w3.org/1999/02/22-rdf-syntax-ns#"
>         xmlns:rdfs="http://www.w3.org/2000/01/rdf-schema#"
>         xmlns:owl ="http://www.w3.org/2002/07/owl#"
>         xmlns:pasta="http://www.food.org/pastaDishes#"
>         xmlns     ="http://www.food.org/food-ex#"
>         xml:base="http://www.food.org/food-ex#"
> >
> ```

Ontology developers usually copy and paste standard namespace declarations from an existing ontology to a new ontology.

## 11.2.3 Ontology Element (owl:Ontology)

The built-in "owl:Ontology" class is used to instantiate individual ontologies. The OWL ontology element envelops the header of an ontology, but not the class, property, and instance assertions that make up the ontology. Although the ontology element (i.e., "<owl:Ontology>") is optional, it is recommended and almost always present. The ontology element provides metadata about the ontology including version information elements, imports elements, and RDF statements (e.g., comments).

| owl:Ontology |
|---|
|  |

The ontology element start tag should include an "rdf:about" attribute. The value, which provides a name or reference for the ontology, is usually null (i.e., "") indicating that the current ontology is being described. Alternatively, a name or reference can be specified. The name of the ontology is the URI of the web document containing the ontology element start tag unless an "xml:base" attribute is being used. The ontology header ends with an "</owl:Ontology>" end tag.

The primary purpose of the ontology element is to provide ontology-level metadata including specifying versioning information and ontologies to import. A human-readable name for the ontology should be provided with an "rdfs:label" property. The ontology element is used in ontology (Tbox) files and instance (Abox) files.

# Chapter 11 – Encoding an OWL Ontology

> The typical syntax of an OWL ontology declaration is:
>
> <owl:Ontology rdf:about="**optionalOntologyNameOrReference**">
> </owl:Ontology>
>
> where **optionalOntologyNameOrReference** is either "" (indicating the current file) or a specified URI.

Recommended practice is to provide RDFS comments and a label describing the ontology. Comments are specified using the "rdfs:comment" element described in section 9.5.4.2. A label is specified using the "rdfs:label" element description in section 9.5.4.1.

> An example of an OWL ontology declaration is:
>
> <owl:Ontology rdf:about="">
>     <rdfs:label>Restaurant Menu</rdfs:label>
>     <rdfs:comment>This ontology describes the basic concepts that are used to represent a restaurant's menus</rdfs:comment>
> </owl:Ontology>

The ontology element typically includes properties for specifying version information, ontologies to be imported, and documentation.

## 11.2.3.1 Versioning Information

Ontology specifications often evolve into new versions. The resulting changes can invalidate existing applications. Human and software users of an ontology should be provided with explicit versioning information within the "owl:Ontology" element so that they know which version to use.

OWL provides versioning information using a variety of statements including versioning text, indications of prior versions of the ontology, statements about compatibility with previous versions, and declarations of deprecation.

OWL provides explicit versioning information to indicate ontology-level versioning, and ontology-level compatibility. It also provides classes and properties for backward-compatibility.

# Section 3 – OWL Lite

Several language constraints are used to provide versioning information as part of the ontology header. Versioning information provides metadata information about the subject ontologies and relates the ontology to other ontologies.

### 11.2.3.1.1 Version Information (owl:versionInfo)

An "owl:versionInfo" property provides a string that gives information about the ontology's version. Instead of just descriptive words, Revision Control System (RCS) and Concurrent Version System (CVS) keywords can be provided in the string.

The "owl:versionInfo" statement is a predefined property for associating a text string with an ontology. The value of the property provides a human-readable description (see Figure 11-4). The "owl:versionInfo" property does not contribute to the logical meaning of the ontology, it is merely a documentation comment. The "owl:versionInfo" property is normally used for describing ontologies. However, it can be used to describe any OWL construct (e.g., class).

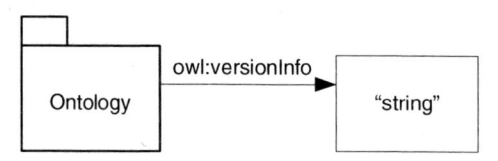

Figure 11-4. versionInfo Property

---

The typical syntax of a versionInfo property is:

<owl:versionInfo>**versionText**</owl:versionInfo>

where **versionText** is versioning information text or RCS/CVS keywords.

---

An example of using the versionInfo property with text is:

```
<owl:Ontology>
        <owl:versionInfo>This is the first draft of the restaurant menu ontology, created 1/1/2005</owl:versionInfo>
</owl:Ontology>
```

# Chapter 11 – Encoding an OWL Ontology

**RCS/CVS Keywords**

A commonly used convention is to provide RCS/CVS keywords as the values of the "owl:versionInfo" property.

---

The format of the RCS/CVS keyword value is:

<versionInfo>$Id: **filename, versionNumber date time owner** Exp$</versionInfo>

where: **filename** is the name of the ontology file (without path information), **versionNumber** is the version number (e.g., "1.2"), **date** is the last saved date, **time** is the last saved time, and **owner** is the file owner.

---

An example of using the versionInfo property with an RCS/CVS keyword set value is:

<owl:versionInfo>$Id: restaurantMenu-ont.owl,v 1.2 2004/08/30 12:34:56 llacy Exp $</owl:versionInfo>

In this example, the version information is provided using RCS/CVS keywords.

The RCS/CVS keywords would be interpreted as:

filename = "RestaurantOntology-ont.owl"
version number = "v 1.2"
last saved date = "2004/08/30"
last saved time = "12:34:56"
owner = "llacy"

---

The best practice is to include an "owl:versionInfo" property in each OWL document. One way to use the "owl:versionInfo" property is to leverage Dublin Core metadata standards. The value of the "owl:versionInfo" property is not interpreted. It is merely intended for human consumption in the current version. However, it may eventually evolve into parseable Dublin Core items. The "owl:versionInfo" property provides information for versioning systems. It is basically a glorified comment. The property can apply to classes, properties, and other ontologies.

The "owl:versionInfo" property can be used with any "owl:Thing" and its value must be an "rdfs:Literal".

Section 3 – OWL Lite

**11.2.3.1.1.1 Indicating an Earlier Version (owl:priorVersion)**

As new versions of an ontology are developed, explicit references to previous versions are needed. The "owl:priorVersion" property relates a newer version of an ontology to a previous version of the ontology (see Figure 11-5). This supports tracking an ontology's version history. The value of the "owl:priorVersion" property identifies the ontology.

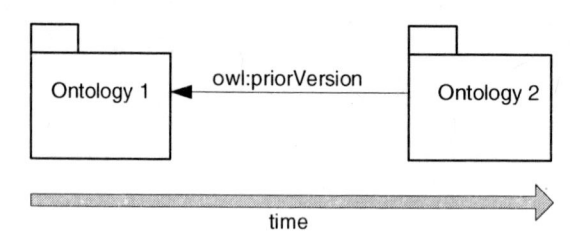

Figure 11-5. priorVersion Property

---

The typical syntax of the priorVersion property is:

<owl:priorVersion rdf:resource="**priorOntURI**"/>

where **priorOntURI** is the identifier of a prior version of the described ontology.

---

An example of using the priorVersion property is:

<owl:Ontology rdf:about="">
    <owl:priorVersion rdf:resource="http://www.food.org/pasta0603-ont"/>
</owl:Ontology>

---

The ontology identified in the "owl:priorVersion" property value is an earlier version of the ontology being described. Change occurs for some reason, and different versions of an ontology are likely not compatible with each other in the areas where they are different. The incompatibility could be minor (e.g., value differences) or major (e.g., removal of classes).

# Chapter 11 – Encoding an OWL Ontology

If an ontology has errors, you could look at a previous version. The "owl:priorVersion" property can only be applied to ontology instances and only identifies another ontology instance.

The "owl:priorVersion" property can be used with any "owl:Ontology" and its value must be an instance of an "owl:Ontology".

### 11.2.3.1.1.2 Backward Compatible Ontologies (owl:backwardCompatibleWith)

As new versions of an ontology are developed, changes may result in the new version being incompatible with an earlier version. However, if the new version is still compatible (all constructs have the same meaning), it should be explicitly stated with the "owl:backwardCompatibleWith" property. The "owl:backwardCompatibleWith" property is a subproperty of "owl:priorVersion" that relates two compatible ontologies. The property identifies previous versions that the described ontology is compatible with (see Figure 11-6). You cannot assume compatibility with previous versions (default is incompatibility). Being compatible means that all identical identifiers have the same interpretation.

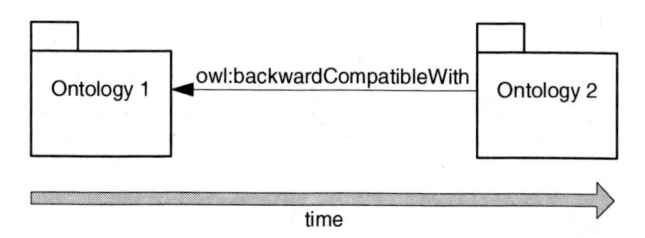

Figure 11-6. backwardCompatibleWith Property

---

The typical syntax of the backwardCompatibleWith property is:

<owl:backwardCompatibleWith rdf:resource="**olderOntURI**"/>

where **olderOntURI** is the URI of an older ontology that the current ontology is backward compatible with

---

# Section 3 – OWL Lite

---

An example of specifying a backward compatible ontology is:

```
<owl:Ontology rdf:about="">
    <owl:backwardCompatibleWith rdf:resource="http://www.KnightOwlRestaurant.com/Menu062204-ont"/>
        <rdfs:comment>added new menu items since 06/22/04 version</rdfs:comment>
</owl:Ontology>
```

---

Imagine software or an agent going to a location and encountering a new version of an ontology that it has committed to in the past. If the "owl:backwardCompatibleWith" property identifies the earlier version, the software can be safely updated with namespace and imports references to the new version.

The "owl:backwardCompatibleWith" property can be used with any "owl:Ontology" and its value must be an instance of an "owl:Ontology".

### 11.2.3.1.1.3 Incompatible Ontologies (owl:incompatibleWith)

New versions of ontologies will evolve that differ in semantics from earlier versions. The "owl:incompatibleWith" property identifies previous versions of the ontology that the new ontology supersedes and is inconsistent with.

---

The typical syntax for declaring an ontology to be incompatible is:

`<owl:incompatibleWith rdf:resource="`**`olderOntURI`**`"/>`

where **olderOntURI** is the URIref of the older ontology.

---

An example of the use of the owl:incompatibleWith property is:

```
<owl:Ontology rdf:about="">
    <owl:incompatibleWith rdf:resource=" http://www.KnightOwlRestaurant.com/Menu062204-ont"/>
        <rdfs:comment>added new menu items</rdfs:comment>
</owl:Ontology>
```

If a new ontology replaces an existing ontology, explicitly state whether applications can upgrade to the new version without changes. By virtue of encoding an ontology, it is newer than existing ontologies.

The "owl:incompatibleWith" property identifies an incompatible (normally predecessor) ontology (see Figure 11-7). It is used to explicitly state incompatibility and provides hints to authors of importing applications. The "owl:incompatibleWith" property is a subproperty of "owl:priorVersion". Whenever you generate a new version of an ontology, you should indicate if changes make the new version incompatible with the old version

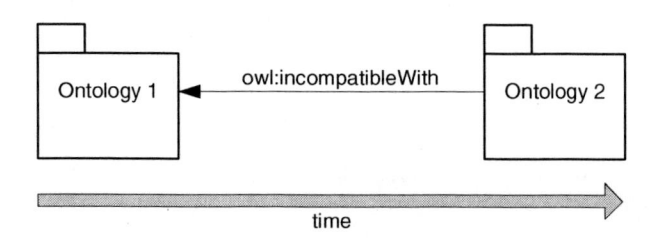

Figure 11-7. incompatibleWith Property

The "owl:incompatibleWith" property can be used with any "owl:Ontology" and its value must be an instance of an "owl:Ontology".

### 11.2.3.1.1.4 Deprecating Classes (owl:DeprecatedClass)

The "owl:DeprecatedClass" class is a predefined class that indicates that a specified class is nearing "end of life" and that changes should occur in software that commits to the ontology and uses the class.

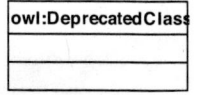

Since there are no semantics associated with a deprecated class specification, it is basically a glorified comment. However, tools might generate a warning when encountering a deprecated class.

OWL provides versioning support for constructs other than ontologies. As ontologies evolve, the descriptions and their classes and properties change. As we define new classes and properties, some will no longer be needed.

## Section 3 – OWL Lite

Sometimes, a class is no longer needed, but remains to support backward compatibility. The Java programming language has a concept for identifying classes that are "going out of business".

Developers of new ontologies should not reference a deprecated class. Maintainers of an ontology that uses a class that has been updated should upgrade to the newly defined class.

OWL includes a pre-defined class called "owl:DeprecatedClass" to specify classes being deprecated. The "owl:DeprecatedClass" class indicates that member classes will be changing in a future release that will be incompatible with the current meaning. This should signal authors that use the ontology that changes may be needed. Users must interpret the treatment of deprecated classes.

Deprecation supports short-term backward-compatibility and signals long term incompatibility. Deprecation eases migration to a new version for existing applications.

---

The typical syntax for identifying an owl:DeprecatedClass class is:

<owl:DeprecatedClass rdf:about="**oldClassName**">

where **oldClassName** is the URIref of the class being deprecated.

---

An example of specifying a deprecated class is:

```
<owl:DeprecatedClass rdf:about="#Pie">
        <rdfs:comment> use the new DessertPie class to avoid confusion with PizzaPie</rdfs:comment>
</owl:DeprecatedClass>
```

---

The deprecated class construct announces the newer version, explicitly stating incompatibility. The best practice is to provide a comment for human readers, indicating the preferred replacement class.

The "owl:DeprecatedClass" is a subclass of "rdfs:Class". Instances (classes) of "owl:DeprecatedClass" are members of a group whose use is discouraged in new documents that are compliant with the ontology.

## 11.2.3.1.1.5 Deprecating Properties (owl:DeprecatedProperty)

The "owl:DeprecatedProperty" class is used to identify properties that will no longer be supported in future versions of the ontology. Similar to "owl:DeprecatedClass", OWL provides an "owl:DeprecatedProperty" class to indicate a property that will be "going out of business".

The "owl:DeprecatedProperty" class is a subclass of the "rdf:Property" class. If an ontology author deprecates a property, they are indicating that the property should not be used in new documents that use the ontology that contains the deprecated property. Deprecation supports backward compatibility.

---

The typical syntax for deprecating a property is:

<owl:DeprecatedProperty rdf:about="**oldPropertyName**">

where **oldPropertyName** is the URIref of the deprecated property.

---

An example of the use of the deprecatedProperty property is:

```
<owl:DeprecatedProperty rdf:about="#cost">
        <rdfs:comment>use menuPrice to avoid confusion with inventory ontology property</rdfs:comment>
</owl:DeprecatedProperty>
```

---

Deprecated properties support backward compatibility by keeping the retiring property in the ontology. However, they indicate that the deprecated property may no longer be supported in future releases of the ontology.

If a tool encounters a deprecated property, it may provide a warning. If you encounter a deprecated property, you should migrate to the newly recommended property instead of continuing to use the deprecated property.

Section 3 – OWL Lite

#### 11.2.3.1.1.6 Versioning Summary

Versioning constructs do not provide additional semantics and are not intended for use by inferencing engines. Table 11-2 summarizes the elements used to provide versioning metadata for OWL ontologies.

Table 11-2. Versioning Constructs

| Construct | Purpose |
|---|---|
| owl:versionInfo | Provides version information |
| owl:priorVersion | Identifies an earlier version of the subject ontology |
| owl:backwardCompatibleWith | Identifies an earlier version that is compatible with the subject ontology |
| owl:incompatibleWith | Identifies an earlier version that is incompatible with the subject ontology |
| owl:DeprecatedClass | Identifies a class that should no longer be used |
| owl:DeprecatedProperty | Identifies a property that should no longer be used |

### 11.2.3.2 Importing Ontologies (owl:imports)

One of the biggest strengths of OWL is the ability while defining an ontology to reference and extend other ontologies. Just as hyperlinks created the web of information, relating ontologies will create a distributed web of semantic descriptions.

External ontologies are referenced and extended by importing them into the current ontology. This concept is similar to the include-style mechanism used in programming languages.

# Chapter 11 – Encoding an OWL Ontology

The "owl:imports" construct (see Figure 11-8) introduces dependencies because the importing ontology is dependent on the imported ontology. Otherwise, there would be no reason to perform the import operation. Imports statements are made within the ontology element of the importing ontology.

The "owl:imports" property is an ontology property used to specify the URI of an external OWL ontology whose assertions apply to the ontology that is currently being described (importing ontology).

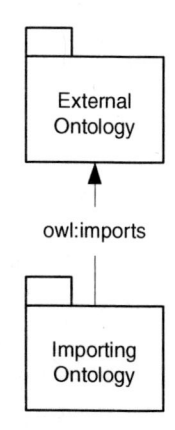

Figure 11-8. Imports Relationship

---

The typical syntax of the imports property is:

`<owl:imports rdf:resource="URIofOntologyToBeImported"/>`

where **URIofOntologyToBeImported** is the URI location of the ontology being imported.

---

An example of using imports is:

`<owl:imports rdf:resource="http://www.agriculturalUniversity.edu/ontologies/fruit-ont"/>`

---

The OWL vocabulary does not need to be imported and importing it is discouraged in the OWL documentation.

The imports statement is a composition mechanism. The ability to extend other ontology supports incremental and distributed descriptions.

# Section 3 – OWL Lite

## Namespace and Imports Differences

There is a major difference between imports declarations and namespace declarations. Normally, there is a namespace declaration for each ontology being imported. Namespace declarations identify prefix abbreviations for identifying identifiers. Namespace declarations do not include the meaning of the ontologies at the location specified by the URI. The "owl:imports" statement does not provide a shorthand notation for referring to the identifiers from the imported documents.

Some imported ontologies will not provide any new names. Those that do need corresponding namespace declarations in order to have shorthand prefix references. There is normally a one-to-one correspondence between an imports statement and a namespace declaration. The namespace declaration provides a shortcut to reference resources in the imported OWL ontologies.

The "owl:imports" property specifies that all the assertions of the ontology identified by the property value are included in the current ontology. The namespace reference does not imply that any terms are imported. The imports statement does not set up shorthand notation for names the way a namespace reference does.

---

An example of the same URIref being used within a namespace declaration and an imports statement is:

```
<rdf:RDF
        xmlns:xsd ="http://www.w3.org/2001/XMLSchema#"
        xmlns:rdf ="http://www.w3.org/1999/02/22-rdf-syntax-ns#"
        xmlns:rdfs="http://www.w3.org/2000/01/rdf-schema#"
        xmlns:owl ="http://www.w3.org/2002/07/owl#"
        xmlns:pasta="http://www.food.org/pastaDishes#"
        xmlns     ="http://www.food.org/food-ex#"
        xml:base="http://www.food.org/food-ex#"
>

<owl:Ontology rdf:about="">
        <owl:imports rdf:resource="http://www.food.org/pastaDishes"/>
</owl:Ontology>
```

## Chapter 11 – Encoding an OWL Ontology

**Imports Rules**

OWL allows multiple import statements. The "owl:imports" statements are transitive (see Figure 11-9). That means that if ontology A imports ontology B, and ontology B imports ontology C, then it is as if ontology A imports both ontologies B and C. There is no effect from an ontology importing itself, which means that cycles are allowed. If two ontologies import each other, they are equivalent.

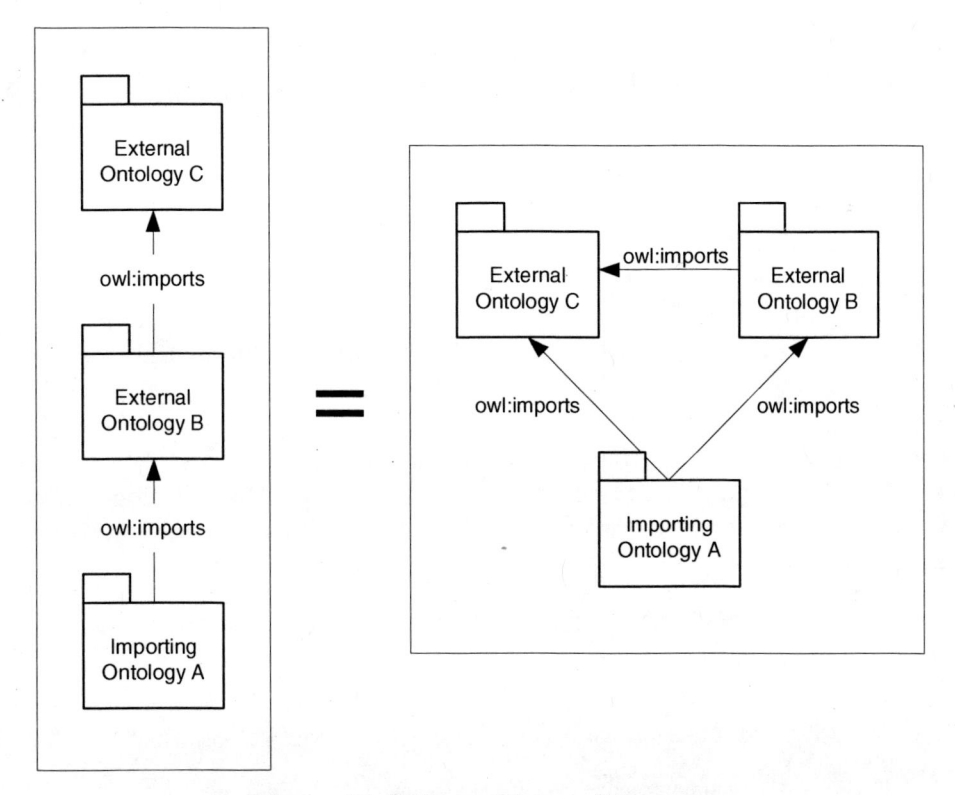

Figure 11-9. Transitivity of Imports

OWL tools read imported ontologies and consider them as part of the importing ontology. Tools depend on the ability to access imported ontologies and the imported ontologies being valid.

## Section 3 – OWL Lite

If ontology A imports ontology B, then ontology A includes all of B's assertions (by reference). Therefore, when the reasoner encounters the import statement, it should read in the imported information and treat it as if it was part of the specification currently being read.

At runtime, Semantic Web applications may not find an ontology at the specified URI. The lack of availability of the missing ontology's axioms may prevent the use of the importing ontology.

The "owl:imports" property can be used with any "owl:Ontology" and its value must be an instance of "owl:Ontology".

### 11.2.3.3 Ontology Element Summary

The Ontology element provides metadata about the ontology including information about the ontology, its versioning, its name, descriptive comments, and any imported ontologies. The versioning information helps manage multiple versions or ontologies.

The name used to reference the ontology to a human reader should be provided by an "rdfs:label" property. Descriptive comments about the ontology should be provided in "rdfs:comment" properties. The "owl:imports" ontology properties indicate dependencies on statements from other OWL ontologies.

```
An example of a complete ontology element is:

<Ontology rdf:about="">
        <owl:versionInfo>$Id: restaurantMenu-ont.owl,v 1.2 2004/10/24 12:34:56 llacy Exp $</owl:versionInfo>
        <rdfs:comment>Restaurant Menu ontology</rdfs:comment>
        <owl:imports rdf:resource="http://www.restaurant.com/2004/08/food-ont"/>
        <owl:priorVersion rdf:resource="http://www.restaurant.com/2004/07/Menu-ont"/>
        <owl:incompatibleWith rdf:resource="http://www.restaurant.com/2004/06/Menu-ont"/>
        <owl:backwardCompatibleWith rdf:resource="http://www.restaurant.com/2004/07/Menu-ont"/>
</Ontology>
```

## 11.2.4 OWL Header Summary

Headers do not change that often and usually you can copy and paste from an existing ontology. The OWL file header includes the RDF namespace envelope and the ontology element. OWL headers typically include a start tag, namespace declarations, and an "owl:Ontology" element. Figure 11-10 shows a conceptual organization of header classes and properties.

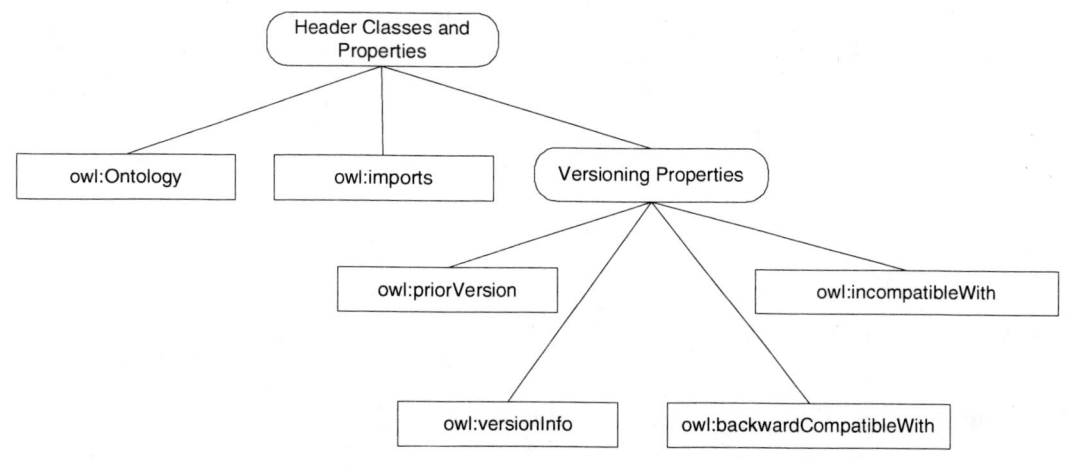

Figure 11-10. Header Concepts

## 11.3 Body

The body of an ontology is normally made up of class and property statements. However, any legal OWL Lite statement could be made. The order of axioms in OWL files is normally unimportant. Forward references are okay. Statements that occur together can be assumed to be conjunctive (i.e., assumed to be connected by an "AND").

Some information representation systems have a closed world assumption. Under the closed-world assumption, anything that cannot be inferred by the existing statements is assumed to be false. This assumption is used as part of some inferencing systems.

Unfortunately, the web is too large and dynamic to use this assumption. Unlike bounded AI problems, the web is vast, and we cannot assume we have all the facts. Instead, OWL makes an open-world assumption. That means that just because something is not specified, you cannot assume it to be false; it might be specified somewhere on the web.

OWL treats classes and properties as first class concepts. Ontologies are used to define classes and properties. OWL classes describe part of what is called the "object domain". These classes are internally implemented as members of "owl:Class", which is a subclass of "rdfs:Class". A class represents a subset of the universe that contains all objects of that type. Values in OWL are either XMLS datatype values (datatype domain) or object instances (object domain). Most of the emphasis in OWL is on classes that describe the object domain. OWL classes define a set of individuals that share the same properties. Properties define relationships between resources and either other resources or datatype values.

## *11.4 Footer - Closing Tag*

OWL ontology files end with a closing RDF tag: "</rdf:RDF>".

> The typical syntax for the closing RDF tag is:
>
> </rdf:RDF>

## *11.5 OWL Encoding Summary*

OWL ontologies are specified through statements in files. These files begin with header information that provide namespaces, versioning information, and import statements. The body of an OWL file contains the statements about classes, properties, and their relationships. The file ends with a footer.

The next chapter describes how basic OWL Lite classes and properties are encoded in OWL.

# 12 Defining Basic OWL Lite Classes and Properties

Classes are the basic building blocks that represent domains in OWL. The OWL class concept is a richer specialization (subclass) of the "rdfs:Class" concept. There are two basic types of OWL Lite classes: simple named classes and predefined classes. OWL Lite also provides several types of properties.

## 12.1 Defining a Simple Named Class (owl:Class)

OWL classes define basic concepts. Typically, one of the first steps in defining an ontology is to identify simple named classes. A simple named class is defined using the "owl:Class" element and the class name (URIref) of the new class. A class is given a name (URIref) with the "rdf:ID" attribute. OWL Lite classes are defined by associating a resource with the "owl:Class" type, normally using the typedNode syntax.

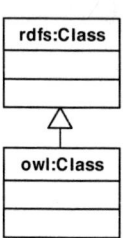

---

The typical syntax of a simple owl:Class element is:

`<owl:Class rdf:ID="`**classname**`"/>`

where **classname** is the name of the simple class being defined.

---

The best practice is to name classes with upper CamelCase (e.g., "Food", "Menu" "KeyLimePie"). Upper CamelCase is also known as Pascal case.

---

An example of defining a simple named class is to define a kind of thing called KeyLimePie.

`<owl:Class rdf:ID="KeyLimePie"/>`

This asserts that there is a class known as KeyLimePie. An example with the recommended rdfs:label and rdfs:comment properties is:

```
<owl:Class rdf:ID="KeyLimePie">
        <rdfs:label>Key Lime Pie</rdfs:label>
        <rdfs:label>custard-style pie made with the juice of Key limes</rdfs:label>
</owl:Class>
```

Section 3 – OWL Lite

---

The "rdfs:label" and "rdfs:comment" properties should be used in "owl:Class" specifications. The "xml:lang" attribute can be used to provide multilingual descriptions of the class. The "rdf:ID" attribute signals that a new resource (in this case class) is being defined. That resource is used by properties for reference and by individuals to declare membership.

Specifying a class with the "owl:Class" construct only supplies a name. No other information about the class can be assumed until further descriptions (e.g., property restrictions, subclass declaration) are provided. Classes can be referenced internally by their URIref fragment (e.g., "#classname"), and externally by full URIrefs.

If there are multiple class descriptions, the intersection of the restrictions defines the set of individuals belonging to the class. Things known about a class can be assumed to be true about the class's individuals.

## 12.2 Predefined OWL Classes (Extreme Classes)

In addition to providing a way to define classes, OWL provides some predefined classes. OWL's list of predefined classes includes "owl:Thing" and "owl:Nothing". These "extreme" classes are used for making statements that apply to all or no instances.

### 12.2.1 Thing Class (owl:Thing)

The "owl:Thing" class is a pre-defined class that is the most general class in OWL. The "owl:Thing" class provides a root class (superclass) for all classes. Therefore, every individual is a member of "owl:Thing" and every class is a subclass of the "owl:Thing" class.

| owl:Thing |
| --- |
|  |

The "owl:Thing" class is equal to the union of any class and its complement. You can use the "owl:Thing" class to make global assertions because everything that applies to a superclass applies to its subclasses, and every class is a subclass to "owl:Thing", so everything about "owl:Thing" applies to "everything".

Since all resources are members of the "owl:Thing" class, an alternate to the rdf:resource="URIref" syntax is to include the object itself through a typed node syntax item using "<owl:Thing rdf:about="individualURIref"/>".

168

## 12.2.2 Nothing Class (owl:Nothing)

The nothing class is a predefined OWL class that is the subclass of all classes. The "owl:Nothing" class is a pre-defined empty class that has no member individuals.

## *12.3 Describing OWL Lite Properties*

RDF introduced the concept of simple properties ("rdf:Property"). Properties associate values with individuals. In OWL, the primary intention of properties is to relate subject individuals to either a datatype value or another individual object. OWL defines classes of properties to represent the varieties of property specifications.

Recall that properties are binary relations among individuals or from individuals to values and enable the specification of facts (attribute/value pairs). Properties are used to make statements about all members or a class or about specific individuals in a class. Properties relate instances of a domain to instances of a range

There are four disjoint types of properties in OWL Lite. Each type has an associated "rdf:Property" subclass (see Figure 12-1) for describing properties that:
- relate objects to datatype values (Datatype properties),
- relate objects to other objects (Object properties),
- describe objects (Annotation properties), and
- relate ontologies to ontologies (Ontology properties).

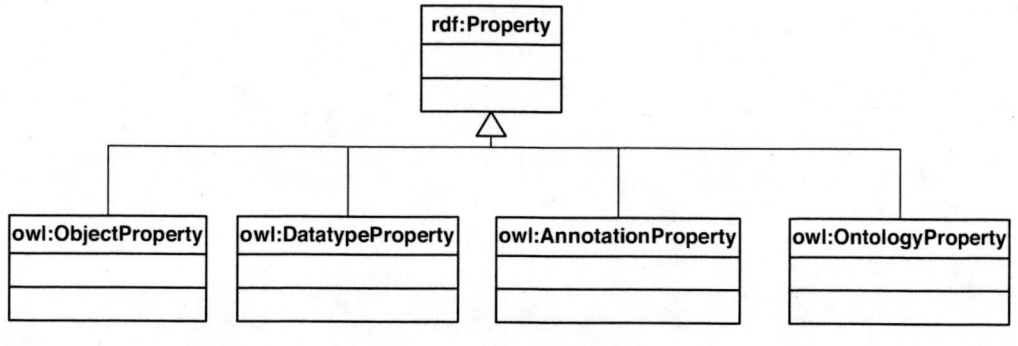

Figure 12-1. Property Types

Section 3 – OWL Lite

## 12.3.1 Datatype Properties (owl:DatatypeProperty)

The "owl:DatatypeProperty" class is a subclass of the "rdf:Property" class used to identify a property whose value is associated with a datatype. OWL datatype properties support "data-valued" relations of instances.

| owl:DatatypeProperty |
|---|
|  |
|  |

The values of "owl:DatatypeProperty" properties are literals, rather than resources. Datatype properties relate instances to values that belong to datatypes. The datatypes can be strings or simple XMLS datatypes. OWL uses a subset of the predefined XMLS datatypes. Datatypes are referenced using the URI reference for the datatype relative to the XMLS URI *"http://www.w3.org/2001/XMLSchema".*

---

A datatype property can be specified in the following pattern:

<owl:DatatypeProperty rdf:ID="**propertyname**"/>

where **propertyname** is the name of the datatype property being defined.

---

An example of specifying a datatype property along with associated domain and range values is:

```
<owl:DatatypeProperty rdf:ID="restaurantClosingTime">
     <rdfs:domain rdf:resource="#Restaurant"/>
     <rdf:range rdf:resource="&xsd;time"/>
</owl:DatatypeProperty>
```

---

The value of a datatype property may be either an untyped literal or a typed literal.

---

An example of using a datatype property with an untyped literal is:

```
<rest:Restaurant rdf:ID="JoesPizza">
     <faxNumber>4075551234</faxNumber>
</rest:Restaurant>
```

## Chapter 12 – Defining Basic OWL Lite Classes and Properties

Datatype values are expressed using RDF/XML syntax, but have special meaning in OWL. The datatype attribute marries a string representation of the value with an explicit declaration or the XMLS datatype. When the string representation of the value is parsed, the value is interpreted based on the specified XMLS datatypes.

---

An example of using a datatype property with a typed literal value is:

<restaurantClosingTime rdf:datatype="&xsd;time">21:00:00+01:00</restaurantClosingTime>

---

XML Schema datatypes describe part of what is called the "datatype domain". These datatypes are referenced using their URIs. They are considered members of the "rdfs:Datatype" class.

The XML Schema types do not have unique URIrefs. However, many tools recognize the use of the XML namespace for representing its datatypes. XML Schema defines a datatype hierarchy. XMLS datatypes are integrated into the OWL class hierarchy. Reasoners use the datatype property to interpret a statement's datatype value.

### 12.3.2 Object Properties (owl:ObjectProperty)

The "owl:ObjectProperty" class is used to identify a property whose value is a reference to an individual (as opposed to a datatype value). Object properties support "individual-valued" properties. The value of an object property is a resource (rather than a string literal).

| owl:ObjectProperty |
| --- |
|  |
|  |

---

The typical syntax for specifying an ObjectProperty is:

<owl:ObjectProperty rdf:ID="**propertyName**"/>

where **propertyName** is the name of the object property being defined.

---

Adding information about an existing object property is accomplished using the "rdf:about" attribute to reference the object property. The best practice is to name object properties using lower Camel Case.

171

## Section 3 – OWL Lite

---

The following specification example shows how an object Property (ownedBy) can be specified.

`<owl:ObjectProperty rdf:ID="ownedBy"/>`

---

An example of using the specified objectProperty ownedBy is:

```
<Person rdf:ID="person123">
      <personName>Jason Relles<personName>
</Person>

<Restaurant rdf:ID="KnightOwlRestaurant">
      <rdfs:label>Knight Owl Restaurant</rdfs:label>
      <ownedBy rdf:resource="#person123"/>
</Restaurant>
```

---

The "owl:ObjectProperty" class supports a reasoner by pointing to a resource containing the value of a particular property. This is used in answering queries.

For example, suppose a query answerer was responding to a query of "What is the name (personName) of the owner (ownedBy) of the Knight Owl Restaurant?" Once the query engine found the Restaurant instance "Restaurant123", named "Knight Owl Restaurant", it could follow the ownedBy object property to the "person123" instance and return the value of the personName property (Jason Relles) as the answer to the query.

### 12.3.3 Annotation Properties (owl:AnnotationProperty)

| owl:AnnotationProperty |
|---|
|  |
|  |

Annotation properties are a special type of property that describe a construct. OWL defines the "owl:AnnotationProperty" class for representing annotation properties. The pre-defined OWL annotation properties are: "rdfs:label", "rdfs:comment", "rdfs:seeAlso", "rdfs:isDefinedBy", and "owl:versionInfo".

---

The typical syntax for specifying that a property is an annotation property is:

<owl:AnnotationProperty rdf:about="**uriREF**">

where **uriREF** is the uriRef of the annotation property.

---

An example of defining an Annotation Property is:

<owl:AnnotationProperty rdf:about="&rest;reviewer"/>

---

In OWL Lite and OWL DL, the domain of an annotation property must be a named class, property, individual, or ontology. The range must be an individual, data literal, or URIref.

### 12.3.4 Ontology properties (owl:OntologyProperty)

| owl:OntologyProperty |
|---|
|  |
|  |

An ontology property is a property that relates two ontologies (instances of the "owl:Ontology" class). The "owl:OntologyProperty" class formalizes the concept of ontology properties. The ontology properties predefined by OWL are: "owl:imports", "owl:backwardCompatibleWith", "owl:incompatibleWith", and "owl:priorVersion".

173

Section 3 – OWL Lite

## 12.4 Basic OWL Lite Classes and Properties Summary

Basic classes can be defined with the "owl:Class" construct. OWL includes two predefined classes: "owl:Thing", the root class of all individuals, and "owl:Nothing", a class with no members. OWL defines four types of properties. OWL datatype properties support atomic datatype values. Object properties are used to define properties with resources as values. Annotation properties provide additional information about constructs. Ontology properties relate ontologies. The next chapter describes how OWL Lite property characteristics are encoded.

Figure 12-2 shows the relationship of OWL Lite class and property concepts.

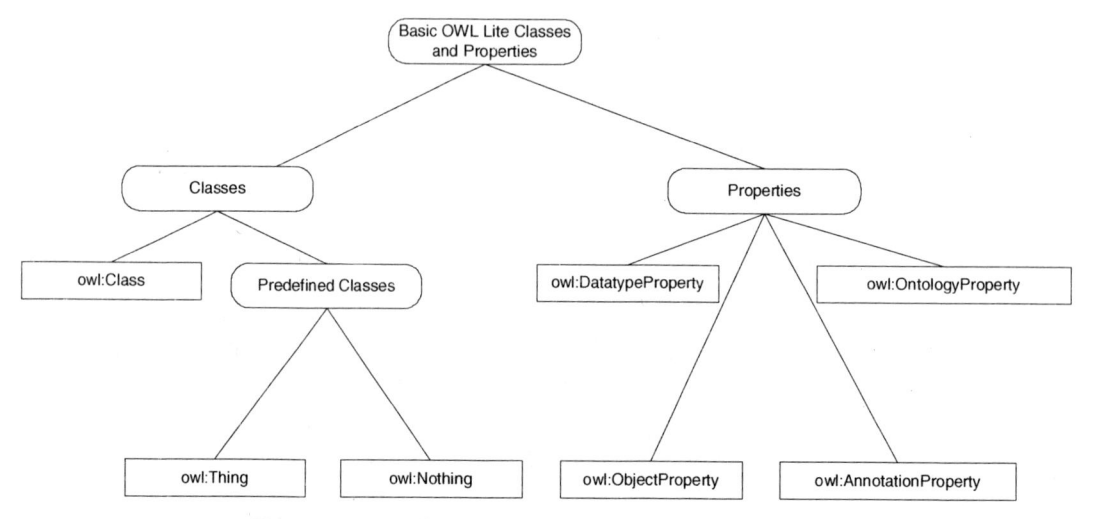

Figure 12-2. OWL Lite Classes and Properties

# 13 Describing OWL Lite Property Characteristics

The previous chapter described the specification of properties. Besides simply defining a property, we may want to provide additional information about the property. There are several types of statements that can be made about a property. These statements include properties (metaproperties) that describe the property and classes for making general statements about properties.

The following sections describe methods for describing properties and their relationships to classes including global restrictions, relating properties, inference shortcuts, and local property restrictions.

## 13.1 Defining Global Property Restrictions

OWL can be used to globally restrict properties. A global property restriction applies to all uses of a property, not just when describing individuals of a particular class. The two types of global property restrictions in OWL (in addition to the "rdfs:domain" and "rdfs:range" restrictions provided by RDFS) are functional properties and inverse functional properties.

### 13.1.1 Functional Property (owl:FunctionalProperty)

Often times, there should be only a single value associated with a property (e.g., "currentPrice", "primaryLocation").  ✓ FunctionalProperty

A functional property can have at most one (unique) value for a particular subject individual (see Figure 13-1). However, there is no requirement to have a property value. Both object properties and datatype properties can be identified as "functional" properties. A property is a functional property if any values for a particular object must be the same.

Figure 13-1. Functional Property

175

## Section 3 – OWL Lite

---

The typical syntax for identifying an object property as a functional property is:

```
<owl:ObjectProperty rdf:ID="propertyName">
        <rdf:type rdf:resource="&owl;FunctionalProperty"/>
</owl:ObjectProperty>
```

where **propertyName** is the name of the functional property.

---

The following states that the price property is functional, i.e., a MenuDish resource can have at most one value for the hasPrice property:

```
<owl:ObjectProperty rdf:ID="hasPrice">
        <rdf:type rdf:resource="&owl;FunctionalProperty"/>
</owl:ObjectProperty>
```

---

The typedNode syntax for functional properties is discouraged because a property is normally first and foremost an object property or a datatype property. Therefore, the functional property designation should occur within the property definition as an "rdf:type" property.

If more than one statement about a resource is made with the same functional property, the objects can be assumed to be the same. Property characteristics support consuming applications such as reasoners. If a reasoner finds a value for a functional property, it can stop looking for values because it knows there is only one value. If validating software finds more than one value for the property for a given object, the assertions have created an illegal condition.

For example, "hasFavoriteRestaurant" may be stated to be a functional property. From this, a reasoner may deduce that no individual may have more than one favorite restaurant. However, this does not imply that every person must have a favorite restaurant.

Since a given instance can only have one value for a functional property, we can infer that two items are the same if they are both values for a functional property associated with the same subject resource.

# Chapter 13 – Describing OWL Lite Property Characteristics

## 13.1.2 Inverse Functional Property (owl:inverseFunctionalProperty)

The opposite (inverse) relationship of a functional property is an inverse functional property. The concept is similar to a "key" field in a RDBMS.

☑ InverseFunctionalProperty

The "owl:InverseFunctionalProperty" designation is used to identify object properties whose values uniquely identify the subject instance of the property. In other words, if you know the value of the inverse functional property, you know which subject it belongs to.

---

The typical syntax of an inverse functional property is:

```
<rdf:ObjectProperty rdf:ID="propertyName">
    <rdf:type rdf:resource="&owl;InverseFunctionalProperty"/>
</rdf:ObjectProperty>
```

or using the typedNode syntax:

```
<owl:InverseFunctionalProperty rdf:ID="propertyName"/>
```

where **propertyName** is the name of the property that is being declared to an inverse functional property.

---

An example of defining an inverse functional property is:

```
<owl:InverseFunctional rdf:ID="hasMemberNumber"/>
```

---

A reasoner may encounter two URIrefs that identify resources with the same value for an "owl:InverseFunctionalProperty" property. The reasoner can infer that the two URIrefs are referencing the same individual resources.

The "owl:InverseFunctionalProperty" property is a global constraint and cannot be applied to transitive properties.

177

Section 3 – OWL Lite

Since the value of an inverseFunctional property uniquely identifies the subject, the inverse of an inverseFunctional property is Functional (hence the name). For example, if an inverseFunctional property (e.g., "hasSerialNumber") has an inverse property (e.g., "isSerialNumberFor"), the inverse property can only have at most one value (e.g., a serial number can only be the serial number for 0 or 1 item) (see Figure 13-2). The "owl:InverseFunctionalProperty" class used to represent inverse functional properties is a subclass of the "owl:ObjectProperty" class.

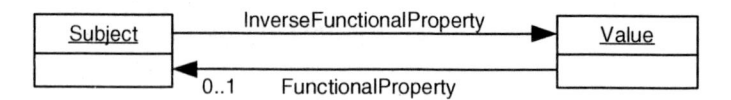

Figure 13-2. InverseFunctionalProperty

## 13.2 Relating Properties

OWL can describe relationships between properties. Two properties can be described as equivalent. Additionally, two properties can be described as the inverse of each other.

### 13.2.1 Stating Property Equivalence (owl:equivalentProperty)

The "owl:equivalentProperty" property can be used to state that two properties are equivalent (have the same property extension). The "owl:equivalentProperty" element is used for specifying the name of the equivalent property. Two properties that are equivalent properties relate a particular subject resource to the same value. Equivalent properties may describe different concepts, yet have the same members.

---

The typical syntax of an equivalent property specification is:

```
<owl:ObjectProperty rdf:ID="property1">
     <owl:equivalentProperty rdf:resource="property2"/>
</owl:ObjectProperty>
```

where **property2** is equivalent to **property1**.

# Chapter 13 – Describing OWL Lite Property Characteristics

> For example, if we wanted to make "menuPrice" a synonym of "menuCost", we could specify the equivalentProperty relationship as below:
>
> ```
> <owl:ObjectProperty rdf:ID="menuPrice">
>     <owl:equivalentProperty rdf:resource="#menuCost"/>
> </owl:ObjectProperty>
> ```

An ontology may exist with one property and another ontology may exist with an equivalent property. Rather than change all property specifications with a global search and replace (possibly invalidating dependent ontologies), an "owl:equivalentProperty" can state equivalence.

The "owl:equivalentProperty" is a subproperty of the "owl:sameAs" property and the "rdfs:subPropertyOf" property. The "owl:equivalentProperty" specification is used in validation and reasoning to "merge" items in their internal symbol tables. It supports ontology joins. Property equivalence means that the equivalent properties are considered subproperties of each other.

The "owl:equivalentProperty" property can be used with any "rdf:Property" and its value must be an instance of "rdf:Property".

## 13.2.2 Identifying Inverse Properties (owl:inverseOf Property)

The "owl:inverseOf" property is used to describe an opposite relationship to the property being described (see Figure 13-3). As described in the RDF chapter, properties are relationships between a domain and a range. An inverse relationship relates members of the range back to the domain. It is all a matter of perspective.

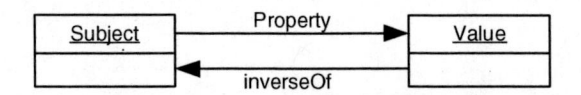

Figure 13-3. inverseOf Property

Only one of the two properties, related by "owl:inverseOf" property needs to be specified as the value because the "owl:inverseOf" property is symmetric.

## Section 3 – OWL Lite

The typical syntax for specifying an inverse property is:

```
<owl:ObjectProperty rdf:ID="property1">
    <owl:inverseOf rdf:resource="property2"/>
</owl:ObjectProperty>
```

where **property1** and **property2** are the URIrefs of the inverse properties.

---

An example of specifying an inverse property is:

```
<owl:ObjectProperty rdf:ID="usedInDish">
    <rdfs:comment>Indicates a dish that the ingredient (subject) is used in</rdfs:comment>
</owl:ObjectProperty>

<owl:ObjectProperty rdf:ID="hasIngredient">
    <rdfs:comment>Indicates an ingredient that the dish (subject) uses</rdfs:comment>
    <owl:inverseOf rdf:resource="#usedInDish"/>
</owl:ObjectProperty>
```

Defining an inverse property relationship provides an inferred "return arc" from the value to the subject. Only object properties can be inverse properties.

---

Using the example above, if we state that:

```
<Ingredient rdf:ID="ingredient345">
    <rdfs:label>avocado</rdfs:label>
</Ingredient>

<MenuItem rdf:ID="item123">
    <rdfs:label>guacamole</rdfs:label>
    <hasIngredient rdf:resource="#ingredient345"/>
</MenuItem>
```

then hasIngredient's inverse property (usedInDish) allows the reasoner to infer that:

```
<Ingredient rdf:about="#ingredient345">
    <usedInDish rdf:resource="#item123"/>
</Ingredient>
```

The "owl:inverseOf" property can be used with any "owl:ObjectProperty" and its value must be an instance of "owl:ObjectProperty".

## 13.3 Inference Shortcuts

OWL statements can describe particular object properties to assist reasoners in making inferences. An object property can be described as transitive or symmetric. This additional information about a property can be specified by making the property a member of a pre-defined OWL class. Belonging to the class can be thought of as a checkmark or flag condition.

### 13.3.1 Transitive Properties (owl:TransitiveProperty)

Designating a property as transitive enables software to perform additional inferencing.  ☑ TransitiveProperty

Recall from geometry that transitivity means that if a transitive function relates X to Y, and Y to Z, then X is related to Z by that same function. In OWL, an object property can be declared transitive. A transitive object property is an object property whose subjects and values can be "chained" together. Transitive properties are commonly used for "relative" relationships (e.g., part/whole, relative size). If a property P is transitive, then if an object X has a value of object Y for property P and if Y has a value of object Z for property P, then you can infer that object X has value object Z for property P (see Figure 13-4).

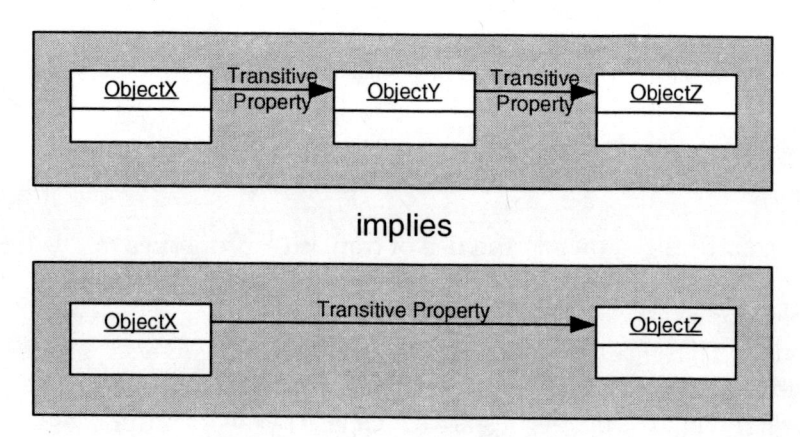

Figure 13-4. Transitive Properties

# Section 3 – OWL Lite

A property is identified as being transitive by making it an instance of the "owl:TransitiveProperty" class.

---

The typical syntax for specifying that a property is transitive is:

```
<ObjectProperty rdf:ID=propertyName>
        <rdf:type rdf:resource="&owl;TransitiveProperty"/>
</ObjectProperty>
```

Alternatively, using the typedNode syntax:

```
<owl:TransitiveProperty rdf:ID="propertyName"/>
```

where **propertyName** is the name of the transitive object property.

---

An example of specifying a transitive property is to specify a transitive smallerThan property is:

```
<owl:TransitiveProperty rdf:ID="smallerThan"/>
```

---

An example of a transitive property being used is:

```
<rest:Restaurant rdf:ID="restaurant123">
        <rest:smallerThan rdf:resource="#restaurant456"/>
</rest:Restaurant>

<rest:Restaurant rdf:ID="restaurant456">
        <rest:smallerThan rdf:resource="#KnightOwlRestaurant"/>
</rest:Restaurant>
```

Given this example, a reasoner can infer that "#restaurant123" is smaller than "#KnightOwlRestaurant".

---

There are several restrictions on the use of transitive properties in OWL Lite. They cannot have local or global cardinality constraints on themselves, their inverses, or their superproperties. This includes functional and inverse functional designations. These restrictions also apply to their inverse properties. The domain and range of a transitive property must match. Only object properties can be transitive. Transitive properties are a subclass of object properties.

## 13.3.2 Symmetric Properties (owl:SymmetricProperty)

Symmetric properties can relate property values back to subject resources (see Figure 13-5).

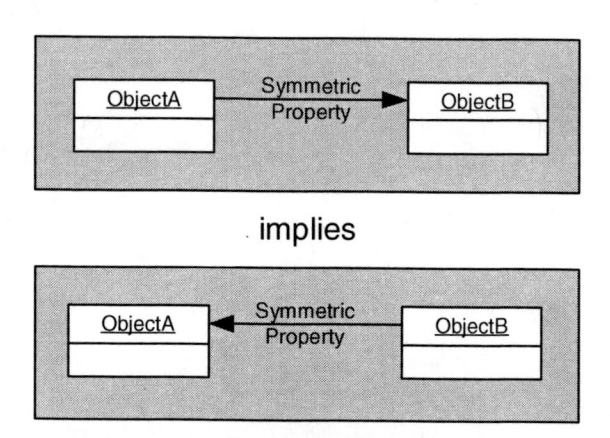

✓ **SymmetricProperty**

Figure 13-5. Symmetric Property

Symmetric properties are a specific type of object property that provide an inference shortcut. Instead of having to specify the property in both directions, only one direction is required. If the domain and range for a symmetric property are restricted, they must be the same.

---

The typical syntax for describing a property named **propertyName** as a symmetric property is:

```
<owl:ObjectProperty rdf:ID="propertyName"/>
    <rdf:type rdf:resource="&owl;SymmetricProperty"/>
</owl:ObjectProperty>
```

Alternatively, the typedNode syntax can be used to define the property as symmetric:

```
<owl:SymmetricProperty rdf:ID="propertyName"/>
```

where **propertyName** is the name of the symmetric property.

Section 3 – OWL Lite

---

This example shows how a property can be specified as a symmetric property using the "rdf:type" property.

```
<owl:ObjectProperty rdf:ID="GoesGoodWith">
    <rdf:type rdf:resource="&owl;SymmetricProperty"/>
</owl:ObjectProperty>
```

or using the typedNode element syntax:

```
<owl:SymmetricProperty rdf:ID="GoesGoodWith"/>
```

---

As an example of using a symmetric property, we specify two "MenuItems": cheese and crackers.

```
<MenuItem rdf:ID="item124">
    <rdfs:label>cheese</rdfs:label>
</MenuItem>

<MenuItem rdf:ID="item123">
    <rdfs:label>crackers</rdfs:label>
    <goesGoodWith rdf:resource="#item124"/>
</MenuItem>
```

From this example, a reasoner can infer that "#item124" goes good with "#item123".

---

A symmetric property implies a relationship in the opposite direction. A reasoner that encounters an instance X that has a symmetric property value of Y can infer that Y has the same property with value X.

With a symmetric property, you only need to specify a relationship in one direction, since the relation in the other direction can be inferred. The domain and range restrictions on a symmetric property should be the same. The "owl:SymmetricProperty" class is a subclass of "owl:ObjectProperty".

## 13.4 Local Property Restrictions (owl:Restriction/owl:onProperty)

Property constraints like "owl:FunctionalProperty" are global, meaning that they apply to all uses of the property. One of the most powerful concepts of RDFS and OWL is the separation of classes and properties. However, there are times when we want to associate property restrictions with particular classes.

# Chapter 13 – Describing OWL Lite Property Characteristics

To define a property restriction that only applies to a particular class extension, a local property restriction is used. A local restriction is defined using an ad-hoc unnamed (anonymous) restriction class of instances that satisfy a specific constraint. The restriction class is defined using the "owl:Restriction" class.

The "owl:Restriction" class has an associated "owl:onProperty" property that identifies the object property or datatype property being restricted. Another property specifies one of the specific types of restrictions/constraints allowed in OWL Lite.

---

The typical syntax of a local property restriction is:

```
<owl:Restriction>
        <owl:onProperty rdf:resource="propertyName"/>
                specificRestriction
</owl:Restriction>
```

where **propertyName** is the URIref of the property being restricted for the particular class, and **specificRestriction** is the detailed description of the particular constraint being placed on the instances of the described class that use the property.

---

Restriction classes are used for validation and to support inferencing. Since the constraints for controlling values of properties are local to the class, they are called local restrictions. A local property restriction can be thought of as limiting the values of a class's properties or as defining a class in terms of its property values. Restrictions are normally related to classes using the "owl:equivalentClass" or "owl:subClassOf" properties described in the next chapter.

The two types of local restrictions that can then be placed on property values are value restrictions (i.e., "owl:allValuesFrom", "owl:someValuesFrom") and cardinality restrictions (i.e., "owl:minCardinality", "owl:maxCardinality", "owl:cardinality") (see Figure 13-6).

## Section 3 – OWL Lite

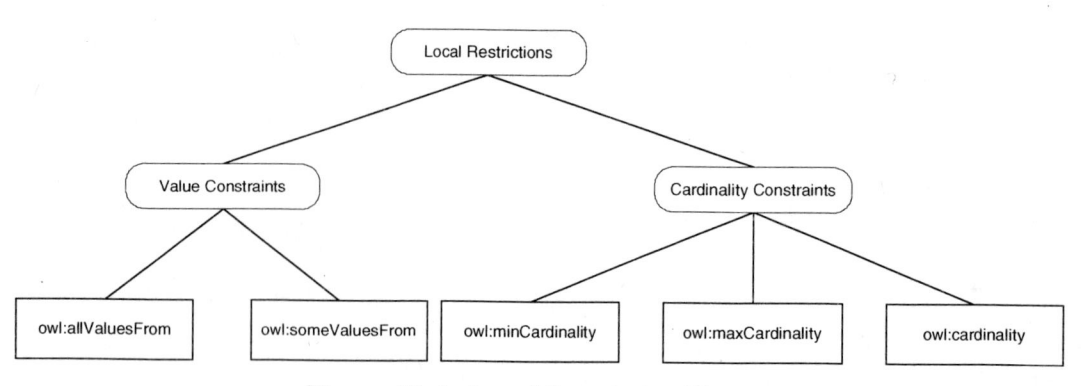

Figure 13-6. Local Restriction Types

The following sections detail each of these five local restriction types.

### 13.4.1 Value Constraints

An OWL Lite value constraint is a restriction on a property's range when used with a specified class. This is different from a global "rdfs:range" restriction that applies to all classes that employ the range restricted property. The two types of OWL Lite value restrictions are "owl:allValuesFrom" and "owl:someValuesFrom".

### 13.4.1.1 Universally Restricting Property Values (owl:allValuesFrom)

The "owl:allValuesFrom" constraint is specified within a restriction. It requires that all property values belong to a particular class.

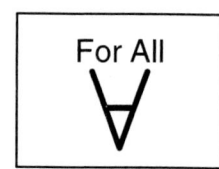

---

The typical syntax of the owl:allValuesFrom property is:

```
<owl:Restriction>
     <owl:onProperty rdf:resource="propertyName"/>
     <owl:allValuesFrom rdf:resource="targetClass"/>
</owl:Restriction>
```

where **propertyName** is the name of the property being restricted and **targetClass** is the class that the property's values must belong to.

# Chapter 13 – Describing OWL Lite Property Characteristics

---

An example of using the restriction is:

```
<owl:Restriction>
        <owl:onProperty rdf:resource="#dishFeeds"/>
        <owl:allValuesFrom rdf:resource="&xsd;nonNegativeInteger"/>
</owl:Restriction>
```

This restriction would constrain members of the class being described to only having non negative integer values for the dishFeeds property.

---

In logic theory, the universal quantifier construct is used to make "blanket" statements about all instances. The "owl:allValuesFrom" constraint insists that all values for a particular property belong to a specified class. In other words, for all uses of the restricted property by members of the described class, the values must belong to the designated class or datatype.

A reasoner can not assume that there are any property instances. If there are no values for the restricted property, the constraint is considered satisfied.

The "owl:allValuesFrom" property can be used with any "owl:Restriction" and its value must be a class expression or datatype.

## 13.4.1.2 Existentially Restricting Properties (owl:someValuesFrom)

Unlike the "owl:allValuesFrom" construct that requires all values to belong to the specified class expression, the "owl:someValuesFrom" property restriction is used to state that at least one value of the restricted property must be an instance of the specified class.

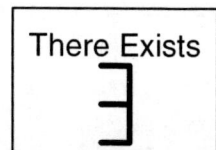

There Exists
∃

---

The typical syntax for defining an existential property restriction is:

```
<owl:Restriction>
        <owl:onProperty rdf:resource="propertyName"/>
        <owl:someValuesFrom rdf:resource="targetClass"/>
</owl:Restriction>
```

which requires at least one value of a particular property named **propertyName** for the restriction class to a class named **targetClass**.

---

187

## Section 3 – OWL Lite

> For example, a restriction can describe the set of things with "Cheese" as their "topping".
>
> ```
> <owl:Restriction>
>         <owl:onProperty rdf:resource="#topping"/>
>         <owl:someValuesFrom rdf:resource="#Cheese"/>
> </owl:Restriction>
> ```

The "owl:someValuesFrom" value restriction is related to the existential quantifier concept in logic theory because every instance of the described class must have at least one value from the specified class. The "owl:someValuesFrom" restriction does not prevent values from other classes.

The "owl:someValuesFrom" restriction is related to the existential quantifier concept from logic theory. In logic theory, the existential quantifier specifies the minimum cardinality of 1.

At least one value of the identified property must be a member of the specified class expression or datatype.

The "owl:someValuesFrom" property can be used with any "owl:Restriction" and its value must be an instance of "rdfs:Class".

### 13.4.2 OWL Lite Restricted Cardinality

In addition to value constraints, OWL Lite properties can be restricted in terms of their cardinality. By default, OWL classes can have an arbitrary number of values associated with a class's properties. A cardinality constraint restricts the number of values a property should have for subject members from a particular class description.

Cardinality constraints are specified as part of property restrictions on classes. They only apply to the property when used with instances of the restricted class. The value of a cardinality value is specified using a non-negative integer (restricted to 0 or 1 in OWL Lite).

## Chapter 13 – Describing OWL Lite Property Characteristics

In OWL Lite, cardinality can be used to require a property (minimum 1), prohibit the use of a property (maximum 0), or to limit the number of occurrences to 0 or 1. In OWL, cardinality does not restrict the syntactic use of a property (e.g., with a maximum of 1), it affects the semantics (e.g., inferring that values are the same). This is because two syntactically different values could be semantically equivalent. Cardinality cannot be specified for transitive properties.

Cardinality values are typically represented with associated "rdf:datatype" attribute values of "&xsd;nonNegativeInteger". The following sections describe the three types of OWL Lite restricted cardinality descriptions: "owl:minCardinality", "owl:maxCardinality", and "owl:cardinality".

### 13.4.2.1 Specifying Minimum Cardinality (owl:minCardinality)

An "owl:minCardinality" restriction on a property means that at least the specified number of distinct values must be associated with members of the restricted class. The data values of "owl:minCardinality" properties must belong to the "nonNegativeInteger" XMLS datatype.

Table 13-1 shows the interpretation of the "owl:minCardinality" value for OWL Lite.

Table 13-1. MinCardinality Value Interpretation

| minCardinality value | Interpretation |
|---|---|
| 0 | Property is optional (default) |
| 1 | Required (at least 1) |

The element syntax for specifying minimum cardinality is:

```
<owl:Restriction>
    <owl:onProperty rdf:resource="propertyName"/>
    <owl:minCardinality rdf:datatype="&xsd;nonNegativeInteger">cardinalityValue</owl:minCardinality>
</owl:Restriction>
```

where **cardinalityValue** is the minimum cardinality for the property named **propertyName**

# Section 3 – OWL Lite

Although the specification of cardinality in an attribute is valid syntax, the element-centric method is more consistent in structure with other restrictions.

---

An example of specifying a minimum cardinality of 0 in a restriction for specifying an optional tax identifier is:

```
<owl:Restriction>
        <owl:onProperty rdf:resource="#taxIdentifier"/>
        <owl:minCardinality rdf:datatype="&xsd;nonNegativeInteger">0</owl:minCardinality>
</owl:Restriction>
```

---

An example of specifying a minimum cardinality of 1 to require items have a price is:

```
<owl:Restriction>
        <owl:onProperty rdf:resource="#hasPrice"/>
        <owl:minCardinality rdf:datatype="&xsd;nonNegativeInteger">1</owl:minCardinality>
</owl:Restriction>
```

---

The "owl:minCardinality" property can be used with any "owl:Restriction" and its value must be a non-negative integer value (0 or 1 in OWL Lite).

## 13.4.2.2 Specifying Maximum Cardinality (owl:maxCardinality)

The "owl:maxCardinality" property limits the number of unique values for a particular class's property. The specified non-negative integer (0 or 1 in OWL Lite) is the maximum number.

---

The typical syntax for specifying the maxCardinality of a property is:

```
<owl:Restriction>
        <owl:onProperty rdf:resource="propertyName"/>
        <owl:maxCardinality rdf:datatype="&xsd;nonNegativeInteger">maxCardinalityValue</owl:maxCardinality>
</owl:Restriction>
```

where the **propertyName** property is being restricted to a cardinality of **maxCardinalityValue**.

> An example of specifying a maximum cardinality of 0 on a partner property (perhaps as part of a sole proprietor class definition) is:
>
> ```
> <owl:Restriction>
>     <owl:onProperty rdf:resource="#hasPartner"/>
>     <owl:maxCardinality rdf:datatype="&xsd;nonNegativeInteger">0</owl:maxCardinality>
> </owl:Restriction>
> ```

Table 13-2 shows the interpretation of the maxCardinality property.

Table 13-2. MaxCardinality Value Interpretation

| maxCardinality Value | Implication |
|---|---|
| 0 | Not allowed |
| 1 | Optional (0 or 1) |

The OWL Lite "owl:maxCardinality" specification can be used to restrict a search. For example, once a query has found a single value for a property whose maximum cardinality is 1, it can terminate searching for other distinct values. The "owl:maxCardinality" property can be used with any "owl:Restriction" and its value must be a non-negative integer value (0 or 1 in OWL Lite).

### 13.4.2.3 Absolute Cardinality (owl:cardinality)

The "owl:cardinality" statement restricts the members of a class to the members with exactly the specified number of property values associated with the member. In OWL Lite, only 0 or 1 can be specified. Therefore, a cardinality of 0 is shorthand for minCardinality=0 and maxCardinality=0 (none allowed). Similarly, a cardinality of 1 means minCardinality=1 and maxCardinality=1 (exactly one is required and permissible). Absolute cardinality is specified in OWL with the "owl:cardinality" attribute on a restriction class specification (attribute syntax) or an "owl:cardinality" element within an "owl:Restriction" class.

## Section 3 – OWL Lite

---

The attribute syntax for defining the absolute cardinality for a property is:

```
<owl:Class rdf:about="className">
    <rdfs:subClassOf>
        <owl:Restriction rdf:datatype="&xsd;nonNegativeInteger" owl:cardinality="cardinalityValue">
            <owl:onProperty rdf:resource="propertyName"/>
        </owl:Restriction>
    </rdfs:subClassOf>
</owl:Class>
```

where **className** is the class whose **propertyName** property has a cardinality of **cardinalityValue**

---

An example of specifying things with a single cheese type (using element syntax) is:

```
<owl:Restriction>
    <owl:onProperty rdf:resource="#hasCheeseType"/>
    <owl:cardinality rdf:datatype="&xsd;nonNegativeInteger">1</owl:cardinality>
</owl:Restriction>
```

---

Table 13-3 shows the interpretation of absolute cardinality property values in OWL Lite.

Table 13-3. Absolute Cardinality Value Interpretation

| cardinality | Interpretation | Same As |
|---|---|---|
| 0 | Not Allowed (keeping something nonsensical from being asserted) | min 0, max 0 |
| 1 | Single Value Required (making sure minimal information is specified) | min 1, max 1 |

The cardinality statement is a shorthand for specifying both minimum and maximum when they have the same value.

The knowledge of cardinality can lead to error identification. If the cardinality is 0 and you find a value, there is an error. If the cardinality is 1, something must be specified and if two items are found, they must be equivalent or there is an error. The "owl:cardinality" property can be used with any "owl:Restriction" and its value must be a non-negative integer value (0 or 1 in OWL Lite).

### 13.4.2.4 OWL Lite Cardinality Summary

Table 13-4 summarizes the meaning of the cardinality elements in OWL Lite whose value is represented by N.

Table 13-4. Cardinality Summary

| Cardinality Type | N = 0 | N = 1 |
|---|---|---|
| Minimum cardinality | Optional (default) 0 or any # allowed | >=1 (required) |
| Maximum cardinality | None allowed | 0 or 1 allowed |
| Cardinality | None allowed | Must be 1 and only 1 |

Table 13-5 indicates the elements to use to achieve a particular OWL Lite functionality.

Table 13-5. Using Appropriate Cardinality Statements and Values

| Desired Functionality | Cardinality Statement | N |
|---|---|---|
| Allow anything (0 or any #) | owl:minCardinality | 0 (default) |
| Require at least one | owl:minCardinality | 1 |
| Do not allow any | owl:maxCardinality | 0 |
| Do not allow any | owl:cardinality (preferred) | 0 |
| Allow 0 or 1 | owl:maxCardinality (or use owl:FunctionalProperty) | 1 |
| Require 1 and only 1 | owl:cardinality | 1 |
| Functional property | owl:minCardinality | 0 (default) |
|  | owl:maxCardinality | 1 |

Section 3 – OWL Lite

## 13.5 OWL Lite Property Characteristics Summary

Figure 13-7 shows a taxonomy of property characteristics that can be defined with OWL.

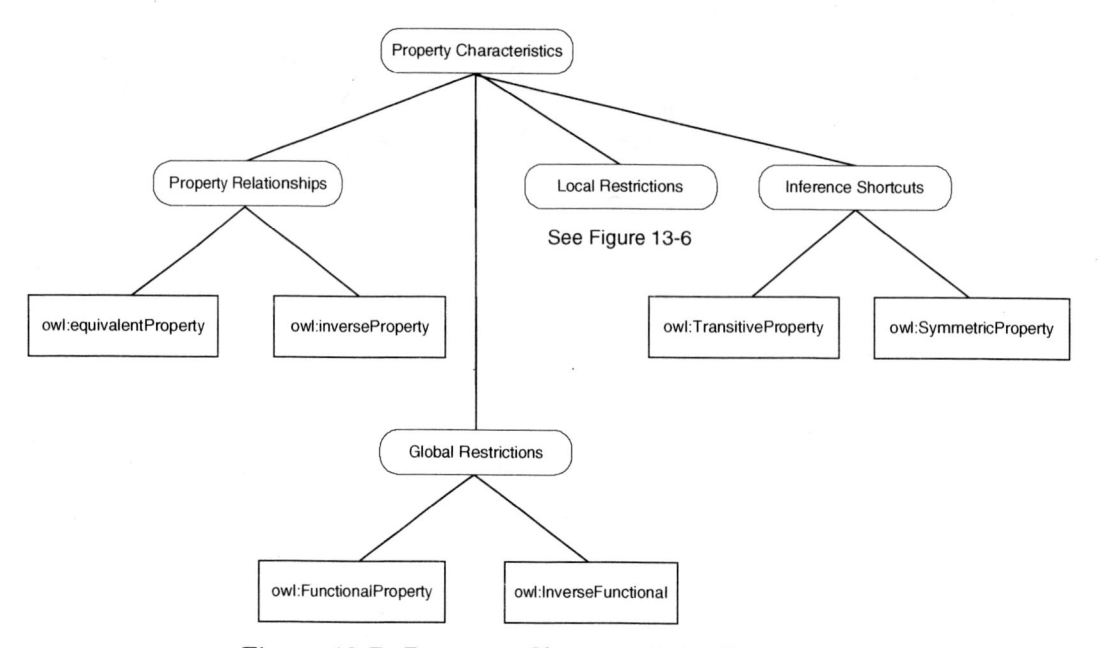

Figure 13-7. Property Characteristics Taxonomy

194

# Chapter 13 – Describing OWL Lite Property Characteristics

Table 13-6 summarizes RDFS and OWL property characteristics.

Table 13-6. Property Characteristic Summary

| Feature | Syntax | Datatype Properties | Object Properties | Scope |
|---|---|---|---|---|
| Global Restrictions | rdfs:domain | X | X | Global |
| | rdfs:range | X | X | |
| | owl:FunctionalProperty | X | X | |
| | owl:InverseFunctionalProperty | | X | |
| Relationships | rdfs:subPropertyOf | X | X | |
| | owl:equivalentProperty | X | X | |
| | owl:inverseOf | | X | |
| Inference Shortcuts | owl:TransitiveProperty | | X | |
| | owl:SymmetricProperty | | X | |
| Property Value Restrictions | owl:allValuesFrom | X | X | Local |
| | owl:someValuesFrom | X | X | |
| Cardinality Restrictions | owl:maxCardinality | X | X | |
| | owl:minCardinality | X | X | |
| | owl:cardinality | X | X | |

Figure 13-8 shows the relationship of the classes used to represent properties.

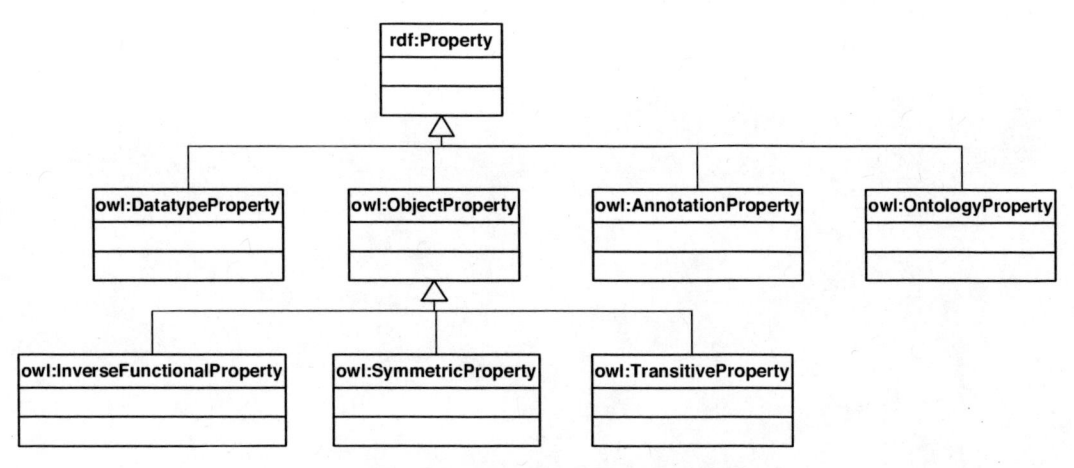

Figure 13-8. Property Relationships

## Section 3 – OWL Lite

OWL Lite supports the description of properties by defining global restrictions, property relationships, inference shortcuts, and local restrictions. Global property restrictions are used to state a property's domain and range and whether a property is functional or inverse functional. Global property relationships specify whether properties are subproperties, equivalent, or inverse. Inference shortcuts identify properties as transitive or symmetric. Local property restrictions relate to values and cardinality. Value constraints require that all or some of the properties values belong to a particular class. Cardinality constraints define the minimum, maximum, or absolute cardinality for a property.

The next chapter describes how derived OWL Lite classes are encoded in OWL.

# 14 Deriving OWL Lite Classes

There are alternative methods for defining OWL classes besides the simple "owl:Class" definition. Properties can define new classes and define relationships between classes. The definition of a class can also be derived from other classes.

Rather than just describing a class by referencing its class name URIref, a class of individuals can be described by a class expression. A class expression is a combination of OWL statements used to describe a class. You can derive a class definition through a subclass relationship, equivalency relationship, intersection, or class expression.

## *14.1 Simple Named Subclass (rdfs:subClassOf)*

A subclass is a class that is a specialization of another class. Specialization is a method for defining a more specific or general class using subsumption and inheritance techniques. The individuals that belong to a subclass are also member individuals of the superclass.

The "rdfs:subClassOf" property identifies the superclass of the class being described. Although the "rdfs:subClassOf" construct is part of the "rdfs:" namespace (see Section 9.5.1.2), it is described here because of its use with "owl:Class" rather than "rdfs:Class".

Subclasses are used to define taxonomies (subsumption hierarchies) of classes. The root classes in the subsumption hierarchy should describe the most general concepts of the domain. A subclass can be defined directly by identifying the superclass's name or through an anonymous restriction class.

Technically, a class is considered to be a subclass of itself. Both classes related in an "rdfs:subClassOf" property must be classes. The value of an "rdfs:subClassOf" property can be either a class name (URIref) or a class expression.

# Section 3 – OWL Lite

---

The typical syntax for defining a subclass is:

```
<owl:Class rdf:ID="SubClassName">
        <rdfs:subClassOf rdf:resource="SuperClassName"/>
</owl:Class>
```

where **SubClassName** is the name of the subclass of the class named **SuperClassName**.

---

The following example shows how SpaghettiDish can be defined as a subclass (specialization) of a PastaDish subclass specification.

```
<owl:Class rdf:ID="SpaghettiDish">
        <rdfs:subClassOf rdf:resource="#PastaDish"/>
</owl:Class>
```

---

The "rdfs:subClassOf" property is a transitive property.

---

The following example illustrates the transitivity of the subClassOf property:

```
<owl:Class rdf:ID="Dessert"/>

<owl:Class rdf:ID="Pie">
        <rdfs:subClassOf rdf:resource="#Dessert"/>
</owl:Class>

<owl:Class rdf:ID="KeyLimePie">
        <rdfs:subClassOf rdf:resource="#Pie"/>
</owl:Class>
```

By making Pie a subclass of Dessert and KeyLimePie a subclass of Pie, by transitivity, we can infer that a KeyLimePie is a subclass of Dessert.

---

Belonging to multiple superclasses is a different concept than the object-oriented notion of multiple inheritance. Multiple inheritance suggests a unique class that inherits from multiple classes. Individuals then belong to that single class. In OWL, the individuals are members of all the classes for which the class is a subclass of.

# Chapter 14 – Deriving OWL Lite Classes

> The following example demonstrates a class being a member of multiple superclasses:
>
> ```
> <owl:Class rdf:ID="Tomato">
>     <rdfs:subClassOf rdf:resource="#Fruit"/>
>     <rdfs:subClassOf rdf:resource="#Vegetable"/>
> </owl:Class>
> ```

As with object-oriented systems, everything that is true about members of the superclass is true about the members of the subclass. Therefore, properties associated with a superclass also apply to the subclass. A reasoner can deduce that an individual member of a subclass is also an individual member of its superclass. For example, a reasoner can infer from the example above that "KeyLimePie" class individuals are also individual members of the "Dessert" class.

The "rdfs:subClassOf" property can be used with a class and its value must be a class or property restriction.

## 14.2 Class Equivalency (owl:equivalentClass)

The "owl:equivalentClass" property is used to identify a synonymous class. The "owl:equivalentClass" property is used to specify that two classes have the same class extension (individual members). Although two classes have the same individual members, they may represent different concepts and be subclasses of different classes. Two classes are equivalent if and only if they are subclasses of each other. The simplest form of specifying the equivalence of classes is to use their names.

> The typical syntax for describing simple class equivalence is:
>
> ```
> <owl:Class rdf:ID="class1">
>     <owl:equivalentClass rdf:resource="class2"/>
> </owl:Class>
> ```
>
> where **class1** is a class whose extension is the same as **class2**

## Section 3 – OWL Lite

A property restriction can be the domain or range of an "owl:equivalentClass" property. However, normally a class identifier is the subject. A class can have multiple "owl:equivalentClass" properties.

---

An example of stating that SodaDrink is equivalentTo PopDrink is:

```
<owl:Class rdf:ID="SodaDrink">
        <owl:equivalentClass rdf:resource="#PopDrink"/>
</owl:Class>
```

---

An example of defining a class by identifying a class extension through a property restriction is:

```
<owl:Class rdf:ID="lunchDish">
       <owl:equivalentClass>
              <owl:Restriction>
                     <owl:onProperty rdf:resource="#onMenu"/>
                     <owl:allValuesFrom rdf:resource="#LunchMenu"/>
              </owl:Restriction>
       </owl:equivalentClass>
</owl:Class>
```

---

The equivalent class concept is important for queries because symbols can be folded together (collapsed) during search. The "owl:equivalentClass" property effectively merges class references in the symbol tables of software performing queries. The "owl:equivalentClass" property can also be used to link ontologies. This is sometimes called a semantic join.

Equivalent classes have the same members (class extension), but may not necessarily represent the same concept. If two classes are equivalent, a reasoner can infer that an individual that belongs to one is also a member of the other (and vice versa).

The "owl:equivalentClass" property can be used with any "owl:Class" and its value must be an instance of an "owl:Class".

## 14.3 OWL Lite Intersection (owl:intersectionOf)

A class can be derived by identifying the intersection of multiple class extensions. The resulting class includes the individuals that belong to all the specified extensions (logical conjunction). It is equivalent to the logical "AND" connector (see Figure 14-1). Intersections are formed in OWL Lite using the "owl:intersectionOf" property.

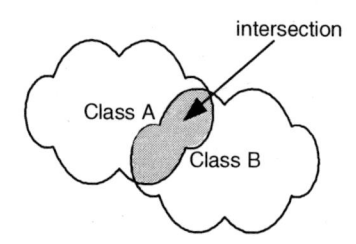

Figure 14-1. Intersection

The intersection is described with a class name and is based on the intersection of a collection of other classes (class descriptions). The class description elements can be a mixture of named classes and restrictions.

---

The typical syntax for specifying a class based on an OWL class intersection is:

```
<owl:Class rdf:ID="ClassName">
      <owl:intersectionOf rdf:parseType="Collection">
            <owl:Class rdf:about="AnotherClass1"/>
            <owl:Class rdf:about="AnotherClass2"/>
      </owl:intersectionOf>
</owl:Class>
```

where **ClassName** is a class defined from the intersection of **AnotherClass1** and **AnotherClass2**.

---

Section 3 – OWL Lite

An example of using the owl:intersectionOf construct is:

```
<owl:Class rdf:ID="FriedFood">
    <owl:intersectionOf rdf:parseType="Collection">
        <owl:Class rdf:about="#MenuDish"/>
        <owl:Restriction>
            <owl:onProperty rdf:resource="#cookingMethod"/>
            <owl:hasValue rdf:resource="#Fry"/>
        </owl:Restriction>
    </owl:intersectionOf>
</owl:Class>
```

## 14.4 Derived OWL Lite Classes Summary

Figure 14-2 shows the three construct that are used to derive OWL Lite classes.

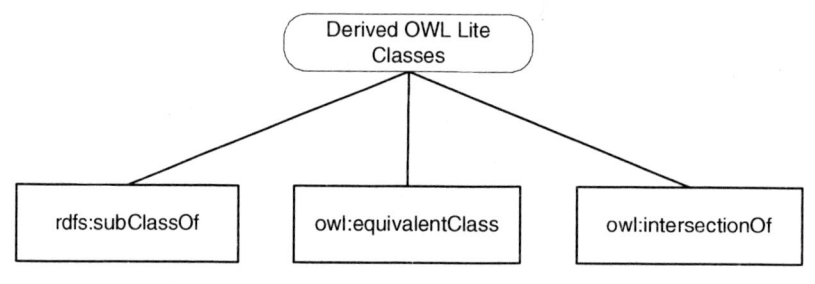

Figure 14-2. OWL Lite Derived Classes

OWL classes can be derived from other classes by defining the relationship between the derived class and other classes. The "rdfs:subClassOf" relationship identifies the derived class as a subset. The "owl:equivalentClass" states that the class extension is the same. The "owl:intersectionOf" property defines a class of individuals that are members of every class specified in the list of classes.

The next chapter describes how class member individuals are encoded in OWL.

# 15 Describing Individuals

OWL individuals are part the ontological primitive layer in the Semantic Web's architecture on top of RDF and RDF/XML (see Figure 15-1). As described in the RDFS chapter (Chapter 9), individuals are members (instances) of user-defined ontological classes.

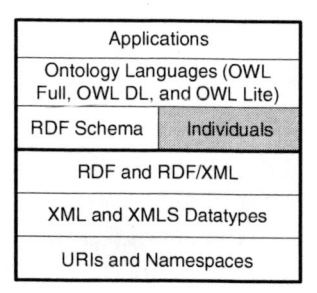

| Applications |
| --- |
| Ontology Languages (OWL Full, OWL DL, and OWL Lite) |
| RDF Schema — Individuals |
| RDF and RDF/XML |
| XML and XMLS Datatypes |
| URIs and Namespaces |

Figure 15-1. Individuals Portion of the Ontological Primitive Layer

This text differentiates between the description of an ontology (vocabulary or Tbox) and individual members (instances or Abox) of user-defined classes that comply with ontologies. A confusing aspect about OWL is that some language constructs (e.g., classes) are themselves instances of classes.

## 15.1 Determining an Individual

Sometimes, it is difficult to identify a resource as an individual. There are key differences between individuals and instances and between individuals and classes.

### 15.1.1 Individual vs. Instance

There is a subtle, yet important difference between instances and individuals. Classes, properties, and other generic concepts can have associated instances. Instances of user-defined ontological classes are described as individuals in this text.

A user-defined OWL class is an instance of the predefined "owl:Class" class. Ontology classes are similar to RDBMS tables and ontology properties are similar to RDBMS fields. The concept of an individual is similar to a record in a relational database management system (RDBMS). Another analogy can be made to object-oriented systems. Ontology individuals are similar to objects in object-oriented systems.

Section 3 – OWL Lite

Individuals are preferably concrete instantiations, not just concepts. For example, a particular pie on a shelf could be considered an individual (an instance of a KeyLimePie class).

## 15.1.2 Class vs. Individual

A common challenge in developing an ontology is determining whether a concept should be represented as a subclass or an individual. In other words, determining whether a concept is related to a class with either a subclass relationship (class) or an "instance of" relationship (individual).

The distinction between a class/subclass and an individual is not always clear. Some concepts represent abstractions that may represent sets (classes) or individuals, depending on the application.

A difficult situation arises when an individual should also be considered a class (which is legal in OWL Full). One person's class may be another person's individual. For example, Key lime pie could be represented as a class and a particular pie on a platter could be considered an individual. To a cookbook, a Key lime pie might seem like an individual, but it is best considered a variety. Sometimes an individual serves as a prototypical instance of a class to represent abstractions.

Individuals should represent actual or virtual objects in the domain of interest. Groups of objects should correspond to class concept sets. In this text, individuals are actual or virtual things, not abstractions that could be considered classes or varieties.

One approach is to focus on the use of the ontology by an application. If the application is treating the information as "data", it may be a candidate for representation as an individual. If the application uses the information to understand the semantics of the data, it may be more appropriately represented as class information.

### 15.1.3 Leaves of a Taxonomy

Individuals often mirror "real world" objects. When you stop having different property attributes (and just have different values) you have often identified an object (individual).

Concepts are often organized into taxonomies. One approach for differentiating between classes and individuals is to make the most specific concepts (leaves of the taxonomical tree) into individuals. However, this assumes that the tree was taken to the most detailed level of resolution to support anticipated applications. Individuals are often used to represent the most specific items represented in a knowledge base. The leaves of the tree should be carefully examined to determine whether they are truly types of things (classes) or actually individuals.

Another method is to identify the lowest level of granularity in the representation. The level of granularity is in turn determined by a potential application of the ontology. Taxonomical concepts (natural hierarchies) from the subject domain should be represented as subclass hierarchies. Individuals are not organized into tree structures, but classes are.

A common heuristic is to consider whether "is a type of" or "is a" more accurately reflects the relationship in the domain. The "is a" relationship is normally represented as an "instance of" relationship between an individual and a class. The "is a type of" relationship is normally represented best as a subclass relationship.

## 15.2 Encoding an Instance File

Whenever possible, separate individual definitions from the ontology classes that they instantiate. The file of individual definitions is often called an instance or artifact file. As you design an ontology for a domain, you must make decisions on how to represent concepts. The primary choices are the class, property, and individual constructs.

Individuals are part of the object domain. The object domain is made up of individuals that instantiate the user-defined classes specified in ontologies. The set of individuals in the instance file correspond to the computer science notion of assertions on individuals (i.e., Abox).

While OWL is needed to describe classes, properties, and their relationships in ontologies, the OWL documentation specifies that RDF is sufficient for representing the associated instance data. Design instance files to minimize the use of OWL constructs whenever possible.

Individual specifications reference classes and properties in ontology files. Although authors should make a distinction between ontologies (Tbox) and instance files containing individuals (Abox), the distinction is transparent to software. Therefore, an instance file conforms to the same encoding requirements as ontologies (see Chapter 11). Instance files are primarily encoded using RDF/XML. They should have a header, body, and footer, just like an ontology file.

## 15.3 Instantiating Individuals

Individuals are preferably specified using RDF/XML in instance datafiles separate from the ontology files. Ontology files are normally fairly static (similar to database schemas), while instance datafiles are often dynamic, similar to RDBMS records. Therefore, the separation helps with version management.

Objects that are members of OWL classes are considered to be part of the "object domain" (as opposed to the datatype domain). The object domain is the set of individuals.

Markup tools should enable those familiar with a domain to easily generate compliant individuals. However, it is important for developers to understand how the data is represented "behind the scenes".

Instances are instantiated with RDF statements. The instances have identifiers specified using the "rdf:ID" attribute. Then the identifiers are used to reference the instance resources. The "rdf:type" property or the typedNode syntax associates an individual with a class.

### 15.3.1 Naming Individuals

Individuals are named using URIrefs. The individual's URIref is assigned with the "rdf:ID" attribute or referenced using the "rdf:about" or "rdf:resource" attributes. With some languages, you can assume that two different names refer to two different items. This is called a unique names assumption. However, since two names (URIrefs) in OWL can be used for the same object, you cannot assume that two names refer to different objects. Therefore, OWL does not have a unique names assumption.

The best practice is to reuse existing instance identifiers from authoritative data whenever possible and practicable. For example, an employee number can serve as part of the "rdf:ID" identifier that represents data about the employee.

### 15.3.2 Joining a Class

An individual is associated with a class using the "rdf:type" property. The typed node syntax can be used to abbreviate the syntax. An individual can belong to multiple classes by specifying multiple "rdf:type" values.

### 15.3.2.1 Instantiating Using RDF Descriptions

One way to create an individual is with the "rdf:Description" element. The creation of a new resource was described in section 8.3.4.1 To associate the resource with a class (make it an individual member) we specify an "rdf:type" property whose value is the user-defined class. The individual is normally named using the "rdf:ID" attribute. However, individuals are not always named, sometimes they are anonymous.

---

The typical syntax for defining an individual using rdf:ID is:

```
<rdf:Description rdf:ID="instanceReference">
     <rdf:type rdf:resource="Class"/>
</rdf:Description>
```

where **instanceReference** is the URIref of the individual being defined and **Class** is the user-defined class that the individual is joining.

---

Section 3 – OWL Lite

### 15.3.2.2 Instantiating Using Class Name

An individual can also be instantiated using the shorthand typedNode syntax (described in Section 8.3.6.1.5). Although only one class can be identified when initially defining the individual with the typed node syntax, additional membership relationships can be specified within the instantiation using the "rdf:type" property.

---

The typedNode syntax for instantiating an individual is:

```
<Class rdf:ID="instanceReference">
</ClassName>
```

where **Class** is the URIref of the class that the individual identified by **instanceReference** belongs to.

---

An example of instantiating an individual using the typedNode syntax with an additional class membership association is :

```
<Restaurant rdf:ID="KnightOwlRestaurant">
    <rdf:type rdf:resource="#SmallBusiness"/>
</Restaurant>
```

---

## 15.4 Describing an Individual

Individuals can be described at the point where they are instantiated or in separate statements. The generation of descriptions of individuals is often automated. Since individuals are resources, properties are defined for individuals using the same approach as making statements about resources (described in section 8.3.3.). In the case of an individual, the subject of the statement is a resource associated with a user-defined class.

### 15.4.1 Associating Property Values at Instantiation

Individuals are assigned attribute/value pairs in the same way that statements are made about resources using RDF/XML syntax. The subject of the statement is the individual.

## Chapter 15 – Describing Individuals

---

The typedNode syntax for associating property values with an individual being instantiated is:

<**ClassName** rdf:ID="identifier">
    instanceProperties
</**ClassName**>

where **ClassName** is the name of the class that the individual belongs to and **instanceProperties** are properties associated with the new individual.

---

An example of specifying information about an individual being instantiated is:

<Restaurant rdf:ID="KnightOwlRestaurant">
    <rest:type>Diner</rest:type>
    <locator:phone>407-555-1212</locator:phone>
</Restaurant>

---

## 15.4.2 Describing Existing Individuals

An existing individual is described by referencing its URIref. Again, this is the same approach as described above, but for resources that are members of user-defined classes.

---

The typical typed node syntax for associating property values with an individual is:

<**ClassName** rdf:about="**identifier**">
    instanceProperties
</**ClassName**>

where **ClassName** is the name of the class that the individual referenced by the **identifier** belongs to and **instanceProperties** are properties associated with the existing individual.

---

An example of specifying information about an existing individual is:

<Restaurant rdf:about="#KnightOwlRestaurant">
    <rest:type>Diner</rest:type>
    <locator:phone>407-555-1212</locator:phone>
</Restaurant>

---

209

Section 3 – OWL Lite

### 15.4.3 Automating Descriptions of Individuals

Individual descriptions normally represent the bulk (by volume) of information representations. Ontologies provide descriptions to help software understand and inference on the individuals. OWL representations are unlikely to replace existing methods for natively representing large knowledge bases. Instead, OWL "views" will likely be published to share the information in those knowledge bases.

Most applications will generate individual data from their legacy proprietary databases. Some applications will generate individual description data in a batch mode, while more dynamic applications will serve up individual descriptions "on the fly". Regardless of the method, it should be transparent to the consuming software application.

## 15.5 Relating Individuals

OWL provides properties for relating individuals to each other. These properties identify equivalency, and differentiate individuals and groups of individuals.

### 15.5.1 Equivalent Individuals (owl:sameAs)

The "owl:sameAs" property is used to specify that two URIrefs refer to the same individual. It can be used to link individuals from different files (map between ontologies).

The distributed nature of the Semantic Web means that distributed information representations will result in authors defining different names for the same individual. Communities often use different methods for naming or referencing individuals. For example, a company might use an employee number for the same individual referenced by the Government using a Social Security Number (SSN). Two individuals can be specified as equivalent using the "owl:sameAs" property.

> The typical syntax for defining equivalent individuals is:
>
> ```
> <ClassName rdf:ID="subjectIndividualURIref">
>         <owl:sameAs rdf:resource="equivIndividualURIref"/>
> </ClassName>
> ```
>
> where **subjectIndividualURIref** is the URIref of the individual equivalent to the resource identified by **equivIndividualURIref**.

> For example, we could state that the following two URI references actually refer to the same restaurant:
>
> ```
> <rdf:Description rdf:about="#restaurant123">
>         <owl:sameAs rdf:resource="#KnightOwlRestaurant"/>
> </rdf:Description>
> ```

The "owl:sameAs" property can be used to "join" different files. It is important for queries to know that resources are the same because information about them can be folded together. An alternative to creating new individuals and specifying that they are the same as others is to add properties to existing individuals.

The "owl:sameAs" property can be used with any "owl:Thing" and its value must be an instance of an "owl:Thing".

### 15.5.2 Differentiating Individuals (owl:differentFrom)

The "owl:differentFrom" property is used to state that two individuals are different (pairwise distinct).

> The typical syntax for declaring a difference between individuals is:
>
> ```
> <owl:differentFrom rdf:resource="differentIndividualURIref"/>
> ```
>
> where **differentIndividualURIref** is the URIref of an individual that is different from the subject individual.

Section 3 – OWL Lite

---

> An example of specifying that two individuals are different is:
>
> ```
> <rest:Restaurant rdf:ID="Restaurant124">
>     <owl:differentFrom rdf:resource="#KnightOwlRestaurant"/>
> </rest:Restaurant>
> ```

The "owl:differentFrom" construct has the opposite meaning of "owl:sameAs". Because of OWL's lack of a unique names assumption, individuals must be explicitly declared to be different. This results in many "owl:differentFrom" statements. The "owl:differentFrom" property is used to specify pairwise disjointness between individuals (specifies that the individuals are not the same object).

The "owl:differentFrom" property supports inferencing. For example, an inference engine will know that "Restaurant124" and "KnightOwlRestaurant" refer to different objects if they are related using the "owl:differentFrom" property. Since RDF and OWL allow multiple names to reference the same object, it is important to be able to specify that two names are not referencing the same object.

The "owl:differentFrom" property can be used with any "owl:Thing" and its value must be an instance of an "owl:Thing".

## 15.5.3 Differentiating Groups of Individuals (owl:AllDifferent/owl:distinctMembers)

Groups of individuals can be differentiated all at once using the predefined "owl:AllDifferent" class. The "owl:distinctMembers" property is used within the class to associate the list of individuals that must be disjoint.

| owl:AllDifferent |
|---|
|  |
|  |

This approach is a shorthand for specifying multiple "owl:differentFrom" properties. Using the "owl:AllDifferent" class with the "owl:distinctMembers" property, several individuals can be specified as separate distinct objects. The end result is explicitly specifying that each item is a different unique thing (mutually distinct).

## Chapter 15 – Describing Individuals

> The typical syntax for declaring several instances to be different is:
>
> ```
> <owl:AllDifferent>
>         <owl:distinctMembers rdf:parseType="Collection">
>                 members
>         </owl:distinctMembers>
> </owl:AllDifferent>
> ```
>
> where **members** is the collection of items being declared disjoint.

> An example of specifying multiple individuals to be different is:
>
> ```
> <owl:AllDifferent>
>         <owl:distinctMembers rdf:parseType="Collection">
>                 <rest:Restaurant rdf:about="#restaurant123"/>
>                 <rest:Restaurant rdf:about="#restaurant456"/>
>                 <rest:Restaurant rdf:about="#KnightOWLRestaurant"/>
>                 <rest:Restaurant rdf:about="#JoesPizzaria"/>
>         </owl:distinctMembers>
> </owl:AllDifferent>
> ```

Instead of having a many "owl:differentFrom" statements, the "owl:AllDifferent" class, along with the "owl:distinctMembers" property can be used. Pairwise disjointness means that items are not the same item. The "owl:distinctMembers" property should only be used with the "owl:AllDifferent" class.

## *15.6 Describing Individuals Summary*

Once an individual has been identified, it can be represented in RDF/XML. Its description should be compliant with an ontology. The same individual can be described with multiple names because there is no unique names assumption in OWL. Individuals are resources that are members of user-defined classes. Individuals can be described as part of their instantiation statement, or in separate statements that reference existing individuals. Individuals can be related to each other to specify equivalence or difference. Groups of individuals can be declared to be different as a group.

## Section 3 – OWL Lite

Figure 15-2 summarizes individual-related concepts.

```
                         Individuals
           ┌─────────────────┼─────────────────┐
  Instantiating Individuals  Describing Individuals  Relating Individuals
        ┌──┴──┐             ┌──┴──┐        ┌──────┼──────┐
                          rdf:ID  rdf:about
    rdf:type  typedNode syntax              owl:sameAs  owl:differentFrom  owl:AllDifferent /
                                                                            owl:distinctMembers
```

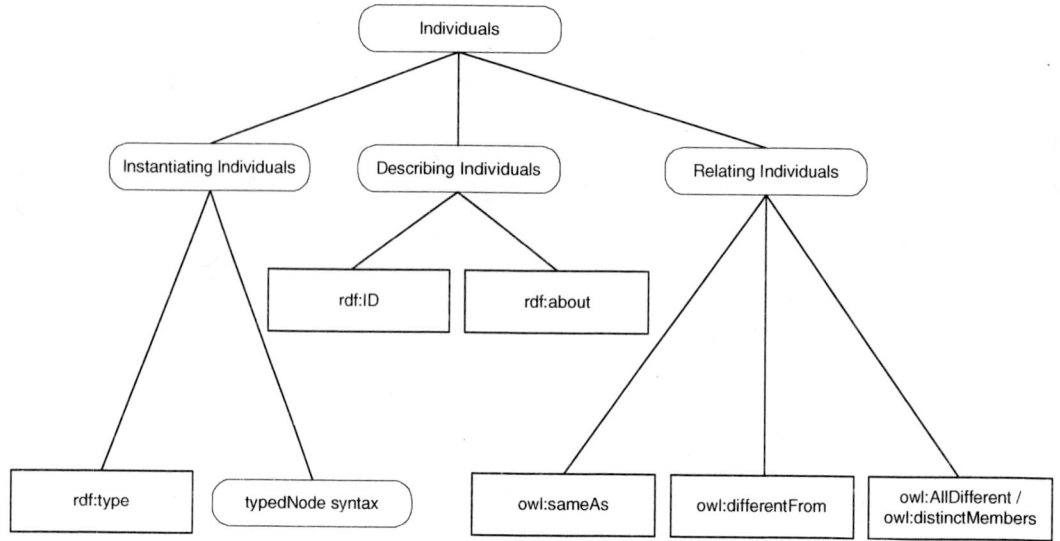

Figure 15-2. Constructs for Describing Individuals

The next chapter summarizes the OWL Lite dialect of the OWL language.

# 16 OWL Lite Summary

OWL ontologies are specified in datafiles using RDF/XML syntax. Ontology files have headers that specify namespaces, versioning information, and other imported ontologies. Ontologies describe classes, properties, and their relationships.

Basic ontological classes can be defined with the "owl:Class" construct. OWL includes two predefined classes: "owl:Thing", the root class of all individuals, and "owl:Nothing", a class with no members. OWL datatype properties support atomic datatype values. Object properties define properties with resources as values. Annotation properties provide additional metadata about a resource. Ontological properties relate ontologies.

OWL Lite supports the description of properties by defining global restrictions, property relationships, inference shortcuts, and local restrictions. Global property restrictions are used to state whether a property is functional or inverse functional. Global property relationships specify whether properties are subproperties, equivalent, or inverse. Inference shortcuts identify properties as transitive or symmetric. Local property restrictions relate to values and cardinality. Value constraints require all or some of the properties values belong to a particular class. Cardinality constraints define the minimum, maximum, or absolute cardinality for a property.

OWL classes can be derived from other classes by defining the relationship between the derived class and other classes. The subclass relationship identifies the derived class as a subset. Class extensions can be equated. Classes also can be described as the instersection of classes.

Individuals are described as instance members of user-defined classes. Individuals can be described within their instantiation statements or in separate statements that reference the individuals. Equivalence and differences between individuals can be stated.

## 16.1 OWL Lite Constructs

Table 16-1 provides a summary of OWL Lite constructs.

Section 3 – OWL Lite

Table 16-1. OWL Lite Constructs

| Construct Group | Construct |
| --- | --- |
| Class/Property Equivalency | owl:equivalentClass |
| | owl:equivalentProperty |
| Individual Equivalency | owl:sameAs |
| | owl:differentFrom |
| | owl:AllDifferent / owl:distinctMembers |
| Property characteristics | owl:inverseOf |
| | owl:TransitiveProperty |
| | owl:SymmetricProperty |
| | owl:FunctionalProperty |
| | owl:InverseFunctionalProperty |
| Property Type Restrictions: | owl:allValuesFrom |
| | owl:someValuesFrom |
| | owl:intersectionOf |
| Restricted Cardinality: | owl:minCardinality (only 0 or 1) |
| | owl:maxCardinality (only 0 or 1) |
| | owl:cardinality (only 0 or 1) |
| Derived Classes | rdfs:subClassOf |
| | owl:equivalentClass |
| Header Ontology Information: | owl:imports |
| | owl:priorVersion |
| | owl:backwardCompatibleWith |
| | owl:incompatibleWith |

## 16.2 OWL Lite Restrictions

OWL Lite uses a subset of OWL Full's constructs and must be used with restrictions compared to OWL DL and OWL Full. The purpose of OWL Lite's restrictions is to place the least requirements on tools while providing basic features including support for classification hierarchies and simple constraints. OWL Lite cannot be considered simply an extension of RDFS because RDFS does not have OWL Lite's restrictions.

To ease the computational burden on OWL DL and OWL Lite compliant tools, values, resources, and constructs can belong to only one type of OWL concept.

## Chapter 16 - OWL Lite Summary

In OWL Lite and OWL DL, all referenced classes must be explicitly typed as OWL classes. Similarly, all URIrefs used as properties must be explicitly typed as OWL properties. OWL Lite and OWL DL also require that classes, datatypes, properties, built-in vocabularies, individuals, and data values must be disjoint. Additionally, properties must be either object properties, datatype properties, annotation properties, or ontology properties. In Figure 16-1, leaf concepts (starred items) designate the constructs that cannot be mixed in OWL Lite.

OWL Lite provides basic ontological constructs for simple, decidable ontologies (e.g., property restrictions). Software tools are available for determining whether a file satisfies the requirement for being considered a valid OWL Lite ontology.

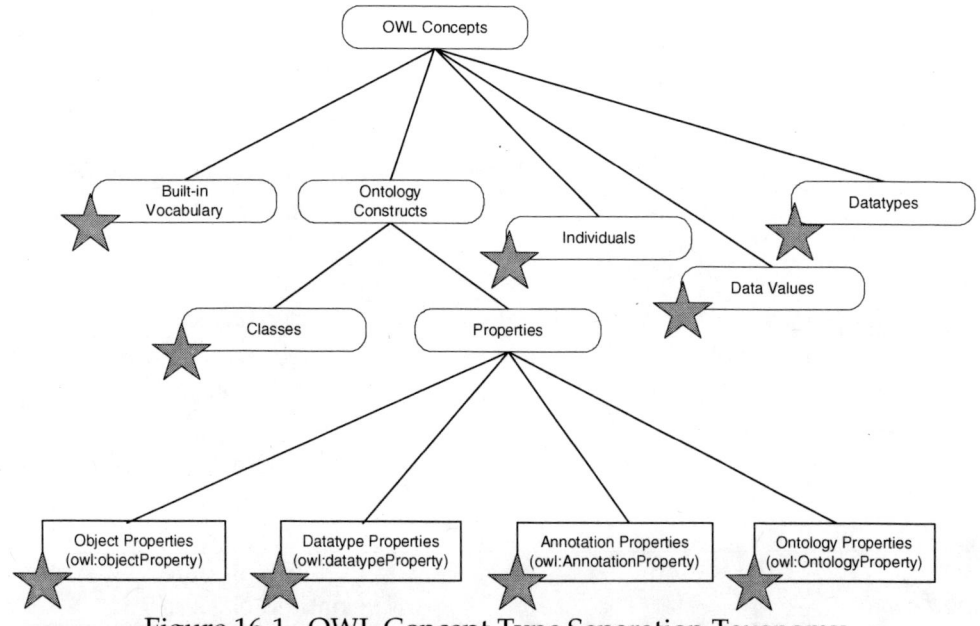

Figure 16-1. OWL Concept Type Separation Taxonomy

While OWL Lite provides extensive support for representing information, additional language constructs are useful. The next section describes the more expressive OWL DL and OWL Full dialects of the OWL language.

# Section 3 – OWL Lite

Table 16-2 summarizes the OWL Lite restrictions.

Table 16-2. OWL Lite Restriction Summary

| Category | Affected OWL Full Construct | Restriction |
|---|---|---|
| Class/Type | rdf:type | Object of statements must be named classes or restrictions |
| Cardinality | owl:minCardinality | Value limited to 0 or 1 |
|  | owl:maxCardinality | Value limited to 0 or 1 |
|  | owl:cardinality | Value limited to 0 or 1 |
| Set Operators | owl:intersectionOf | Used only on lists of length greater than one that contain only named classes and restrictions |
| Derived Classes | owl:equivalentClass | Subject of statements must be named classes |
|  |  | Object of statements must be named classes or restrictions |
|  | rdfs:subClassOf | Subject of statements must be named classes |
|  |  | Object of statements must be named classes or restrictions |
| Local Property Restrictions | owl:allValuesFrom | Object of statements must be named classes or named datatypes |
|  | owl:someValuesFrom | Object of statements must be named classes or named datatypes |
| Global Property Restrictions | rdfs:domain | Object of statements must be named classes |
|  | rdfs:range | Object of statements must be named classes or datatypes |
|  | owl:inverseFunctionalProperty | Cannot be defined for datatype properties |

# Section 4

# OWL DL, OWL Full, and Applications

# Section 4 – OWL DL, OWL Full, and Applications

The previous section described OWL Lite. This section describes OWL DL, OWL Full, OWL Dialect Selection, and the use of OWL information representations.

Chapter 17 – OWL DL – describes the OWL DL dialect, its restrictions, and the remaining OWL constructs.

Chapter 18 – OWL Full – describes the elimination of all restrictions.

Chapter 19 – OWL Dialect Selection – discusses how to select the appropriate dialect.

Chapter 20 – Applications - provides a use case for a Semantic Web enabled application.

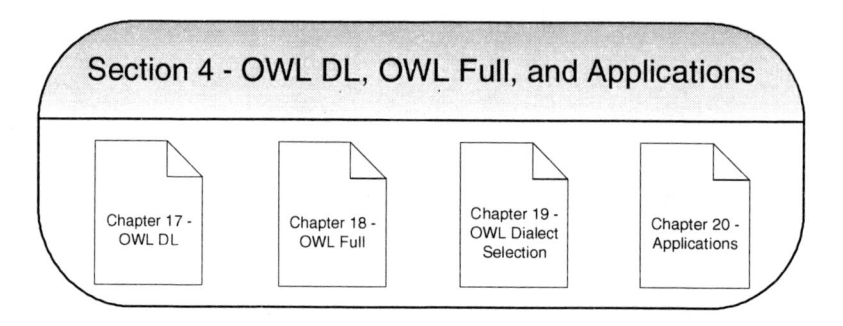

# 17 OWL DL

OWL DL is one of the OWL language dialects (see Figure 17-1). The "DL" in OWL DL stands for Description Logics.

As discussed in Section 3.5.2, DLs are an information representation technique with well-defined semantics that support inferencing.

| Applications |  |
|---|---|
| Ontology Languages (OWL Full, OWL DL, and OWL Lite) ||
| RDF Schema | Individuals |
| RDF and RDF/XML ||
| XML and XMLS Datatypes ||
| URIs and Namespaces ||

Figure 17-1. Ontology Languages Layer

OWL DL contains the whole OWL (Full OWL) vocabulary and has fewer restrictions than OWL Lite. The purpose of OWL DL's restrictions is to support reasoners. These restrictions ensure that reasoning will be computable and decidable.

The description of OWL Lite in the previous section represented a subset of OWL language constructs with certain restrictions on their use. OWL DL adds additional language constructs to OWL Lite and relaxes some restrictions.

This chapter describes OWL DL, a restricted form of OWL, complex classes, required property values, and enumerated data values.

## 17.1 OWL DL Restrictions

OWL DL has fewer restrictions and more constructs than OWL Lite. Table 17-1 summarizes the OWL DL restrictions. As with OWL Lite, an OWL DL class cannot be considered a member (individual instance) of another class.

## Section 4 – OWL DL, OWL Full, and Applications

Table 17-1. OWL DL Restriction Summary

| Affected Constructs | Restrictions |
|---|---|
| owl:cardinality | Cannot be used on a "owl:TransitiveProperty" |
| owl:TransitiveProperty | Cannot have an "owl:cardinality" constraint nor be functional |
| owl:FunctionalProperty | |
| owl:InverseFunctionalProperty | |
| owl:SymmetricProperty | |
| owl:TransitiveProperty | |
| owl:inverseOf | |
| owl:ObjectProperty | Must be disjoint from datatype properties |
| owl:DatatypeProperty | Must be disjoint from object properties |
| | Cannot be inverse functional |
| owl:AnnotationProperty | must belong to the "owl:AnnotationProperty" class and cannot be used in property axioms |
| owl:imports | Cannot import an OWL Full ontology |
| owl:sameAs | Must reference a named individual |
| owl:differentFrom | |
| owl:Class | Cannot be individuals of other classes |
| Class URIref | Must be stated to be a class (type separation) |
| Property URIref | Must be stated to be a property (type separation) |
| Individual URIref | Must belong to a class (type separation) |
| rdf:Property | Must be either "owl:ObjectProperty", "owl:DatatypeProperty", "owl:AnnotationProperty", or "owl:OntologyProperty" |

### 17.1.1 OWL DL Vocabulary

OWL DL has more constructs than OWL Lite because it uses the complete OWL Full vocabulary. Table 17-2 shows the additional constructs.

Table 17-2. Additional Constructs Provided by OWL DL

| Category | Construct | Feature |
|---|---|---|
| Class expression | owl:oneOf | Enumerated classes |
| | owl:disjointWith | Relating classes |
| | owl:unionOf | Boolean combination |
| | owl:complementOf | |
| Enumerated values | owl:dataRange | Enumerated data values |
| Property restrictions | owl:hasValue | Filler information |

Table 17-3 shows the OWL Lite constructs that are less restricted in OWL DL.

Table 17-3. OWL DL Constraint Relaxations

| Category | Construct | Feature |
|---|---|---|
| Class expressions | owl:equivalentClass | Can be applied to class expressions |
| | rdfs:subClassOf | |
| | owl:intersectionOf | Boolean combination |
| Cardinality | owl:minCardinality | Arbitrary values |
| | owl:maxCardinality | |
| | owl:cardinality | |

Users of OWL Lite and OWL DL should not modify RDF, RDFS, or OWL built-in vocabularies.

Restriction classes must be unnamed and must not be members of other classes. They must have an "owl:onProperty" property that identifies either an "owl:DatatypeProperty" or an "owl:ObjectProperty".

Section 4 – OWL DL, OWL Full, and Applications

## 17.2 Complex Classes / Class Expressions

In addition to the added constructs, OWL DL supports complex classes. In Section 12.1, we described the specification of a simple class. More complex class specifications can be described using constructs called class expressions. A class expression is analogous to a mathematical expression, constructed of atomic symbols and anonymous classes in certain allowed patterns. Specifying a class expression does not necessarily mean that any individual belongs to the specified class.

Classes can be described by their name or their contents (by describing an anonymous class). OWL expressions can be formed from:
- class names (URIrefs),
- enumerations,
- property-restrictions, and
- boolean combination of class expressions (see Figure 17-2).

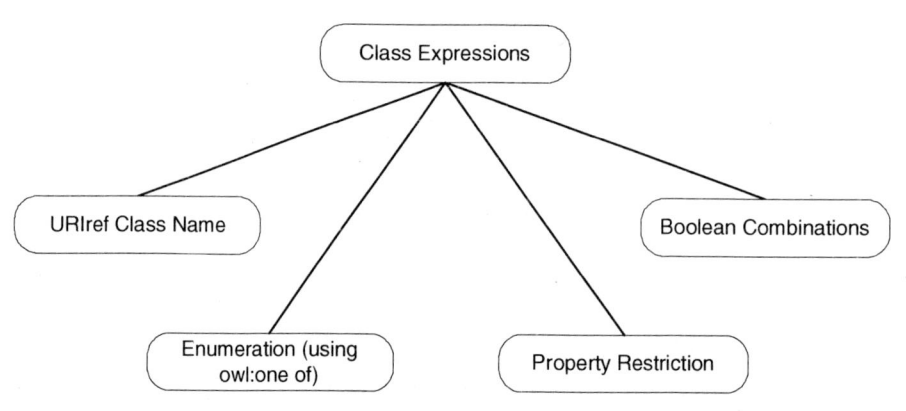

Figure 17-2. Class Expression Components

A class expression describes a set of membership criteria. Individuals that meet the criteria are considered members of the class. This is different from object-oriented systems where objects must be explicitly instantiated from classes.

The types of complex class descriptions that can be defined in OWL DL are enumerated classes, disjoint classes, and Boolean class expressions.

# Chapter 17 – OWL DL

## 17.2.1 Enumerated Classes (owl:oneOf)

An enumeration is a predefined set of members. In OWL DL, enumerated classes can be defined by exhaustively specifying their member individuals.

The value of the "owl:oneOf" property is a list of individuals that exhaustively identifies the class extension. The "Collection" parse type is used to specify the closed list of individuals. No other items can belong to the enumerated class.

---

The typical syntax for the oneOf property is:

```
<owl:Class rdf:ID="className"
    <owl:oneOf rdf:parseType="Collection">
        <classURIref rdf:about="individualURIref"/>
    </owl:one of>
</owl:Class>
```

where **className** is the enumerated class being described, **individualURIref** is the name of an individual in the class extension, and **classURIref** is the name of a class that the individual belongs to.

---

An example of specifying a Days of the Week class is:

```
<owl:Class rdf:ID="DaysOfTheWeek">
    <owl:oneOf rdf:parseType="Collection">
        <hoo:DayOfWeek rdf:about="#Sunday"/>
        <hoo:DayOfWeek rdf:about="#Monday"/>
        <hoo:DayOfWeek rdf:about="#Tuesday"/>
        <hoo:DayOfWeek rdf:about="#Wednesday"/>
        <hoo:DayOfWeek rdf:about="#Thursday"/>
        <hoo:DayOfWeek rdf:about="#Friday"/>
        <hoo:DayOfWeek rdf:about="#Saturday"/>
    </owl:oneOf>
</owl:Class>
```

---

The list of individuals identified by the "owl:oneOf" property must be valid individuals linked to a class. Use enumerated classes when there are a small number of instances that are known a priori. The concept described by the enumerated class should be very stable (e.g., days of the week). The items in the enumerated list are all the members of the defined class. The "owl:oneOf" property can be used with any "owl:Class" and its value must be an instance of an "owl:List".

Section 4 – OWL DL, OWL Full, and Applications

Reasoners can infer the "owl:maxCardinality" of properties whose range is the enumerated class based on the count of the list of members. This assumes that all individuals are distinct.

## 17.2.2 Disjoint Classes (owl:disjointWith)

Classes sometimes describe "either/or" situations. Some individuals are either in one class or another, but not both (see Figure 17-3). The "owl:disjointWith" property is used to distinguish two classes as having no individuals in common (no overlap). An instance of one disjoint class cannot also be a member of a class that it is disjoint with. A class can be disjoint with multiple classes.

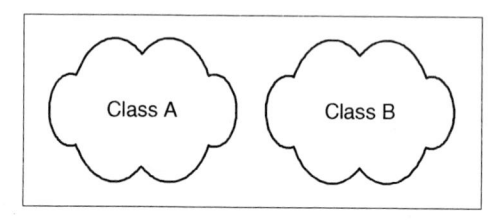

Figure 17-3. Disjoint Classes

---

The typical syntax of the owl:disjointWith property is:

```
<owl:Class rdf:ID="class1URIref">
    <owl:disjointWith rdf:resource="class2URIref"/>
</owl:Class>
```

where **class1URIref** has no instances that overlap with the class identified by **class2URIref**.

---

An example of defining a disjoint class is:

```
<owl:Class rdf:ID="AlcoholicDrink">
    <owl:disjointWith rdf:resource="#NonAlcoholicDrink"/>
</owl:Class>
```

---

Every class is disjoint with the pre-defined "owl:Nothing" class. Strict taxonomies can be defined by specifying unions of disjoint classes. The "owl:disjointWith" property is symmetric.

The "owl:disjointWith" property can be used with any "owl:Class" and its value must be an instance of an "owl:Class".

## 17.2.3 Boolean Class Combinations

Recall that class extensions are sets. As in math, OWL class sets can be manipulated with Boolean combinations using intersection, union, and complement set operators. OWL DL allows arbitrary Boolean combinations of classes and restrictions using the "owl:unionOf", "owl:complementOf", and "owl:intersectionOf" set operators (see Figure 17-4). The operator functions reference named classes and anonymous classes using class expressions.

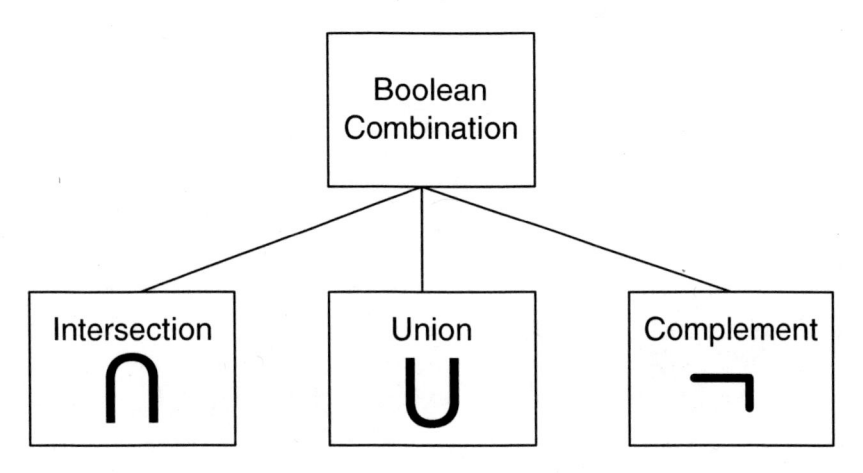

Figure 17-4. Types of Boolean Combinations

### 17.2.3.1 Intersection Property (owl:intersectionOf)

In OWL Full, the OWL Lite restrictions on the "owl:intersectionOf" property are removed. The intersection of multiple classes can define a new class. The application of an "owl:intersectionOf" construct is analogous to a logical conjunction. The class described by the intersection property includes exactly all the individuals that are common to all the identified classes.

## Section 4 – OWL DL, OWL Full, and Applications

The typical syntax of the intersectionOf property is:

```
<owl:Class rdf:ID="ClassReference">
    <owl:intersectionOf rdf:parseType="Collection">
        list of class expressions
    </owl:intersectionOf>
</owl:Class>
```

where **list of class expressions** is a description of classes whose intersection defines the class whose URIref is **ClassReference**.

---

The following example demonstrates the use of the intersectionOf construct to define apple pie ala mode as the intersection of apple pie and ice cream:

```
<owl:Class rdf:ID="ApplePieAlaModeDish">
    <owl:intersectionOf rdf:parseType="Collection">
        <owl:Class rdf:about="#ApplePieDish"/>
        <owl:Class rdf:about="#IceCreamDish"/>
    </owl:intersectionOf>
</owl:Class>
```

An arbitrary number of classes can be identified. The "owl:intersectionOf" property can be used to specify a necessary and sufficient condition. The intersection of classes includes the individuals that belong to both classes (see Figure 17-5). A class intersection is equivalent to an "AND" operation from logic.

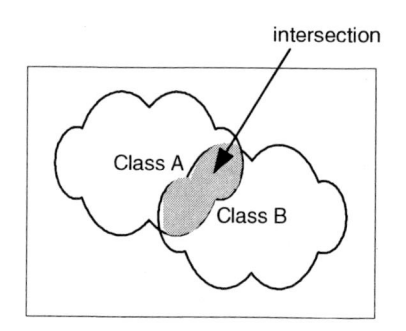

Figure 17-5. Intersection of Classes

The "owl:intersectionOf" property can be used with any "owl:Class" and its value must be an instance of an "rdf:List".

## 17.2.3.2 Union Property (owl:unionOf)

The "owl:unionOf" property describes a class that includes all the members of all the specified classes. The items in the class extension include all the individuals that are in at least one of the listed class extensions of the class descriptions. This is analogous to logical disjunction (the logical "OR" construct).

```
The typical syntax of the unionOf property is:

<owl:Class rdf:ID="ClassReference">
        <owl:unionOf rdf:parseType="Collection">
                list of class expressions
        </owl:unionOf>
</owl:Class>

where the list of class expressions identifies named and anonymous classes, at least one of which must
contain a member individual for it to be considered part of the class whose URIref is ClassReference..
```

```
The following example demonstrates the use of the unionOf construct to specify a Fruit Pies class:

<owl:Class rdf:ID="FruitPies">
        <owl:unionOf rdf:parseType="Collection">
                <owl:Class rdf:about="#ApplePie"/>
                <owl:Class rdf:about="#CherryPie"/>
                <owl:Class rdf:about="#LemonPie"/>
                <owl:Class rdf:about="#KeyLimePie"/>
        </owl:unionOf>
</owl:Class>
```

The "owl:unionOf" property is used to generate the union of the sets identified by the class expressions in the list. If an instance is in the union, it must be in one of the classes in the list. Similarly, if there is an instance of one of the classes, it must be a member of the union. The union of two classes represents all the individuals that are in either or both of the classes (see Figure 17-6).

## Section 4 – OWL DL, OWL Full, and Applications

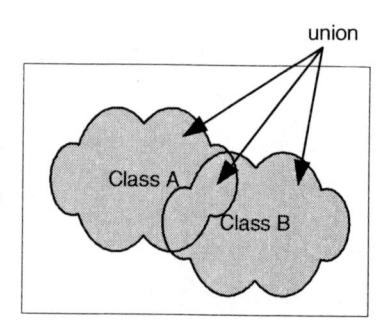

Figure 17-6. Union of Classes

The "owl:unionOf" property can be used with any "owl:Class" and its value must be an instance of an "rdf:List".

### 17.2.3.3 Complement Property (owl:complementOf)

The "owl:complementOf" property relates disjoint classes. The "owl:complementOf" property is used to define a class by identifying all objects that do not belong to a specified class expression (logical negation). The members of the complement class are individuals that are not in the class specified in the object of the statement.

---

The typical syntax for using the complementOf property involves an intersection of a superclass:

```
<owl:Class rdf:ID="classURIref">
    <owl:intersectionOf rdf:parseType="Collection">
        <owl:Class rdf:about="superClass"/>
        <owl:complementOf rdf:parseType="Collection">
            <owl:Class rdf:about="class2URIref"/>
        </owl:complementOf>
    </owl:intersectionOf>
</owl:Class>
```

where **classURIref** is the class being described as being the intersection of a class identified by **class2URIref** and its superclass identified as **superClass**.

## Chapter 17 – OWL DL

> An example of the owl:complementOf property is:
>
> ```
> <owl:Class rdf:ID="MeatDish">
>         <owl:intersectionOf rdf:parseType="Collection">
>                 <owl:Class rdf:about="#MenuDish"/>
>                 <owl:complementOf rdf:resource="#VegetarianDish"/>
>         </owl:intersectionOf>
> </owl:Class>
> ```
>
> The extension of this MeatDish class description contains all #MenuDish individuals that do not belong to the #VegetarianDish class.

Any class expression can be specified within the "owl:complementOf" element including property restrictions. The complement of a class represents the individuals that are not members of the specified class (see Figure 17-7).

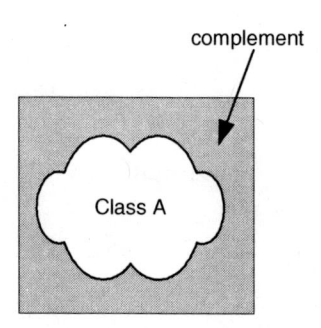

Figure 17-3. Complement of a Class

The difference between "owl:complementOf" and "owl:disjointWith" is that the complement of a class includes everything not in the class. A class that is disjoint with a described class is only known to be part of the described class's complement.

The "owl:complementOf" property can be used with any "owl:Class" and its value must be an instance of an "owl:Class".

# Section 4 – OWL DL, OWL Full, and Applications

### 17.2.3.4 Set Operator Summary

Table 17-5 summarizes the OWL set operations used for specifying classes.

Table 17-1. Set Operator Summary

| Operator | Logical Effect | Resulting Class Contains |
|---|---|---|
| Intersection ∩ | AND | Individuals that are in each identified class |
| Union ∪ | OR | Individuals in at least 1 of the identified classes |
| Complement ¬ | NOT | Individuals not in the specified class |

## 17.3 Requiring a Property Value (owl:hasValue)

The "owl:hasValue" property is a local value restriction that identifies an individual object or a datatype value. To satisfy the "owl:hasValue" constraint, objects must have the identified property and the property's values must include the specified value.

The "owl:hasValue" property can be used to define classes based on the property values of its member individuals. At least one of the individual's property values must be equal to the individual or data value identified by the "owl:hasValue" constraint.

## Chapter 17 – OWL DL

---

The typical syntax of a hasValue local property restriction is:

```
<owl:Restriction>
        <owl:onProperty rdf:resource="propertyURIref"/>
        <owl:hasValue rdf:resource="value"/>
</owl:Restriction>
```

where **propertyURIref** is the property being restricted and **value** is an instance or data value.

---

An example of using the hasValue restriction is:

```
<owl:Class rdf:ID="ChocolatePie">
        <rdfs:subClassOf>
                <owl:Restriction>
                        <owl:onProperty rdf:resource="#hasPieFilling"/>
                        <owl:hasValue rdf:resource="#Chocolate"/>
                </owl:Restriction>
        </rdfs:subClassOf>
</owl:Class>
```

which states that for something to be considered a ChocolatePie individual, it must have a filling property (#hasPieFililng) value of #Chocolate.

---

The "owl:hasValue" property can only be used with an "owl:Restriction" class. The restriction class contains all the individuals whose property has at least one value semantically equal to the "owl:hasValue" property value.

Every individual in the restriction class must have the specified value for the identified property. Each individual of the restricted class does not have to have explicitly stated the property value, because it can be inferred or the same individual may have multiple values for the property.

Unlike the "owl:someValuesFrom" construct that requires a value to be from a specified class, the "owl:hasValue" requires the property have a particular value. Individuals are considered members of the restricted class if they have the specified value for the restricted property.

Section 4 – OWL DL, OWL Full, and Applications

## *17.4 Enumerated Data Values (owl:DataRange)*

Data ranges can be specified using the "owl:oneOf", "rdf:List", "rdf:first", and "rdf:rest" constructs. Statements enumerating data values use the "owl:oneOf" construct like enumerated classes, but with lists of values instead of list of classes.

---

The typical syntax for the oneOf property used for data values is:

```
<owl:DataRange rdf:ID="dataRangeIdentifier">
        <owl:oneOf rdf:parseType="owl:collection">
                list construct
        </owl:oneOf>
</owl:DataRange>
```

where **list construct** is the list construct that enumerates all the possible values for the range named by the URIref **dataRangeIdentifier**.

---

An example of defining an enumerated list representing cup sizes of 10, 12, and 16 ounces is:

```
<owl:DatatypeRange rdf:ID="cupSizeOunces">
     <rdfs:range>
             <owl:DataRange>
                     <owl:oneOf>
                             <rdf:List>
                             <rdf:first>10</rdf:first>
                             <rdf:rest>
                                     <rdf:List>
                                     <rdf:first>12</rdf:first>
                                     <rdf:rest>
                                             <rdf:List>
                                             <rdf:first>16</rdf:first>
                                             <rdf:rest rdf:resource="&rdf;nil"/>
                                             </rdf:List>
                                     </rdf:rest>
                                     </rdf:List>
                             </rdf:rest>
                             </rdf:List>
                     </owl:oneOf>
             </owl:DataRange>
     </rdfs:range>
</owl:DatatypeRange>
```

The example above shows that the list syntax for even a few enumerated data values can be very verbose.

## 17.5 OWL DL Summary

OWL DL is a restricted form of OWL Full. It contains all constructs of the OWL Full language, but their use is restricted. OWL DL extends OWL Lite by adding class expressions, set operations, property value requirements, and enumerated data values.

The next chapter describes the OWL Full dialect of the OWL Language.

# Section 4 – OWL DL, OWL Full, and Applications

# 18 OWL Full

The OWL Full language represents the complete specification of the OWL language. OWL Full can be viewed as an extension of RDF and is part of the logical layer of the Semantic Web architecture (see Figure 18-1).

| Applications |  |
|---|---|
| Ontology Languages (OWL Full, OWL DL, and OWL Lite) ||
| RDF Schema | Individuals |
| RDF and RDF/XML ||
| XML and XMLS Datatypes ||
| URIs and Namespaces ||

Figure 18-1. Ontology Languages Layer

OWL Full allows the ontology developer to say anything about anything, including the RDF, RDFS, and OWL vocabularies themselves. It provides unrestricted use of RDFS constructs, meaning that OWL constructs can be intermingled with any RDFS constructs. Unconstrained RDF documents can be considered OWL Full

## 18.1 OWL Full's Differing Perspective/Relaxation

Like OWL DL, OWL Full supports all OWL constructs. OWL Full relaxes all of the restrictions on OWL DL (listed in section 17.1).

### 18.1.1 Type Separation

Type separation is one of the OWL DL and OWL Lite restrictions that is relaxed in OWL Full. OWL Full does not enforce a strict separation of classes, properties, individuals and data values. OWL Full eliminates restrictions on individuals, classes, and properties.

### 18.1.2 Individuals

Data values are part of the individual domain. In OWL Full, "rdfs:Resource" is equivalent to "owl:Thing". Therefore, all data values are considered individuals.

Section 4 – OWL DL, OWL Full, and Applications

### 18.1.3 Classes as Individuals

In OWL Full, a resource can be considered both a class of individuals and an individual of some other class. Although difficult to visualize, a class can even be a member of its own class extension, which means that it can be an instance of itself.

In OWL Full, "owl:Class" is equivalent to "rdfs:Class". That means that every RDFS class is an OWL class (and vice versa). However, in OWL DL and OWL Lite, "owl:Class" is a subclass of "rdfs:Class", so not all RDF classes are OWL classes in OWL DL and OWL Lite.

### 18.1.4 Properties

In OWL Full, the difference between "owl:ObjectProperty" and "rdf:Property" is removed. The "owl:ObjectProperty" is equivalent to "rdf:Property".

Unlike OWL Lite and OWL DL, object properties and datatype properties do not have to be disjoint in OWL Full. This is because in OWL Full, "owl:ObjectProperty" is equivalent to "rdf:Property". Since "owl:DatatypeProperty" is a subclass of "rdf:Property", in OWL Full "owl:DatatypeProperty" is a subclass of "owl:ObjectProperty".

Since an "owl:DatatypeProperty" is an object property, it can be identified as an "owl:InverseFunctionalProperty". Also, in OWL Full, the global restrictions defined using "rdfs:domain" and "rdfs:range" can have descriptions as values (not just classes and datatypes).

In OWL Full, annotation properties can be used anywhere (without restrictions). Therefore, the use of the "owl:AnnotationProperty" class is not needed in OWL Full.

### 18.1.5 Property Restrictions

As described in Chapter 13, property restrictions define anonymous classes of objects that satisfy the identified constraint. OWL Lite provided value and cardinality property restrictions. The OWL Lite value property restrictions are "owl:someValuesFrom" and "owl:allValuesFrom".

In OWL DL and OWL Full, an additional value restriction ("owl:hasValue") is available and the cardinality values can be arbitrary non-negative integers. OWL Lite cardinality values are restricted to values of either 0 or 1. OWL Full relaxes restrictions on the XMLS datatypes. However, there is no way with OWL syntax to explicitly describe their interpretation.

## 18.2 OWL Full Summary

OWL Full is the complete, unrestricted species of the Web Ontology Language. It is the most expressive OWL species. Restrictions in DL do not affect OWL Full.

The elimination of certain restrictions comes at a price. Inference engines will likely have difficulty supporting the OWL Full language with complete reasoning for features of OWL Full. This is because without the OWL DL restrictions, OWL Full features are available that may violate the constraints of Description Logic reasoners.

The next chapter compares and contrasts the OWL language dialects and addresses dialect selection issues.

# Section 4 – OWL DL, OWL Full, and Applications

# 19 OWL Dialect Selection

Differences between OWL dialects affect an ontology author's choice of language constructs because of the restrictions on their use.

## 19.1 Choosing Your Weapon

OWL ontology developers must select a dialect based on their requirements. Select the most widely supported sufficient dialect. Represent all the information in OWL Lite if possible.

An ontology developed in a more restricted dialect is valid in a less restrictive dialect. OWL Lite ontologies are valid OWL DL ontologies and OWL DL ontologies are valid OWL Full ontologies.

The requirement for meta-modeling features may drive the selection of OWL Full over OWL DL. However, OWL Full reasoning support is less predictable than OWL DL.

The bottom line is to weigh the advantages and disadvantages of the three dialects to support the information representations and application requirements and then select the appropriate dialect.

The choice of OWL dialects reflects a tradeoff between expressiveness (with its complexities) and the availability of software support (resulting from restrictions) (see Figure 19-1). This relationship exists because as the language dialects become more expressive, they require more complex software to support them. Select the most restrictive dialect that meets your requirements to maximize your opportunities to use available tools.

Section 4 – OWL DL, OWL Full, and Applications

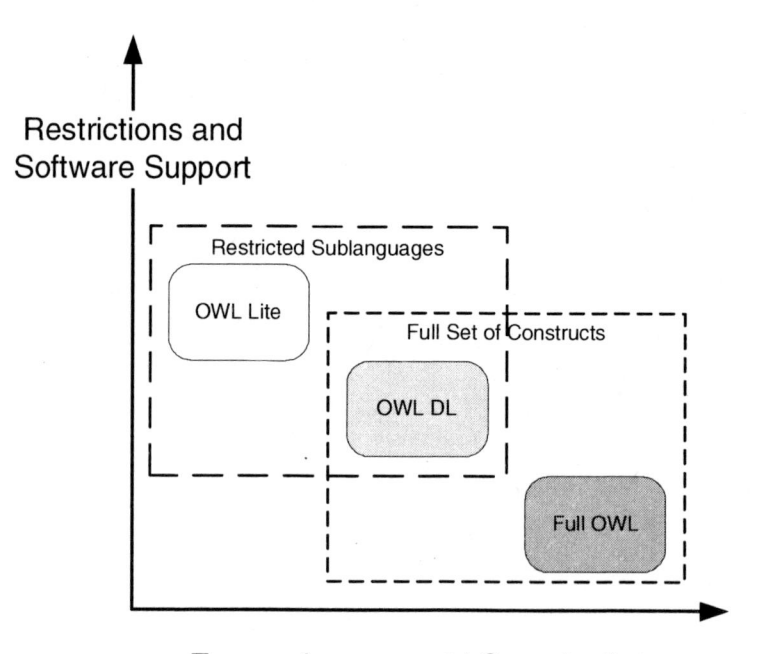

Figure 19-1. OWL Dialects

When opting for either OWL DL or OWL Lite, consider whether the advantages of the choice (e.g., reasoning support) outweigh the restrictions on the use of OWL and RDF constructs.

## 19.2 Migrating XML and RDF Implementations to OWL

As the benefits of OWL are recognized, developers of XML and RDF applications will begin to upgrade their information representations into OWL ontologies and instance data. OWL files are expressed using RDF/XML. However, RDF files are only automatically OWL Full compliant files. You cannot assume that an RDF file meets the OWL Lite or OWL DL restrictions. If OWL Lite or OWL DL is chosen, their restrictions must be satisfied by the XML or RDF statements being migrated. For example, because of type separation requirements, URIrefs of classes, properties, and individuals must be explicitly typed.

OWL DL and OWL Lite restrictions are detailed in Appendix E of the OWL Reference document (see section 10.1.3). XML files can be migrated into RDF/XML by adopting the consistency imposed by RDF/XML. Further modifications can then be performed if OWL Lite or OWL DL compliance is desired. Since OWL Full has no restrictions and is a superset of RDF, it requires no translation from RDF.

## *19.3 Language Selection Summary*

The selection of OWL dialect should be based on the requirements of the application and various constraints on species uses. If an application requires decidability and computability, then OWL DL or OWL Lite should be used. If all the OWL constructs are required, then OWL Full or OWL DL should be used. If all the constructs of OWL are required, but the restrictions imposed by OWL DL can be tolerated, then OWL DL should be used. Table 19-1 summarizes major factors for selecting a dialect.

Table 19-1. Criteria Summary

| Criteria / Requirement | Recommended Species |
| --- | --- |
| Simple taxonomical relationships | OWL Lite |
| Decidability | OWL DL or OWL Lite |
| Maximum expressivity | OWL Full |

## *19.4 Satisfaction of Information Representation Requirements*

The Semantic Web information representation and ontology requirements described in Chapter 2 are fulfilled by OWL. Ontology requirements for specifying semantic relationships are satisfied by various OWL Lite constructs.

Section 4 – OWL DL, OWL Full, and Applications

Table 19-2 shows how the required building blocks identified in section 3.4.1 are satisfied in OWL.

Table 19-2. Supporting Information Representation Building Blocks

| Building Block | OWL Support Description |
|---|---|
| Class | The OWL class construct represents a group or set of individual objects with similar characteristics. Subclass relationships support the definition of a subsumption hierarchy.<br><br>Accomplished through "rdfs:Class" and its subclass "owl:Class" |
| Property | The RDF property construct associates attribute/value pairs with individuals. OWL datatype properties and object properties refine RDF's property concept. Properties can be characterized as being symmetric, transitive, functional, or inverse functional. They can be related through inverse and subproperty relationships.<br><br>Accomplished through "rdf:Property" and its subclasses:<br>• "owl:ObjectProperty",<br>• "owl:DatatypeProperty",<br>• "owl:AnnotationProperty", and<br>• "owl:OntologyProperty" |
| Individual | Instances of user-defined classes are defined as RDF resources associated with classes.<br><br>Accomplished through resources that are individual members of user-defined classes |

244

## Chapter 19 – OWL Dialect Selection

Table 19-3 shows how the required relationships between information representation building blocks identified in section 3.4.2 are implemented in OWL.

Table 19-3. Information Representation Construct Relationships

| Relationship | OWL Support Concepts |
|---|---|
| Relates classes to properties | Restrictions (e.g., rdfs:domain, rdfs:range, owl:Restriction) |
| Relates classes to individuals | Membership (instantiating individuals from classes) accomplished through rdf:type and owl:Class |
| Relates properties to individuals | Property values (implemented as XML elements / attribute values) |

Table 19-4 shows how the semantic relationships described in Section 3.4.3 are supported by OWL constructs.

Table 19-4. Ontology Requirement Satisfaction

| | Relationship | OWL Support Constructs |
|---|---|---|
| = | Synonymy | owl:equivalentClass |
| | | owl:equivalentProperty |
| | | owl:sameAs |
| ≠ | Antonymy | disjoint classes |
| | | owl:differentFrom |
| | | owl:allDifferent / owl:distinctMembers |
| ⩟ | Hyponymy | rdfs:subClassOf |
| | | rdfs:subPropertyOf |
| ◇ | Meronymy / Holonymy | (user-defined properties) |

245

Section 4 – OWL DL, OWL Full, and Applications

Table 19-5 summarizes OWL's support for various ontology language requirements.

Table 19-5. OWL Full Requirement Satisfaction

| Information Representation Requirement | Satisfied by |
| --- | --- |
| Producer descriptions of particular domains | ontologies |
| Distributed representations that can be extended | web-distributed ontologies, importing with "owl:imports" |
| Extending resources | "rdf:about" |
| Work with current development tools | XML syntax |
| Versioning and configuration management | "owl:versionInfo" property, deprecated classes and properties, compatibility properties |
| Semantic join support and synonymy | "owl:sameAs", "owl:equivalentProperty", and "owl:equivalentClass" |
| Modeling primitives | classes, properties, and individuals |
| Leverage open, non-proprietary standards | XML, RDF(S), URIs |
| Distributed representations | URIs, "owl:imports", XML namespaces |
| Extending / reusing ontologies | owl:imports |

## 19.5 OWL Dialect Selection Summary

Table 19-6 summarizes the advantages and disadvantages of the various OWL dialects.

Table 19-6. OWL Dialect Comparison

| Dialect | Advantages | Disadvantages |
|---|---|---|
| OWL Lite | Easy to support with software | Limited expressiveness |
| OWL DL | Decidable | Restricted |
| OWL Full | Very expressive | Not decidable |

Figure 19-2 shows one way to view the relationship between the OWL dialects and RDF.

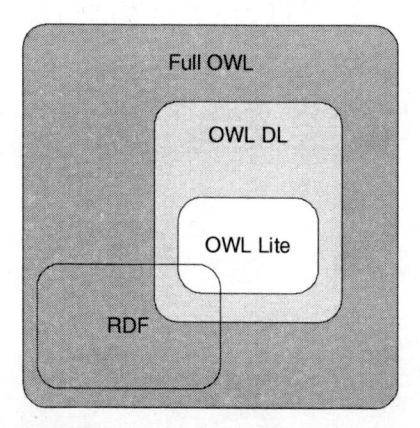

Figure 19-2. OWL Extends RDF

## Section 4 – OWL DL, OWL Full, and Applications

Figure 19-3 shows the relationship of documents using UML class inheritance notation.

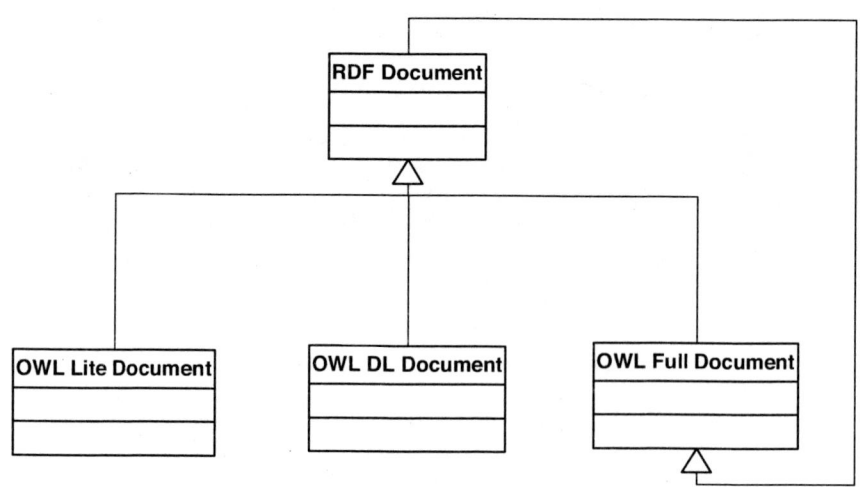

Figure 19-3. RDF Document Relationships

The various OWL language dialects support representing information for use by applications. The next chapter describes how applications can use OWL information representations.

# 20 Applications

The reason we represent information in OWL is to support applications. Applications represent the implementation layer of the Semantic Web layered architecture (see Figure 20-1). The applications include the ontologies and the software to use them.

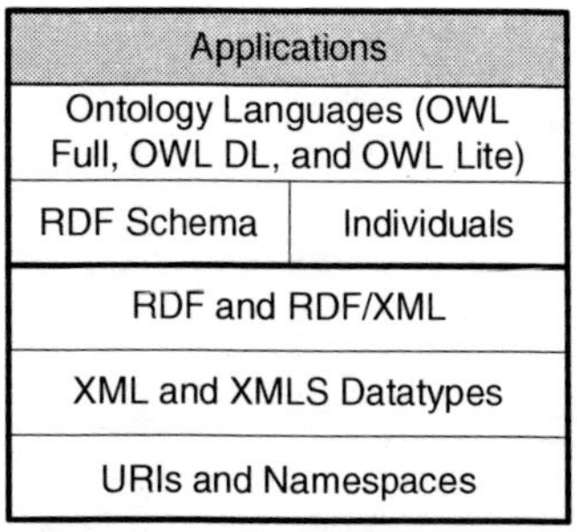

| Applications |||
|---|---|---|
| Ontology Languages (OWL Full, OWL DL, and OWL Lite) ||
| RDF Schema | | Individuals |
| RDF and RDF/XML |||
| XML and XMLS Datatypes |||
| URIs and Namespaces |||

Figure 20-1. Application Layer

As with any software technology, there are normally multiple methods for implementing a particular application. OWL was designed for the web, but could be used in a stand-alone application. On the web, there are multiple uses for OWL with distributed ontologies and instance files.

## *20.1 Application Example*

Figure 20-2 shows one approach for supporting the hungry pie lover query described in Chapter 2. Recall that a customer (named Mark) wants to find an open restaurant serving Key lime pie.

One solution might involve the customer using his personal computer (PC) to enter a search request to a concierge web service provided by a restaurant association. The web service could use OWL data published by individual restaurants to respond to the consumer's query with results. This application is enabled by restaurants posting their menu and hours information in OWL, compliant with ontologies established by the restaurant association.

The following sections present ontologies and sample instance data to support the use case. In this solution, software on the consumer's personal computer requests a search from the restaurant associations concierge web service (1). That service finds the required information by retrieving hour of operation data and menu data that are compliant with the restaurant association's ontologies (2). The service searches the data and performs inferencing (3). The results of the operation are then returned to the consumer's PC software (4).

## Section 4 – OWL DL, OWL Full, and Applications

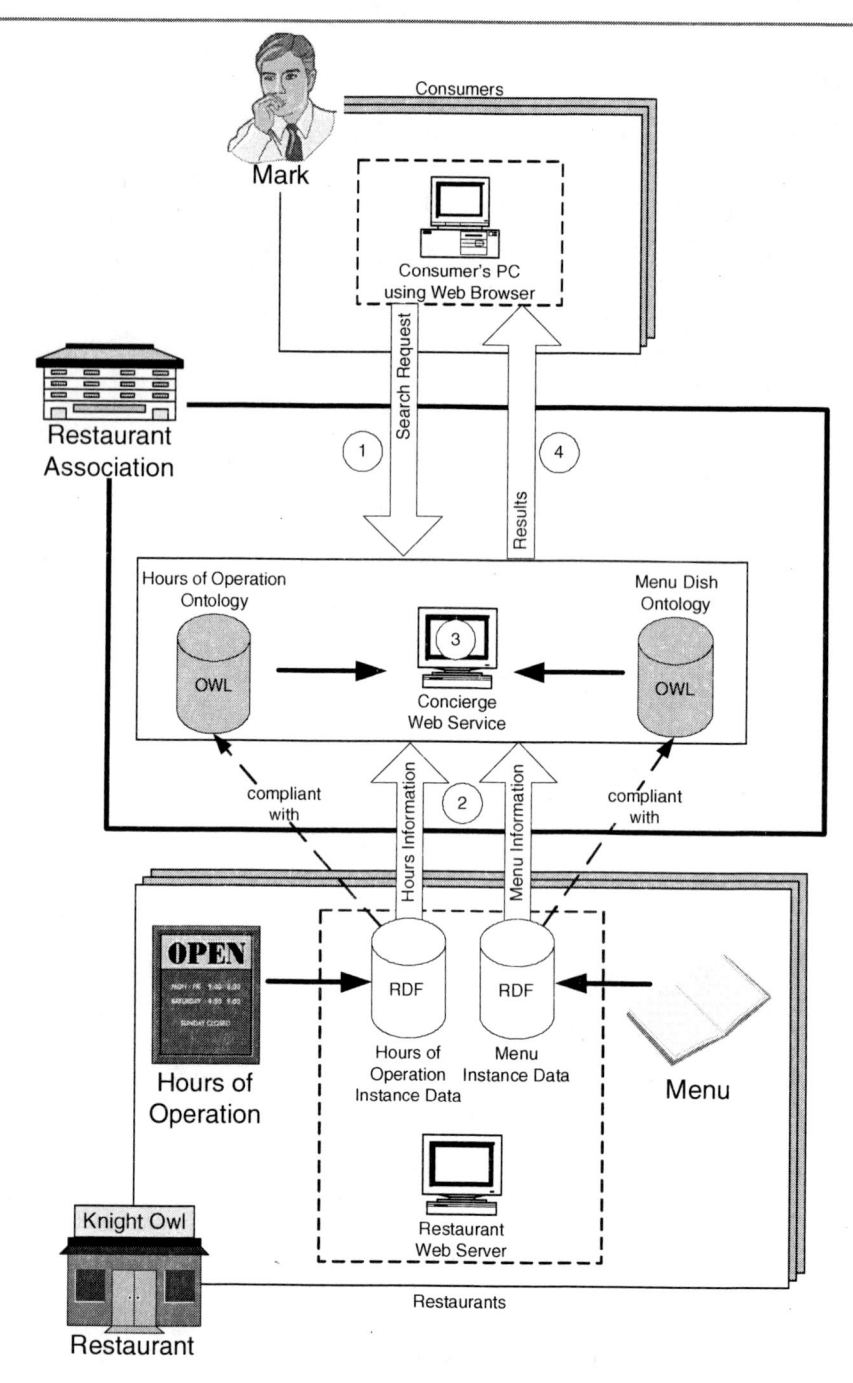

Figure 20-2. Use Case Data Flow Diagram

250

## 20.1.1 OWL Lite Solution

Both an ontology, standardized by the hypothetical restaurant association, and information, represented by restaurants (e.g., the Knight Owl Restaurant) are required for comparison to the consumer's search requirements. The following examples focus on the hours information and assume an OWL Lite solution is desired. Again, examples assume that the typical namespace declarations and entity abbreviations have been specified.

### 20.1.1.1 Ontologies

An "Hours of Operation" ontology could define an "HoursOfOperation" class that is related to a "DailyHours" class by a "hasDailyHours" property. The "DailyHours" class could be related to the "DayOfWeek" class using an "openOn" and "closedOn" property (see Figure 20-3). Hours of operation information is represented in an RDF/XML file that is compliant with the Hours of Operation ontology. For simplicity, the Restaurant class is included in the HOO ontology.

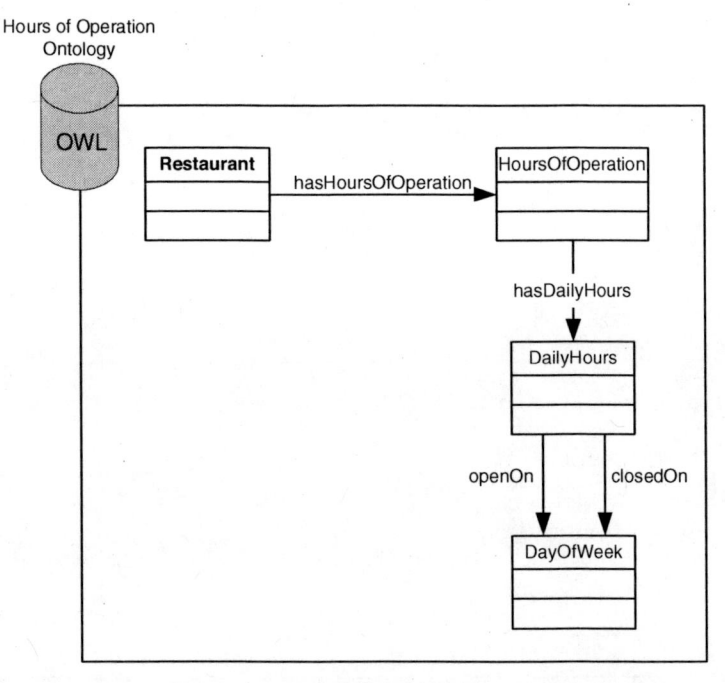

Figure 20-3. Hours of Operation Ontology

# Section 4 – OWL DL, OWL Full, and Applications

As described in section 11.1 above, an ontology file includes a header, body, and footer. The body includes class, property, and individual statements.

The Hours of Operation (HOO) ontology has header information including the XML declaration, entity declarations, RDF start tag, namespace declarations, and an ontology element with version information.

---

This example assumes that the OWL Lite Hours of Operation ontology is at www.restaurant.org and named hoursOfOperation-ont. The header information is:

```
<?xml version="1.0" encoding="UTF-8"?>
<!DOCTYPE rdf:RDF [
<!ENTITY xsd "http://www.w3.org/2001/XMLSchema#">
]>

<rdf:RDF
        xmlns:xsd ="http://www.w3.org/2001/XMLSchema#"
        xmlns:rdf ="http://www.w3.org/1999/02/22-rdf-syntax-ns#"
        xmlns:rdfs="http://www.w3.org/2000/01/rdf-schema#"
        xmlns:owl ="http://www.w3.org/2002/07/owl#"
        xmlns     ="http://www.restaurant.org/hoursOfOperation-ont#"
        xml:base="http://www.restaurant.org/hoursOfOperation-ont#"
>

<owl:Ontology rdf:about="">
        <rdfs:label>Hours of Operation Ontology</rdfs:label>
        <rdfs:comment>This ontology is used as an example for various OWL constructs</rdfs:comment>
        <owl:versionInfo>$Id: hoursOfOperation-ont.owl,v 1.2 2004/11/02 12:34:56 llacy Exp $</owl:versionInfo>
</owl:Ontology>
```

---

The Hours of Operation (HOO) ontology contains classes to represent concepts.

---

The class definition constructs in the OWL Lite Hours of Operation ontology are:

```
<owl:Class rdf:ID="Restaurant"/>
<owl:Class rdf:ID="HoursOfOperation"/>
<owl:Class rdf:ID="DailyHours">
        <rdfs:label>Daily Hours</rdfs:label>
        <rdfs:comment>represents a set of opening hours for specified days of the week</rdfs:comment>
</owl:Class>

<owl:Class rdf:ID="DayOfWeek"/>
```

# Chapter 20 - Applications

The HOO properties relate a restaurant's information.

A listing of the property definition constructs in the OWL Lite Hours Ontology is:

```
<owl:DatatypeProperty rdf:ID="openingTime">
      <rdfs:range rdf:resource="&xsd;time"/>
</owl:DatatypeProperty>

<owl:DatatypeProperty rdf:ID="closingTime">
      <rdfs:range rdf:resource="&xsd;time"/>
</owl:DatatypeProperty>

<owl:ObjectProperty rdf:ID="openOn">
      <rdfs:range rdf:resource="#DayOfWeek"/>
</owl:ObjectProperty>

<owl:ObjectProperty rdf:ID="closedOn">
      <rdfs:range rdf:resource="#DayOfWeek"/>
</owl:ObjectProperty>

<owl:DatatypeProperty rdf:ID="effectiveDate">
      <rdfs:range rdf:resource="&xsd;date"/>
</owl:DatatypeProperty>

<owl:ObjectProperty rdf:ID="hasDailyHours">
      <rdfs:range rdf:resource="#DailyHours"/>
</owl:ObjectProperty>

<owl:ObjectProperty rdf:ID="hasHoursOfOperation">
      <rdfs:range rdf:resource="#HoursOfOperation"/>
</owl:ObjectProperty>
```

Restaurant Association

## Section 4 – OWL DL, OWL Full, and Applications

Although instance files normally define individuals, some instances may need to be predefined as part of the ontology.

---

Instance data definition as part of the HOO ontology might be the individuals representing the days of the week.

```
<DayOfWeek rdf:ID="Sunday">
        <rdfs:label>Sunday</rdfs:label>
</DayOfWeek>

<DayOfWeek rdf:ID="Monday">
        <rdfs:label>Monday</rdfs:label>
</DayOfWeek>

<DayOfWeek rdf:ID="Tuesday">
        <rdfs:label>Tuesday</rdfs:label>
</DayOfWeek>

<DayOfWeek rdf:ID="Wednesday">
        <rdfs:label>Wednesday</rdfs:label>
</DayOfWeek>

<DayOfWeek rdf:ID="Thursday">
        <rdfs:label>Thursday</rdfs:label>
</DayOfWeek>

<DayOfWeek rdf:ID="Friday">
        <rdfs:label>Friday</rdfs:label>
</DayOfWeek>

<DayOfWeek rdf:ID="Saturday">
        <rdfs:label>Saturday</rdfs:label>
</DayOfWeek>
```

Chapter 20 - Applications

## 20.1.1.2 Hours of Operation Individuals

Information about the individual restaurant's hours is needed to perform the query. The instance data contains references to the ontology. Figure 20-4 shows the relationship of the hours related individual information to the HOO ontology.

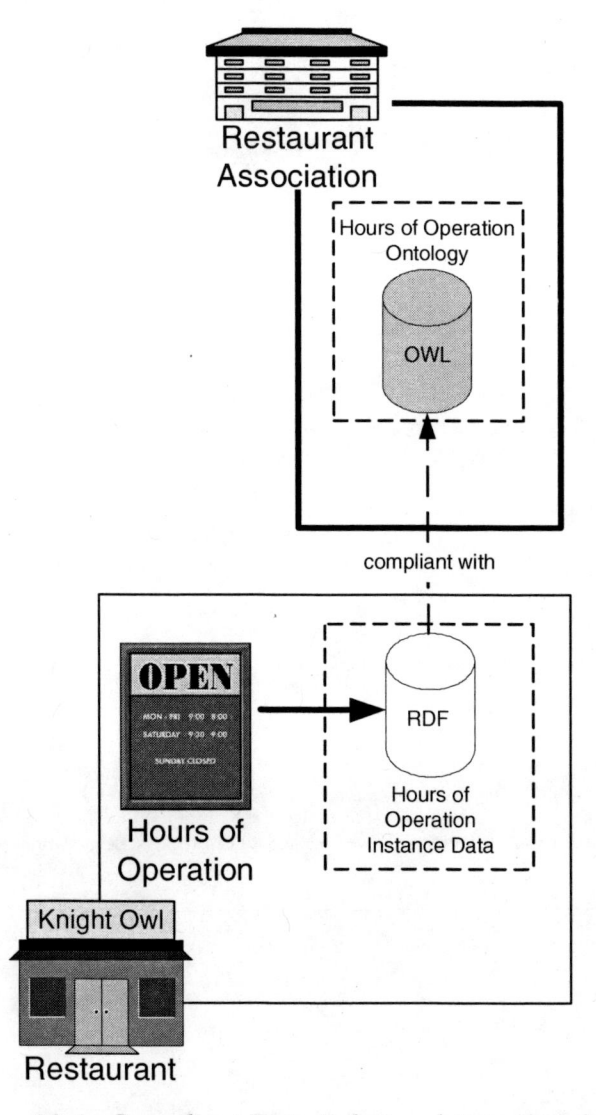

Figure 20-4. Compliant Data Relationship to Ontology

255

# Section 4 – OWL DL, OWL Full, and Applications

Example hours of operation data for the sample application are: "Effective 4/1/2004, the Knight Owl Restaurant's hours are: Sunday closed, Monday through Friday 9am to 8pm, and Saturday 9:30am to 9pm" (see Figure 20-5).

Figure 20-5. Sample Open Hours

---

The following RDF data could specify the hours of operation for the Knight Owl restaurant:

```
<?xml version="1.0"?>
<!DOCTYPE rdf:RDF [
<!ENTITY hoo "http://www.restaurant.org/hoursOfOperation-ont">
<!ENTITY xsd "http://www.w3.org/2001/XMLSchema#">
]>

<rdf:RDF
        xmlns:xsd ="http://www.w3.org/2001/XMLSchema#"
        xmlns:rdf ="http://www.w3.org/1999/02/22-rdf-syntax-ns#"
        xmlns:rdfs="http://www.w3.org/2000/01/rdf-schema#"
        xmlns:owl ="http://www.w3.org/2002/07/owl#"
        xmlns:hoo="http://www.restaurant.org/hoursOfOperation-ont#"
        xmlns     ="http://www.restaurant.org/hoursOfOperation-ont#"
        xml:base="http://www.restaurant.org/hoursOfOperation-ont#"
>

<owl:Ontology rdf:about="">
        <rdfs:label>Hours of Operation Information for the Knight Owl Restaurant</rdfs:label>
        <owl:imports rdf:resource="http://www.restaurant.org/hoursOfOperation-ont"/>
</owl:Ontology>
```

## Chapter 20 - Applications

```
<hoo:DailyHours rdf:ID="KOWeekdayHours040104">
        <hoo:openOn rdf:resource="&hoo;#Monday"/>
        <hoo:openOn rdf:resource="&hoo;#Tuesday"/>
        <hoo:openOn rdf:resource="&hoo;#Wednesday"/>
        <hoo:openOn rdf:resource="&hoo;#Thursday"/>
        <hoo:openOn rdf:resource="&hoo;#Friday"/>
        <hoo:openingTime rdf:datatype="&xsd;time">09:00:00+8</hoo:openingTime>
        <hoo:closingTime rdf:datatype="&xsd;time">20:00:00+8</hoo:closingTime>
</hoo:DailyHours>

<hoo:DailyHours rdf:ID="KOSaturdayHours040104">
        <hoo:openOn rdf:resource="&hoo;#Saturday"/>
        <hoo:openingTime rdf:datatype="&xsd;time">09:30:00+8</hoo:openingTime>
        <hoo:closingTime rdf:datatype="&xsd;time">21:00:00+8</hoo:closingTime>
</hoo:DailyHours>

<hoo:DailyHours rdf:ID="KOSundayHours040104">
        <hoo:closedOn rdf:resource="&hoo;#Sunday"/>
</hoo:DailyHours>

<hoo:Restaurant rdf:ID="KORest">
        <hoo:hasHoursOfOperation rdf:resource="#KORestHOO040104"/>
</hoo:Restaurant>

<hoo:HoursOfOperation rdf:ID="KORestHOO040104">
        <hoo:hasDailyHours rdf:resource="#KOWeekdayHours040104"/>
        <hoo:hasDailyHours rdf:resource="#KOSaturdayHours040104"/>
        <hoo:hasDailyHours rdf:resource="#KOSundayHours040104"/>
        <hoo:effectiveDate rdf:datatype="&xsd;date">2004-04-01</hoo:effectiveDate>
</hoo:HoursOfOperation>

</rdf:RDF>
```

The example above assumes that the restaurant association provides a web service that takes search requests for menu items and time of day. It also assumes that the association maintains a registry of restaurant OWL information. The registry allows the application to easily access the hours of operation and menus that correspond to the published ontologies for the restaurants.

Unlike an XML implementation, the OWL representation supports future applications that may want to leverage the ontologies developed for this application.

Section 4 – OWL DL, OWL Full, and Applications

## 20.2 Supporting Applications

The purpose of representing information in OWL is to support application functionality. By providing a consistent method for representing information and explicitly providing semantics, new and exciting Semantic Web application will emerge. For these applications to work properly, OWL must be used correctly and its features used consistently.

### 20.2.1 Inappropriate Applications

OWL is not the best choice for every information representation challenge. OWL suffers from many of the same challenges as XML, as well as challenges related to reasoning on a web scale.

Since OWL is relatively new, it will take some time before a large established base of software supports the manipulation of OWL information representations. It will also take time to develop a workforce conversant in OWL. However, since OWL represents a logical evolution of XML and Description Logics, software professionals and their tools will likely quickly rise to the occasion.

As with XML, OWL may have performance issues due to the verbosity of the markup used to describe content. This may be especially problematic for applications with real-time requirements that require access to marked up data.

Although the reasoning features of OWL are very powerful, it is difficult to scale reasoning on a web-scale. OWL has limited support for describing rules and research continues on rules extensions to OWL.

Because of OWL's XML-based syntax, it does not make sense to use OWL for representing certain types of data (e.g., digital video). However, the meta-data used to describe these media files is easily represented using OWL.

### 20.2.2 Appropriate Applications

A common challenge with technologies like the Semantic Web is to identify the niche of appropriate applications. Appropriate applications should leverage OWL's strengths as an ontology language for providing a web-ready object-oriented information representation with an open vendor-neutral language.

OWL is well suited for representing many types of information representation solutions. Applications that provide information on their servers for access by software applications and human readers are good candidates for OWL. Also, applications characterized by well-defined object-oriented domains that can be described with text, and are described on distributed web servers should be considered for OWL information representations. Taxonomical relationships are easily described in OWL using the subclass relationships.

Each potential application must be individually examined to determine its appropriateness for an OWL representation.

## *20.3 Applications Summary*

Ultimately, the success of OWL will hinge on the benefits of applications that leverage OWL's features. OWL provides the language features to represent the required information.

As with any new technology, there are appropriate and inappropriate uses. Each situation must be analyzed to determine the "value add" provided by OWL. As adoption of OWL continues, new applications will form the next evolution of the web – the Semantic Web.

# Section 4 – OWL DL, OWL Full, and Applications

# Acronyms

| | |
|---|---|
| AI | Artificial Intelligence |
| API | Application Programming Interface |
| COI | Community of Interest |
| COTS | Commercial Off-The-Shelf |
| CVS | Concurrent Versions System |
| DAML | DARPA Agent Markup Language |
| DAML+OIL | DARPA Agent Markup Language + Ontology Interface Layer |
| DARPA | Defense Advanced Research Projects Agency |
| DC | Dublin Core |
| DIF | Data Interchange Format |
| DL | Description Logic |
| DNS | Domain Name Service |
| DoD | Department of Defense |
| DRC | Dynamics Research Corporation |
| DTD | Document Type Definition |
| EU | European Union |
| FCG | Foreign Clearance Guide |
| FTP | File Transfer Protocol |
| HTML | HyperText Markup Language |
| HTTP | HyperText Transfer Protocol |
| IANA | Internet Assigned Numbers Authority |
| ISBN | International Standard Book Number |
| ISO | International Organization for Standardization |
| IT | Information Technology |
| NLP | Natural Language Processing |
| OIL | Ontology Inference Layer |
| OO | Object-Oriented |
| OOP | Object-Oriented Programming |
| PC | Personal Computer |
| RCS | Revision Control System |
| RDBMS | Relational Database Management System |
| RDF | Resource Description Framework |
| RDFS | Resource Description Framework Schema |
| RFC | Request for Comment |
| ROI | Return On Investment |
| SGML | Standard Generalized Markup Language |

# Acronyms

| | |
|---|---|
| SOAP | Simple Object Access Protocol |
| TCP/IP | Transmission Control Protocol / Internet Protocol |
| UML | Unified Modeling Language |
| URI | Uniform Resource Identifier |
| URL | Uniform Resource Locator |
| URN | Uniform Resource Name |
| UTF | UCS Transformation Format |
| UTF | Unicode Transformation Format |
| W3C | World-Wide Web Consortium |
| XHTML | Extensible Hypertext Markup Language |
| XML | Extensible Markup Language |
| XMLS | XML Schema |
| XSD | XML Schema Definition |

# Glossary

The following glossary defines terms used in this text and terms found in OWL documentation and related literature. The definitions provided are in the context of this text.

| | |
|---|---|
| Abox | assertional component – facts associated with the terminological vocabulary (Tbox) |
| absolute URI | a URI that begins with a scheme identification, followed by a colon, and then a string that is interpreted based on the identified scheme |
| agent | autonomous software whose purpose is to accomplish a user's goal |
| anonymous class | class declaration with no associated identifier, often used within another declaration |
| antonymy | semantic relation between concepts that can express opposite meanings |
| assertion | authored statement that may or may not be true. |
| attribute | specific XML syntactic construct associated with an XML element, best used to provide metadata about the element's value |
| axiom | statement whose truth is assumed to be self-evident |
| camel case | capitalization rule used to represent multiple words combined together into a single word with original concatenated words started with an uppercase letter (e.g., keyLimePie) |

# Glossary

| | |
|---|---|
| cardinality | restriction on the number of unique values that a property can have for a particular individual |
| class description | specification of a set of member individuals using either a class name or by specifying the class extension |
| class extension | set of individuals (class instances) associated with a class |
| closed world assumption | assumption that anything that is not stated is false |
| community of interest | organization or group of individuals with a common interest in a particular subject or domain |
| complement | elements of a set that are not elements of the specified subset |
| computable | something that can be computed by an algorithm |
| conceptual completeness | situation in which all conclusions are computable |
| conceptualization | abstract or simplified model of a domain |
| conjunction | statements connected with a logical "AND" |
| container | grouping of resources treated as a single resource |
| data range | datatype identifier or set of data values |
| datatype | combination of distinct values, lexical representations, and properties that describe the values and representations |
| decidability | condition of a software system where computations are expected to finish in finite time |

# Glossary

| | |
|---|---|
| Description Logic | information representation technique tailored for expressing knowledge about concepts, concept hierarchies, properties (called slots), and values (called fillers) |
| Description Logic terminology | collection of concept descriptions |
| disjoint | sets with no shared members |
| disjunction | statements connected with a logical "OR" |
| domain | specific subject area or area of knowledge. |
| domain ontology | ontology that describes a particular subject matter with statements about concepts from the domain |
| element | a specific XML syntactic construct |
| entail | infer a logical consequent |
| entailment | inferred statement |
| enumeration | exhaustive list of possible values |
| epistemology | philosophical theory of knowledge |
| Extensible Markup Language (XML) | metalanguage used to define and use markup tags |
| extralogical | something with no impact on semantics |
| first order logic | language describing the truth of mathematical expressions |
| fragment | (see fragment identifier) |
| fragment identifier | optional portion of a URIref that follows the "#" separator and identifies part of a resource |

# Glossary

| | |
|---|---|
| full URIref | URIref formed by appending a QName's local name to the namespace URI associated with the QName's prefix |
| functional property | property that can have at most one (unique) value for each instance |
| generalization | process of creating a more general concept by abstracting common descriptions from more specific concepts |
| holonymy | semantic relation between a whole and its parts (see meronymy) |
| HTML | HyperText Markup Language – formatting language used on the web |
| individual | instance of a user-defined class |
| inference | determination of a new statement from existing statements |
| injective property | property with only one possible subject per object |
| instance | an object that belongs to a class. |
| intersection | set of members shared by other sets |
| inverse | property relationship that is reversed (turned backward) in direction |
| inverse-functional | property whose object uniquely identifies the subject individual (similar to a key in a relational database) |
| knowledge base | combination of an ontology and a set of individuals that comply with the ontology |
| literal | primitive value type in RDF that typically represents a string of characters |

# Glossary

| | |
|---|---|
| lower camel case | camel case term with initial letter not capitalized (see camel case) |
| markup | tagging information added to text used by parsing software |
| mereology | formal theory of meronymy (part-whole relations) |
| meronymy | semantic relationship between a part and the whole that includes it (see holonymy) |
| metadata | data about data |
| normative | definitive / official |
| ontological commitment | agreement to use a use the vocabulary specified by an ontology |
| ontology | an OWL-encoded web-distributed vocabulary of declarative formalisms describing a model of a domain |
| ontology property | property that relates two ontologies |
| Pascal case | (see upper camel case) |
| predicate | RDF statement property |
| primitive | low-level object used to compose higher-level objects |
| property | specific attribute used to describe a resource |
| property restriction | constraints that specify a class containing individuals that satisfy the constraints |
| QName | (see qualified name) |
| qualified name (QName) | namespace URI reference separated from a local name with a colon |

# Glossary

| | |
|---|---|
| reasoning | using logical induction or deduction to infer new conclusions from statements |
| referent | thing described in an "rdf:about" attribute. |
| reification | referencing a statement as data |
| relative URI reference | URI references that inherit their scheme name from the base URI (see absolute URI) |
| resource | any physical object or virtual concept that is identified by a URI |
| restriction class | anonymous class containing individuals that satisfy a set of constraints |
| Semantic Web | next generation of the current web in which computers can interpret the meaning of web content because of explicit semantics provided in markup |
| Semantic Web service | web service defined and described by Semantic Web ontologies |
| semantics | meaning of a text string in a language |
| serialization | encoding structured data into a linear datafile format for storage and interchange purposes |
| specialization | process of defining a more specific concept from a general concept (see generalization) |
| statement | RDF expression that identifies a subject resource, a property (attribute), and provides the value for that property for the subject resource |
| striped syntax | alternating property/value pairs in which a value (object of a statement) becomes the subject of a subsequent statement |

# Glossary

| | |
|---|---|
| subclass | specialization of a class |
| subject | resource that an RDF statement describes |
| subproperty | specialization of a property |
| symmetric | relation S for which from xSy we can infer ySx |
| syntax | structure of strings in a language specified by a grammar |
| Tbox | terminological component – vocabulary with associated facts (Abox) |
| transitive | relation T for which if xTy and yTz, we can infer xTz |
| triple | representation of an RDF statement consisting of just the property, the subject resource identifier, and the property value (in that order) |
| type separation | requirement that something cannot belong to more than one of the specified types |
| typed node syntax | abbreviated alternative representation that uses the value of a type property as the XML tag name when instantiating an instance of a class |
| union | set of all members that belong to either or both of the specified sets |
| unique names assumption | two different names refer to two different items |
| universal quantifier | logical quantifier that asserts that something is true for all members of a specified class |
| Uniform Resource Identifier (URI) | string of characters used to refer to a resource |

# Glossary

| | |
|---|---|
| Uniform Resource Locator (URL) | subset of URIs that indicate the resource's primary access mechanism |
| upper camel case | camel case notation with initial letter capitalized |
| upper ontology | general (domain-independent) ontology |
| URI reference | string of characters that represents a URI |
| URI scheme | text string (e.g., "http") that precedes the colon in a URI and indicate how to interpret the remainder of the URI |
| vertical ontology | domain-specific ontology |

# Recommended Reading

The W3C documents on XML, RDF, RDF/XML, RDFS, and OWL are identified in sections 6.1, 7.1.3, 8.1.2, 9.1, and 10.1.3. In addition to these authoritative documents, the following exceptional books and articles were extremely useful in developing this text. They help describe the Semantic Web, ontologies, and RDF(S).

| | |
|---|---|
| | *Weaving the Web: The Original Design and Ultimate Destiny of the World Wide Web* by Tim Berners-Lee, HarperBusiness; 1st edition (November 7, 2000), ISBN: 006251587X |
| | "The Semantic Web", *Scientific American*, May 2001, by Tim Berners-Lee, James Hendler and Ora Lassila. |
| | *The Semantic Web : A Guide to the Future of XML, Web Services, and Knowledge Management* by Michael C. Daconta, Leo J. Obrst, and Kevin T. Smith, Wiley; (May 19, 2003), ISBN: 0471432571 |
| | *Spinning the Semantic Web: Bringing the World Wide Web to Its Full Potential* by Dieter Fensel (Editor), Wolfgang Wahlster, Henry Lieberman, James Hendler, The MIT Press; (November 15, 2002), ISBN: 0262062321 |
| | The Emerging Semantic Web - Selected Papers from the first Semantic Web Working Symposium Edited by Isabel Cruz, Stefan Decker, Jerome Euzenat, Deborah McGuinness 2002 IOS Press, ISBN: 1586032550 |
| | *Ontologies: A Silver Bullet for Knowledge Management and Electronic Commerce* by Dieter Fensel, Michael L. Brodie, Springer-Verlag; 2nd Rev edition (December 1, 2003), ISBN: 3540003029 |
| | *Practical RDF* by Shelley Powers, O'Reilly; 1 edition (July 2003), ISBN: 0596002637 |

Direct links for purchasing some of these items can be found at: http://www.lacydatasystems.com/owlbook/recomread.htm

# Reference Acknowledgements

Gruber quote Reprinted from Knowledge Acquisition, Vol. 5, T. Gruber, "A Translation Approach to Portable Ontology Specifications", Pages No. 199-220, Copyright (1993), with permission from Elsevier.

Scripture taken from the HOLY BIBLE, NEW INTERNATIONAL VERSION®. NIV®. Copyright©1973, 1978, 1984 by International Bible Society. Used by permission of Zondervan. All rights reserved.

The Mikael Nilsson quote was used by permission of the author and publisher.

Photos of Tim Berners-Lee and Dr. James Hendler were provided by the subjects.

OWL documentation and other W3C documents are covered by Copyright © 1994-2004 W3C ® (Massachusetts Institute of Technology, European Research Consortium for Informatics and Mathematics, Keio University), All Rights Reserved.

Some clipart provided by www.GifArt.com

The following is a list of W3C terms claimed as a trademark or generic term by MIT, ERCIM, and/or Keio on behalf of the W3C:
- W3C®, World Wide Web Consortium (registered in numerous countries)
- HTML (generic), HyperText Markup Language
- HTTP (generic), Hypertext Transfer Protocol
- Metadata (generic)
- RDF (generic), Resource Description Framework
- XHTML (generic), The Extensible HyperText Markup Language
- XML (generic), Extensible Markup Language
- XSL (generic), Extensible Stylesheet Language

"METADATA" is a trademark of the Metadata Company. This text uses the term "metadata" to describe data about data.

# Appendix – Language Construct Description Index and Cross Reference

Table A-1. RDF Construct Descriptions in RDF Documentation

| Construct | This Text | RDF/XML[1] | RDFS[2] | RDF Primer |
|---|---|---|---|---|
| rdf:_n (numbered properties) | 8.3.6.3.1.1 | 2.15 | 5.15 | 4.1 |
| rdf:about | 8.3.4.2 | 2.14 | | 3.1 |
| rdf:Alt | 8.3.6.3.4 | 2.15 | 5.1.4 | 4.1 |
| rdf:Bag | 8.3.6.3.2 | 2.15 | 5.1.2 | 4.1 |
| rdf:datatype (attribute) | 8.3.6.1.4 | 2.9 | | 3.1 |
| rdf:Description | 8.3.3 | | | 4.2 |
| rdf:first | 8.3.6.4.2 | | 5.2.2 | 4.2 |
| rdf:ID | 8.3.4.1 | 2.14, 2.17 | | 3.2 |
| rdf:li | 8.3.6.3.1.2 | 2.15 | | 4.1 |
| rdf:List | 8.3.6.4.1 | | 5.2.1 | 4.2 |
| rdf:nil | 8.3.6.4.4 | | 5.2.4 | 4.2 |
| rdf:parseType="Collection" | 8.3.6.4 | 2.16 | | 4.2 |
| rdf:parseType="Literal" | 8.3.6.1.3 | 2.8 | | 4.5 |
| rdf:parseType="Resource" | 8.3.6.1.1 | 2.11 | | 4.4 |
| rdf:Property | 9.3.2.4 | | 2.6 | 5.2 |
| rdf:RDF | 8.3.1 | 2.6 | | 3.1 |
| rdf:resource (attribute) | 8.3.6.2 | 2.14 | | 3.1 |
| rdf:rest | 8.3.6.4.3 | | 5.2.3 | 4.2 |
| rdf:Seq | 8.3.6.3.3 | 2.15 | 5.1.3 | 4.1 |
| rdf:type | 8.3.6.1.5 | 2.13 | 3.3 | 3.2 |
| rdf:value | 8.3.6.1.2 | | 5.4.3 | 4.2 |
| rdf:XMLLiteral | 9.3.2.7 | | 2.5 | 2.4 |

[1] RDF/XML = RDF/XML Syntax Specification (Revised)
[2] RDFS = RDF Vocabulary Description Language 1.0: RDF Schema

# Appendix

Table A-2. RDFS and XML Construct Descriptions in RDF Documentation

| Construct | This Text | RDF/XML[1] | RDFS[2] | RDF Primer |
|---|---|---|---|---|
| rdfs:Class | 9.3.2.5 | | 2.2 | 5.1 |
| rdfs:comment | 9.5.4.2 | | 3.7 | 5.4 |
| rdfs:Container | 9.5.3.1 | | 5.1.1 | |
| rdfs:ContainerMembershipProperty | 9.5.3.2 | | 5.1.5 | |
| rdfs:Datatype (class) | 9.3.2.8 | 2.9 | 2.4 | 5.2 |
| rdfs:domain | 9.5.1.5 | | 3.2 | 5.2 |
| rdfs:isDefinedBy | 9.5.2.2 | | 5.4.2 | 5.4 |
| rdfs:label | 9.5.4.1 | | 3.6 | 5.4 |
| rdfs:Literal | 9.3.2.6 | | 2.3 | |
| rdfs:member | 9.5.3.3 | | 5.1.6 | |
| rdfs:range | 9.5.1.4 | | 3.1 | 5.2 |
| rdfs:Resource (class) | 9.3.2.3 | | 2.1 | 5.1 |
| rdfs:seeAlso | 9.5.2.1 | | 5.4.1 | 5.4 |
| rdfs:subClassOf | 9.5.1.2, 14.1 | | 3.4 | 5.1 |
| rdfs:subPropertyOf | 9.5.1.3 | | 3.5 | 5.2 |
| xml:base | 5.4 | 2.14 | | |
| xml:lang | 6.1.5.1 | 2.7 | | |
| xmlns | 5.3 | | | App. B |

[1]RDF/XML = RDF/XML Syntax Specification (Revised)
[2]RDFS = RDF Vocabulary Description Language 1.0: RDF Schema

## Appendix

Table A-3. RDFS and XML Construct Descriptions in OWL Documentation

| Construct | This Text | OWL Guide[1] | OWL Reference[2] |
|---|---|---|---|
| rdfs:Class | 9.3.2.5 | | 3.1 |
| rdfs:comment | 9.5.4.2 | 2.2. | 7.1 |
| rdfs:Container | 9.5.3.1 | | |
| rdfs:ContainerMembershipProperty | 9.5.3.2 | | |
| rdfs:Datatype (class) | 9.3.2.8 | 3.2.2. | |
| rdfs:domain | 9.5.1.5 | 3.2.1. | 4.1.2 |
| rdfs:isDefinedBy | 9.5.2.2 | | 7.1 |
| rdfs:label | 9.5.4.1 | 3.1.1. | 7.1 |
| rdfs:Literal | 9.3.2.6 | 3.3. | 6.1 |
| rdfs:member | 9.5.3.3 | | |
| rdfs:range | 9.5.1.4 | 3.2.1. | 4.1.3 |
| rdfs:Resource (class) | 9.3.2.3 | | 8.1 |
| rdfs:seeAlso | 9.5.2.1 | | 7.1 |
| rdfs:subClassOf | 9.5.1.2, 14.1 | 3.1.1. | 3.2.1 |
| rdfs:subPropertyOf | 9.5.1.3 | 3.2.1. | 4.1.1 |
| xml:base | 5.4 | 2.2 | 7.2 |
| xml:lang | 6.1.5.1 | | |
| xmlns | 5.3 | 3.1.1 | |

[1] OWL Guide = OWL Web Ontology Language Guide
[2] OWL Reference = OWL Web Ontology Language Reference

# Appendix

Table A-4. OWL Class Construct Descriptions in OWL Documentation

| OWL Class | This Text | OWL Overview[1] | OWL Guide[2] | OWL Ref.[3] | OWL Sem.[4] |
|---|---|---|---|---|---|
| AllDifferent | 15.5.3 | 3.2 | 4.3 | 5.2.3 | 5.2 |
| AnnotationProperty | 12.3.3 | 3.9 | 2.2 | 7.1 | 3.3 |
| Class | 12.1 | 3.1 | 3.1.1 | 3.2 | 3.3 |
| DataRange | 17.4 | | | 6.2 | 3.2 |
| DatatypeProperty | 12.3.1 | 3.1 | 3.2.2 | 4 | 3.3 |
| DeprecatedClass | 11.2.3.1.1.4 | | 6 | 7.4.5 | 3.3 |
| DeprecatedProperty | 11.2.3.1.1.5 | | 6 | 7.4.5 | 3.3 |
| FunctionalProperty | 13.1.1 | 3.3 | 3.3. | 4.3.1 | 3.3 |
| Nothing | 12.2.2 | 3.1 | 3.1.1. | 3.1 | 3.2 |
| ObjectProperty | 12.3.2 | 3.1 | 3.2.1. | 4 | 3.3 |
| Ontology | 11.2.3 | | 2.2. | 7.2 | 3.4 |
| OntologyProperty | 12.3.4 | | | 7.2 | 3.2 |
| Restriction | 13.4 | 3.4 | 3.4. | 3.1.2 | 3.2 |
| SymmetricProperty | 13.3.2 | 3.3 | 3.3. | 4.4.2 | 3.3 |
| Thing | 12.2.1 | 3.1 | 3.1.1. | 3.1 | 3.2 |
| TransitiveProperty | 13.3.1 | 3.3 | 3.3. | 4.4.1 | 3.3 |

[1]OWL Overview = OWL Web Ontology Language Overview
[2]OWL Guide = OWL Web Ontology Language Guide
[3]OWL Ref. = OWL Web Ontology Language Reference
[4]OWL Sem. = OWL Web Ontology Language Semantics and Abstract Syntax

# Appendix

Table A-5. OWL Property Construct Descriptions in OWL Documentation

| OWL Property | This Text | OWL Over.[1] | OWL Guide[2] | OWL Ref.[3] | OWL Sem.[4] |
|---|---|---|---|---|---|
| allValuesFrom | 13.4.1.1 | 3.4 | 3.4.1 | 3.1.2.1.1 | 3.2 |
| backwardCompatibleWith | 11.2.3.1.1.2 |  | 6 | 7.4.3 | 4.1 |
| cardinality | 13.4.2.3 | 3.5, 4 | 3.4.2 | 3.1.2.2.3 | 3.2 |
| complementOf | 17.2.3.3 | 4 | 5.1.3 | 3.1.3.3 | 3.2 |
| differentFrom | 15.5.2 | 3.2 | 4.3. | 5.2.2 | 3.3 |
| disjointWith | 17.2.2 | 4 | 5.3. | 3.2.4 | 3.3 |
| distinctMembers | 15.5.3 | 3.2 | 4.3. |  | 5.2 |
| equivalentClass | 14.2 | 3.2 | 4.1. | 3.2.2 | 3.3 |
| equivalentProperty | 13.2.1 | 3.2 | 4.1. | 4.2.1 | 3.3 |
| hasValue | 17.3 | 4 | 3.4.3. | 3.1.2.1.3 | 3.2 |
| imports | 11.2.3.2 |  | 2.2. | 7.3 | 3.4 |
| incompatibleWith | 11.2.3.1.1.3 |  | 6 | 7.4.4 |  |
| intersectionOf | 14.3 (Lite), 17.2.3.1 (Full) | 3.6, 4 | 5.1.1. | 3.1.3.1 | 3.2 |
| inverseFunctionalProperty | 13.1.2 | 3.3 | 3.3. | 4.3.2 | 3.3 |
| inverseOf | 13.2.2 | 3.3 | 3.3. | 4.2.2 | 3.3 |
| maxCardinality | 13.4.2.2 | 3.5, 4 | 3.4.2. | 3.1.2.2.1 | 3.2 |
| minCardinality | 13.4.2.1 | 3.5, 4 | 3.4.2. | 3.1.2.2.2 | 3.2 |
| oneOf | 17.2.1 | 4 | 5.2 | 3.1.1 | 3.2 |
| onProperty | 13.4 | 3.4 | 3.4. | 3.1.2 | 3.2 |
| priorVersion | 11.2.3.1.1.1 |  | 6 | 7.4.2 |  |
| sameAs | 15.5.1 | 3.2 | 4.2. | 5.2.1 | 3.3 |
| someValuesFrom | 13.4.1.1 | 3.4 | 3.4.1. | 3.1.2.1.2 | 3.2 |
| unionOf | 17.2.3.2 | 4 | 5.1.2. | 3.1.3.2 | 3.2 |
| versionInfo | 11.2.3.1.1 |  | 6 | 7.4.1 |  |

[1] OWL Overv. = OWL Web Ontology Language Overview
[2] OWL Guide = OWL Web Ontology Language Guide
[3] OWL Ref. = OWL Web Ontology Language Reference
[4] OWL Sem. = OWL Web Ontology Language Semantics and Abstract Syntax

Appendix

Table A-6. RDF(S) Property Domains and Ranges

| Property | Domain | Range |
|---|---|---|
| rdf:type | &rdfs;Resource | &rdfs;Class |
| rdfs:subClassOf | &rdfs;Class | &rdfs;Class |
| rdfs:subPropertyOf | &rdf;Property | &rdf;Property |
| rdfs:domain | &rdf;Property | &rdfs;Class |
| rdfs:range | &rdf;Property | &rdfs;Class |
| rdfs:label | &rdfs;Resource | &rdfs;Literal |
| rdfs:comment | &rdfs;Resource | &rdfs;Literal |
| rdfs:member | &rdfs;Resource | &rdfs;Resource |
| rdf:first | &rdf;List | &rdfs;Resource |
| rdf:rest | &rdf;List | &rdf;List |
| rdfs:seeAlso | &rdfs;Resource | &rdfs;Resource |
| rdfs:isDefinedBy | &rdfs;Resource | &rdfs;Resource |
| rdf:value | &rdfs;Resource | &rdfs;Resource |

Table A-7. OWL Property Domains and Ranges

| OWL Property | Domain | Range |
|---|---|---|
| allValuesFrom | &owl;Restriction | &rdfs;Class |
| backwardCompatibleWith | &owl;Ontology | &owl;Ontology |
| cardinality | &owl;Restriction | &xsd;nonNegativeInteger |
| complementOf | &owl;Class | &owl;Class |
| differentFrom | &owl;Thing | &owl;Thing |
| disjointWith | &owl;Class | &owl;Class |
| distinctMembers | &owl;AllDifferent | &rdf;List |
| equivalentClass | &owl;Class | &owl;Class |
| equivalentProperty | &rdf;Property | &rdf;Property |
| hasValue | &owl;Restriction | (none) |
| imports | &owl;Ontology | &owl;Ontology |
| incompatibleWith | &owl;Ontology | &owl;Ontology |
| intersectionOf | &owl;Class | &rdf;List |
| inverseOf | &owl;ObjectProperty | &owl;ObjectProperty |
| maxCardinality | &owl;Restriction | &xsd;nonNegativeInteger |
| minCardinality | &owl;Restriction | &xsd;nonNegativeInteger |
| oneOf | &owl;Class | &rdf;List |
| onProperty | &owl;Restriction | &rdf;Property |
| priorVersion | &owl;Ontology | &owl;Ontology |
| sameAs | &owl;Thing | &owl;Thing |
| someValuesFrom | &owl;Restriction | &rdfs;Class |
| unionOf | &owl;Class | &rdf;List |
| versionInfo | (none) | (none) |

# Index

&rdf;nil .................................................. 106
Abox ...................................................... 25
agent software ..................................... 21
AI .......................................................... 26
Berners-Lee, Tim . 1, 15, 23, 43, 44, 134
class ...................................................... 33
conceptualization ............................... 27
Connolly, Dan ................................... 134
DAML+OIL ......................................... 16
DARPA ..................................... 1, 16, 21
DTDs .................................................... 70
European Union ................................. 16
explicit semantics ................................. 6
finding ................................................... 5
Foreign Clearance Guide .................. 22
Gruber, Thomas .................................. 27
Hendler, Dr. James ................. 134, 135
HTML .......................... 1, 2, 4, 8, 17, 19
HTTP ...................................................... 1
literals .................................................. 80
McGuiness, Deborah .......................... 26
NLP ........................................................ 4
OIL ...................................................... 135
ontologies ........................... 16, 19, 21, 25
OWL DL .................................... 138, 221
OWL Full .................................. 138, 237
OWL Lite ........................................... 138
owl:AllDifferent ............................... 212
owl:allValuesFrom ........................... 186
owl:AnnotationProperty ................. 173
owl:backwardCompatibleWith ..... 155
owl:cardinality .................................. 191
owl:Class ........................................... 167
owl:complementOf .......................... 230
owl:DataRange ................................. 234
owl:DatatypeProperty ..................... 170

owl:DeprecatedClass ....................... 157
owl:DeprecatedProperty ................. 159
owl:differentFrom ............................ 211
owl:disjointWith .............................. 226
owl:distinctMembers ....................... 212
owl:equivalentClass ................ 185, 199
owl:equivalentProperty .................. 178
owl:FunctionalProperty .................. 175
owl:hasValue .................................... 232
owl:imports ...................................... 160
owl:incompatibleWith .................... 156
owl:intersectionOf .................. 201, 227
owl:inverseFunctionalProperty .... 177
owl:inverseOf Property .................. 179
owl:maxCardinality ......................... 190
owl:minCardinality ......................... 189
owl:Nothing ..................................... 169
owl:ObjectProperty ......................... 171
owl:oneOf ......................................... 225
owl:onProperty ................................ 184
owl:Ontology ................................... 150
owl:OntologyProperty .................... 173
owl:priorVersion .............................. 154
owl:Restriction ................................. 184
owl:sameAs ...................................... 210
owl:someValuesFrom ...................... 187
owl:subClassOf ................................ 185
owl:SymmetricProperty .................. 183
owl:Thing ......................................... 168
owl:TransitiveProperty ................... 181
owl:unionOf ..................................... 229
owl:versionInfo ................................ 152
property ............................................... 33
QNames ............................................... 57
Qualified Names ................................ 57
RDF/XML ........................................... 83

# Index

rdf:_n .................................................. 96
rdf:about ............................................. 89
rdf:Alt ................................................ 101
rdf:Bag ................................................ 99
rdf:datatype ......................................... 91
rdf:Description ..................................... 86
rdf:first ............................................... 104
rdf:ID .................................................. 88
rdf:li ................................................... 97
rdf:List ............................................... 103
rdf:parseType="Collection" .......... 102
rdf:parseType="Literal" .................. 90
rdf:parseType="Resource" ........... 107
rdf:Property ............................. 115, 169
rdf:RDF .............................................. 85
rdf:resource ........................................ 95
rdf:rest ............................................... 106
rdf:Seq ............................................... 100
rdf:type ........................................ 92, 118
rdf:value ............................................ 107
rdf:XMLLiteral ................................. 116
rdfs:Class .......................................... 115
rdfs:comment ................................... 129
rdfs:Container .................................. 126
rdfs:ContainerMembershipProperty
    ...................................................... 127
rdfs:Datatype ................................... 116
rdfs:domain ...................................... 123
rdfs:isDefinedBy ............................. 125

rdfs:label .......................................... 128
rdfs:Literal ....................................... 115
rdfs:member .................................... 127
rdfs:range ......................................... 120
rdfs:Resource .................................. 115
rdfs:seeAlso ..................................... 125
rdfs:subClassOf ....................... 118, 197
rdfs:subPropertyOf ........................ 120
Semantic Web 1, 6, 7, 12, 16, 18, 20,
    21, 22, 23, 25, 26, 43, 44, 45, 49, 50,
    60, 61, 71, 73, 75, 92, 111, 131, 132,
    133, 134, 137, 140, 203, 210, 237,
    243, 249, 258, 259
Tbox .................................................... 25
typedNode syntax ............ 93, 176, 206
Uniform Resource Identifiers .......... 44
Uniform Resource Locators .............. 1
Uniform Resource Names ................ 51
URI References ................................. 53
W3C 2, 16, 43, 44, 45, 46, 62, 63, 64,
    65, 69, 75, 76, 111, 133, 134, 135, 140
World Wide Web ................................ 1
XML 2, 3, 8, 17, 19, 43, 45, 56, 57, 61,
    62, 65
XML Schema ...................................... 69
xml:base ............................................. 58
xml:lang ............................................. 66
xmlns .................................................. 56
XMLS .................................................. 69

ISBN 1412034448-5